PREPARATION
FOR ART

PREPARATION

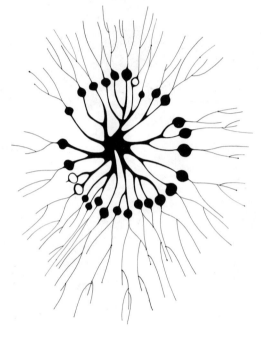

Illustrated by Jean Ray Laury

FOR ART

June King McFee
Stanford University

WADSWORTH PUBLISHING COMPANY, INC.
SAN FRANCISCO

L.C. CAT. CARD NO.: 61–5915
PRINTED IN THE UNITED STATES OF AMERICA.

**To Malcolm
and John**

FOREWORD

June King McFee believes that a *preparation for art* for prospective teachers has to create more than a simple enthusiasm for art expression in the classroom.

Her zest for studying art education in the light of recent research in cultural anthropology, in psychology, and in our complex American social environment is catching—and stimulating. She writes for the teachers who are never through learning and for the new teachers we will need in our national effort to improve the relevance of our instruction.

Her breadth of scholarship will help to preserve and to enhance the place of the visual arts in general education. But it will do this not just because she shows the relationship of art to science and psychology, the dominating disciplines of our era. Rather, she clarifies the distinctive qualities of art experiences and of art works in the life of the individual and of the community.

Visual and plastic arts are media of personal expression. They are also instruments for perceptual education by means of which children's creative powers are matured and extended. Perceptual education is also the basis for aesthetic awareness of one's home and community environment with its potentialities for maintaining and improving the cultural values man produces.

Art has created human values; and cultures of all times and places on earth have created works of art. The author sets out to describe in what manner these aspects of art bear upon the painting of five-year-olds, or upon the way in which a first year teacher or a veteran of three decades may set the educational stage for the art experiences of children.

I believe her book to be a major achievement, creating a

theory of art education and presenting with it a comprehensive pattern of activities through which teachers and others who work with children will be able to realize in practice the aesthetic accomplishments which the author helps us to visualize.

Frederick M. Logan

PREFACE

Art is a form of language necessary for the progress of humanity and the maintenance of civilization. That art fulfills a basic human need must be recognized before you can determine the way it is to be presented to children, whether this presentation takes the form of recreation, education, or rehabilitation in the home, the church, or the school. In *Preparation for Art,* cultural anthropology and recent research in psychology are integrated with the practice of teaching art. Emphasis, you will find, is on the individual child as he responds to an art task.

In Part One, a theory is developed to help you understand the behavior of children in art. The theory serves as a framework in which differences among children can be identified. The information in Part One is a guide for solving the problems in real situations, discussed in Part Two. The premise is a simple one: if you understand the variables within a group of children, you can more successfully help each child develop his creative potential.

Interest in art, in human behavior in art, and in art as a part of culture have provided the stimulation for this writing. These interests have been developed in the author through challenging associations. Her early motivation in art came from a mother whose great love of beauty in many forms led to their sharing of inspection of Puget Sound tide pools, the Pacific Coast rain forests, and the work of the artists who interpreted them. The author owes much to the influence of the Seattle Art Museum and the talented artists of the Thirties and Forties whose work inspired her. A year of concentrated study with the Ukrainian sculptor Alexander Archipenko opened many new avenues of expression and furthered her intellectual analysis of the nature of art. A period of study under the French Purist, Amédée Ozenfant, at the University of Washington led to greater control of expression and deeper study of design.

Experience in teaching broadened the author's interest in art to include a study of its psychological and cultural implications. Inspired teachers played a most important role. Many persons on the staff of the Stanford University School of Education and the Department of Art, most notably Professors Pauline Snedden Sears and George D. Spindler, contributed greatly to the author's training in relating art to the social sciences.

Several leaders in the field of education have reviewed the manuscript at various stages of its development. For guidance, criticism, and encouragement, the author is indebted to Frederick M. Logan of the University of Wisconsin, Mayo Bryce of the United States Office of Education, Ralph Beelke, Secretary of the National Art Education Association, Jerome Hausman of Ohio State University, Frank Bach of Central Washington College of Education, Doris Standerfer of San Jose State College, Reid Hastie of the University of Minnesota, and Paul H. Mussen of the Department of Psychology of the University of California. The author's husband, Malcolm McFee, has been most helpful in evaluating the anthropological data.

Several individuals and organizations gave permission to use children's art works: Arthur Perry Newcomb, Jr., Yvonne Whitehurst Seidel, Al Zelver for the Japanese children's prints, the Palo Alto Public Schools, and the Palo Alto Art Club.

The case studies in this book are actual cases, but names and details are changed to preserve the anonymity of the children and adults involved.

The author is particularly indebted to Jean Ray Laury, the artist whose talent in expressing ideas in highly creative ways contributes so much to the book. Lucille Just, the editor, has been of inestimable help in the clarification and organization of the materials. Finally the author wishes to express her gratitude to her parents, her husband, and her son, who in so many ways have contributed to the development of this book.

CONTENTS

FOREWORD BY FREDERICK M. LOGAN   vii

PREFACE   ix

1 Your Preparation for Art   **3**

     Attitudes About Art   *4*
     The Function of the Book   *5*
     The Scope of Art Education   *6*
     Using Research in Art Education   *10*

PART ONE
THE FOUNDATIONS OF ART EDUCATION

2 Art in Culture   **17**

     What Is Culture?   *17*
     What Is Art?   *18*
     Functions of Art in Culture   *20*
     Separation of Fine and Applied Arts   *27*
     Sources of Taste   *28*
     Learning Art in Balinese Culture   *30*
     Learning Art in Western Culture   *33*

3 Children's Individual Differences in Art   **37**

     Perception as Information-Handling   *38*
     Organization of the Perception-Delineation Theory   *40*
     Readiness: Response Sets   *42*
         Prior Learning   *43*
         Cognitive and Visual Learning   *46*
         Orientation to Space   *50*
         Rigidity-Flexibility   *54*

Implications for Practice   *56*
Related Activities   *65*

4   Individual Differences in Development in Art   71

Growth and Development   *72*
Perceptual Development   *78*
Culture as a Factor in Children's Perceptual Growth   *84*
Implications for Practice   *91*
Related Activities   *96*

5   Environmental Factors in Children's Work   101

Motivation   *102*
Threat and Non-threat   *102*
Success and Failure Experience   *104*
Discontinuity   *106*
Child-Rearing Practices and Art Education   *109*
Changing American Core Values and Values in Art Education   *113*
Implications for Practice   *121*
Related Activities   *125*

6   The Creative Process   129

Personality Traits Related to Creativity   *131*
Past Experiences   *138*
Implications for Practice   *140*
Related Activities   *143*

7   Theories of Child Art   147

Perception-Delineation   *147*
Other Theories of Child Art   *151*
Naïve Realism   *151*
Intellectualist Theory   *153*
Perceptual Theory   *155*
Haptic and Visual Theory   *156*
Developmental Stages   *156*
Implications for Practice   *160*

PART TWO
THE ART CURRICULUM
IN THE ELEMENTARY SCHOOL

8 Establishing Objectives for Art Activities   169

Difficulties in Establishing Objectives   169
Objectives from Society   171
Philosophical Sources of Objectives   175
Objectives Derived from the Nature of the Pupils   176
Objectives from the Field of Art   177
The History of Art Education in the United States   179

9 Organizing the Learning Experience   185

Planning for Individual Differences   185
Classroom Learning Experience   191
Training in Art   203
Evaluation   206

10 Scope and Sequence of an Art Program   213

The Primary Years: Art Learning Activities   214
The Primary Years: Self-Directed Art   226
The Primary Years: Integrated Art   227
The Intermediate Years: Art Learning Activities   230
The Intermediate Years: Self-Directed Art   237
The Intermediate Years: Integrated Art   238

11 Design for the Classroom Teacher   243

The Nature of Design   243
Psychological Basis for Design   245
Principles of Design   249
Elements of Design   257
Design Activities   268

12 Classroom Procedures for New Teachers   273

The Art Consultant   273
Tools and Materials   275
Basic Art Materials   281
Related Tasks for Part Two   299

13 Summary: Perception-Delineation and Art Education Practice   303

Point I: Readiness   *303*
Point II: The Psychological Environment   *306*
Point III: Information-Handling   *308*
Point IV: Creativity and Delineation   *309*
Conclusion   *311*

SUGGESTIONS FOR FURTHER READING   313

GLOSSARY   317

INDEX OF AUTHORS   321

INDEX OF SUBJECTS   323

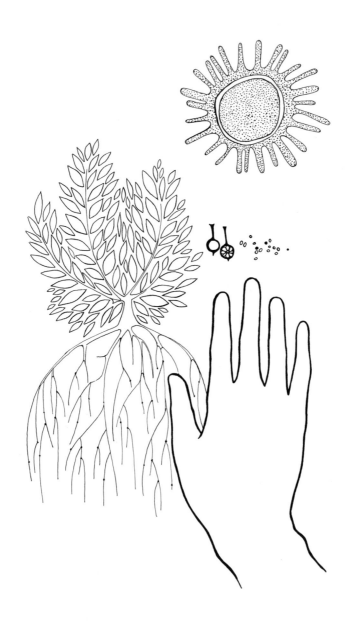

1

Your Preparation for Art

This book is designed for you who are concerned with the art activities of children. Its purpose is to help you to be more effective in guiding their experiences in art—in school, in recreation and guidance centers, and at home.

Two assumptions are basic to the ideas developed in the book: (1) people who have enjoyed creative activities in art can best lead children into creative expression; (2) those who experience creativity and who also understand the nature of the creative process and children's individual differences will be more effective teachers.

Art activity courses will give you experience in creative work. The theory and research described in this book will help you to understand this experience. With this knowledge you will have a sounder basis for understanding children as they explore art. The title *Preparation for Art* means just that. This book's goal is to prepare you to become a professional person who understands human behavior in art and art education from its foundations.

Related activities are suggested at the end of appropriate chapters to make the information have more meaning. A glossary at the end of the book provides definitions of technical terms. A bibliography of selected foundations material will also be found at the end of the book. After each chapter are listed the research materials and references that apply to that chapter.

ATTITUDES ABOUT ART

Many people do not think of themselves as artists, yet they design and create; they make aesthetic judgments many times a day. If you lack confidence in your own ability, you may feel timid about trying to develop children's abilities. This book is planned to accompany an art activities course, so that *you can understand more about what lies behind the ways you feel about art*. This guided experience should help you become more confident in teaching art.

A young teacher-in-training found that finger painting was very repulsive to her. She was able to pour the starch on the paper and sift powder paint into it. Then she just sat looking at the "mess," unwilling to put her carefully groomed hands into it. Finally she covered her eyes with one hand and slapped the other hand into the paint. The instructor, observing this girl's difficulty, praised her for being willing to try something she so obviously disliked. Later in a conference the girl and her instructor discussed childhood training and its relationship to cleanliness attitudes. The student was encouraged to be patient with herself, to use materials she felt comfortable with until she had some success, then gradually to try those that seemed "messy" to her.

Elementary school teachers have been observed introducing a medium they have negative feelings about. Without realizing it, by the expressions on their faces and the way they handle the medium, the teachers communicate to the children their dislike for it. Such an introduction will hardly encourage children to use the medium freely. *This is the reason why it is so important for teachers to explore art for themselves as well as for teaching*.

Why do some of us have these mixed feelings about art? How does a person's past experience help to determine his present attitudes? What real use does art have in the life of a child? These are some of the questions you may be asking as you strive to prepare yourself as a professional person.

THE FUNCTION OF THE BOOK

This book is focused on the role of the elementary school classroom teacher. What is said, however, is useful to those of you who work with children in art in other situations. The purpose is to raise the professional level of your activity. By knowing *why* you do the things you do, you will be able to make intelligent judgments about the art experiences you give children.

You and your art instructor—each has a specific role to play. Your role is to be as receptive as possible to new ideas, to be patient when you find yourself resisting, to experience or to study what is suggested, and to take time to let new ideas fit into what you already know before you pass judgment on them. Your instructor has had experience with children, with many art media, and with problems of classroom procedure. Furthermore, as an artist in his own right, familiar with the art heritage we share, he has much to contribute to your understanding of the vitality and importance of art for living. He will lead and encourage you as you learn about elementary school art activities.

The contribution of this book to your training is to interpret suitable information from research that applies to art education. Accounts of investigations in psychology and anthropology have been selected to help you in your own creative development and in your work with children. The materials apply both to you and to the children. Because you are preparing to be *professional* teachers, it is necessary to describe the research to you as well as to help you interpret it for possible uses in the classroom.

A good teacher does not work by formulas, memorizing methods and using them no matter how the situation changes. The most exciting things about teaching are the differences among children, the changes in the group from day to day, and the challenges to the professional teacher in responding to them.

THE PROFESSIONAL TEACHER

A professional person will not simply accept the word of an authority. He wants to know how the authority arrived at his conclusions. He evaluates different kinds of evidence. Those of you who are advanced students will use the bibliographies and go to the original sources to evaluate these materials. Others of you can derive directives for teaching from the available summaries and their interpretations. Because the situations in which you work will constantly change, and because each of you is a distinct individual, we will only make suggestions about how you might use the information. Many possibilities for good teaching can evolve from the ideas presented here. Your instructor will show you some of them. His interpretations may differ from those you read here. It is good to have more than one point of view from which to make your own judgments. Most important, the sources of your information should be as reliable as possible.

THE SCOPE OF ART EDUCATION

Art education is not a distinct discipline since it is linked with many fields. First of all it is art, a basic form of *communication.* The symbols on this page, the alphabet, started out as pictographs —pictures with which man symbolized what he thought, felt, and experienced. Language and art have both developed with the history of man. Both are necessary for civilized life. Children have to learn both forms of communication in order to operate successfully as civilized human beings. For this reason we shall study art as it functions in man's life. Anthropology will contribute to our understanding of art as it has functioned in the lives of man collectively and as it operates in our lives and in the lives of our pupils.

The production and the appreciation of art are kinds of human behavior. The broad study of behavior—psychology—is applicable here, with special emphasis on individual differences in perception, creativity, and growth and development. In order to teach we ourselves have to learn; we have to understand how and why we learn as we do. Psychology—the study of the individual— cannot be separated from anthropology—the study of the group. Our attitudes about art have evolved from our culture, our background of experience. For this reason we study behavior from both psychological and anthropological points of view. All of your college courses in general psychology and anthropology are pertinent to art education.

Art education is also vitally concerned with the elementary curriculum, the planning and sequence of meaningful experiences that help children develop their means of visual communication. Some kinds of communication can be taught; others must be discovered by the children. Children's awareness in all subjects can be sharpened by their study of art.

We are concerned with the relationship of art in school to art in the home and community. As a consumer, each person must make choices, many of which depend on art judgments. As a citizen, each person's contribution to community planning is affected by his aesthetic viewpoint. As a member of a democratic society, each person is concerned with preserving a philosophy of individuality that can be enriched by art experiences.

Art education is much more than an isolated study of skills. Initially, it is an activity of children in their individual reactions to their environment. It is a language that enriches the entire curriculum. The teacher's use of art should be based on an understanding of its foundations, combined with practical experience in creative activity. Figure 1–1 is an outline of the major fields that contribute to the area called *art education.* One book cannot cover so vast a subject. This book derives its information from the fields listed, with special emphasis on the psychological and anthropological implications for practice in art. Suggested supplementary books are listed in the appendix. For those of you who are particularly inquisitive about certain areas, this outline and the bibliographical materials listed at the end of each chapter should be useful.

THE ROLE OF THE CLASSROOM TEACHER

The major role of the classroom teacher is to prepare children to deal creatively and effectively with the challenges of life. As they learn about their environment, children can see the beauty and order that is in it—in nature and in man's artistic creations. They can learn how to make it more beautiful and orderly. The teacher's role is to serve as a catalyst in whose presence children

The Place of Art	The Areas of Study	The Functions of Art and Art Education
. . . in the world (from the past to the present, a vast growing phenomenon)	world history art history archaeology aesthetics art criticism	to communicate man's individual and collective experience
. . . in the school (an organized, purposeful community)	philosophy of education educational theory and research psychology of —creativity —perception —individual differences —motivation —learning cultural anthropology	to transmit knowledge, skills, and values from one generation to the next to improve the environment to motivate and educate individuals
. . . in the child (a questioning, developing, complex being)	drawing painting designing imprinting building weaving modeling sculpturing inlaying art of other people art in our own lives	to provide opportunities for developing —avenues of expression and communication —independent aesthetic judgment —understanding of the cultural heritage —increased perceptual awareness —more uses of the creative potential

FIGURE **1–1. THE SCOPE OF ART EDUCATION**
This chart traces art from its appearance as a cultural phenomenon, through its integration into the school situation, toward a meaningful entity for the child.

are exposed to many art forms, giving them experiences through which they can develop their own sensitivity for making artistic judgments. Just as we cannot know what scientific judgments our children will have to make as adults, so we do not know what kinds of aesthetic judgments they will have to make. We *can* give them a basis for judgment by exposing them to what has already been done and by giving them opportunities for creative expression in art. Creative problem-solving ability is crucial in both science and art.

CONCEPTS OF TEACHING

The concept of teaching is often limited to its traditional role —making children learn a specific body of knowledge. *Teaching in its broader sense means giving children opportunities and experiences that will enable them to understand, to relate, to interpret new information.* Of the many school situations providing such opportunities, two are described here. In the first, the teacher's role is focused on developing an environment so full of interesting things that the children have to search out information in order to know how to deal with it. In the second, the teacher works with problems that the children see and want to work on, feeding in the learning of information, materials, and skills as needed.

1. A third grade class should know how to do many kinds of print-making for many activities during the year. When the children arrive one morning, they see the room alive with print-making equipment, all within the range of third grade children, but allowing for many differences in ability. There are potatoes to cut, linoleum blocks, cutting tools, old inner tubes, assorted erasers, brayers, inks, boards, plastic cement, interesting varieties of paper and cloth. The variety in the environment is the source of motivation. The task is to test and explore what the different media will do, with the teacher serving as a resource person, helping when a child can't solve a problem alone. To do this kind of teaching the teacher should know a great deal about the children in order to select appropriate materials. He should know how many kinds of choices they can tolerate, how skilled they are in working on their own, how much instruction they will need to get them started. He should understand the effects of failure and frustration on those pupils who will need special encouragement.

2. The teacher guides the children in a discussion of what they like or don't like about their classroom from the standpoint of beauty and what they might like to do to improve it. Together they do problem-solving. They investigate the way others have solved similar problems. They suggest what they would like to do and, another matter, what is practical to do. The teacher contributes information about materials to carry out their ideas and

gives assistance in developing skills as needed. The teacher has to understand the children to know if they can set realistic goals for themselves, what kinds of tasks they can handle, and what kind of resource information will be helpful to them in solving their problems.

The teacher, if he is flexible, can shift the teaching situation as needed. He must understand himself as well as the children. All of us cannot work in the same degree of complexity. Some of us are not able to teach effectively with more than three kinds of classroom activities going on at once. Others can manage a great deal more and can have the class operating in as many activities as there are children. Adaptability should develop with experience.

These are only two of the teaching methods that you may find effective. To use them and to develop new ideas for teaching, you need a basis from which to decide whether or not you are helping your pupils to develop attitudes of value to them.

USING RESEARCH IN ART EDUCATION

The purpose of Part One of this book is to give you a better basis for making decisions in teaching art. In the classroom you are constantly asking yourself questions such as these:

1. What kinds of art experiences will have meaning for this particular group of children?

2. How can I motivate the children who appear to differ in many ways from the rest of the group? Why are they different?

3. What should I expect the children at this level to achieve? What experiences should come first, which later?

4. Are the established objectives realistic for these children? How can the children be helped to reach their goals?

If the teacher has sound information about the kinds of individual differences he is likely to encounter, he can more easily make intelligent decisions. If he understands something about the nature of creativity and about the perceptual process, he is in a better position to evaluate possible activities for his class. He can decide whether the activities will encourage or inhibit the development of creativity, perceptual abilities, and aesthetic judgment.

In order to help you make such decisions, this book presents a new approach to art education. It is based on a foundation of research in experimental psychology and the behavioral sciences. The study of this research was done with the elementary teacher and the art consultant in mind. The research studies were selected for the soundness of their procedures, and their applicability to children as well as to adults. New directives for classroom procedures in art emerge. They should contribute to the teacher's effectiveness in the classroom.

A scientist, to be systematic, must test each change as he makes it. This is a slow process. We teachers have our pupils to teach *now*, with all the problems of individual differences to solve *now*—we cannot wait.[1] To do the best job of teaching, we use as many scientific directives as we can. There is always a gap between what is tested and the problems we have to solve. The obligation of the teaching profession is to be aware of and to utilize the research that is already available.

USES OF THEORY

The label "theory" can be attached to several kinds of ideas. Anyone who makes an observation and generalizes about its nature, source, or function, can say he has a "theory," even though he does not test or analyze his assumption extensively. In scientific terminology, this kind of hunch is more a hypothesis than a theory. Although such a hypothesis can be useful it must be distinguished from a theory which is developed from well-controlled experimental evidence or from extensive clinical or logical analysis.

The function of a theory is to help us organize numerous pieces of related evidence into a workable tool for dealing with problems. Scattered research that is not related to other research can do little to help us deal with complex problems like child behavior in art. Theory is necessary in understanding behavior that is complex, but the theory is always subject to change as new experiments are made.

A theory in the behavioral sciences is usually part of a larger body of theoretical study and research. The perception-delineation theory (P-D) presented in this book is eclectic. Many pertinent studies have contributed to its formation. Its roots are in Gestalt or "field" psychology.[2] The field (like the field in the physical sciences) means a whole situation, the parts of which are dynamically interdependent (the development and function of one of the parts is dependent on the development and function of all the other parts). More recent studies of personality and perception that contribute to P-D utilize association theory (which stresses the relationships learned in past experience) and theories of personality in culture.[3]

The material in this book is based on the premise that, while scientific means may not completely explain people's behavior, they will reveal certain patterns and consistencies from which a theoretical model of human behavior can be built. From a study of human behavior will come a better understanding of the child— one of the most wonderful and complex things in the world. It is with this model in mind that we begin to explore the differences you will find in children and in their art. In Part One we will study the foundations of art education; in Part Two we will apply them to the classroom.

REFERENCES

1. J. W. Tilton, *An Educational Psychology of Learning* (New York: The Macmillan Company, 1951), p. 7.

2. Kurt Lewin, *Dynamic Theory of Personality* (New York: McGraw-Hill Book Company, 1935).

3. Jerome S. Bruner, "Personality Dynamics and the Process of Perceiving," in *Perception: An Approach to Personality,* edited by Robert R. Blake and Glenn V. Ramsey. Copyright 1951 The Ronald Press Company.

PART ONE

THE FOUNDATIONS
OF ART EDUCATION

Teachers can increase their effectiveness in art education by understanding their own attitudes as well as the behavior of children. Part One of this book provides information that is applicable to people of any age, though the emphasis is on the child as he creates an art form.

Chapter 2 describes the function of art in culture. Chapters 3 through 6 explore the kinds of individual differences in art behavior found among children. Chapter 7 reviews the existing theories of child art in terms of the perception-delineation theory and research, and summarizes the findings so that they can be applied in practice.

2

Art in Culture

Art is one of man's means of communication—of sharing his experience with others. Art can communicate qualities of experience that cannot be put into words. By sharing experience, through verbal language and through art, man is able to build social groups and develop culture. To understand children's art we must first understand the functions of art in culture.

WHAT IS CULTURE?

Culture is the pattern of interaction within a given group of people. The pattern is determined by the people's shared values, beliefs, and opinions on acceptable behavior. Within the pattern people have roles to play and work to do. The culture in part determines how children are trained and how beliefs and values are maintained from generation to generation. Culture includes education, religion, science, art, folklore, and social organization.

The term *culture* is used some of the time to describe a very large society such as "Western culture." Among the nations of Western Europe and the Americas, and the peoples from these areas in other parts of the world, there are traditionally shared beliefs and values that differentiate them as a whole from other large cultural groups. *Culture* is also used to describe small, some-

17

what isolated or homogeneous groups where the similarities among the people are more evident. In talking about American culture, we refer to the *core* culture, meaning those values and beliefs shared in some degree by a majority of Americans. Different regional, ethnic, and religious groups within the whole are called subcultures. These people share the core culture in part but also have a nucleus of values and beliefs and ways of behaving that set them apart. Almost everyone is, in some way, part of the core culture and part of one or more subcultures. A given family, because of the background and experience of the two parents, may represent several subcultures.

Differences in values and beliefs are expressed through language and art forms such as dress, architecture, and decoration. Without verbal and visual means of sharing these ideas, cultures could not evolve. While there are nonliterate societies (those without written language), there are no societies that are without art forms, however primitive, for communicating ideas.[1]

WHAT IS ART?

Art, like man, is a complex changing phenomenon, difficult to define. Anthropologist Melville Herskovits says art can be thought of as "any embellishment of ordinary living that is achieved with competence and has describable form." [2] The describable form may be very primitive or very complex, depending on the art tradition of the culture and the ability of the individual artist. Art in

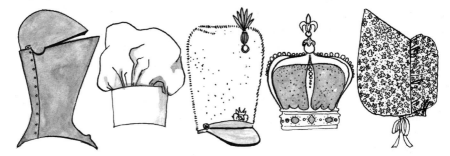

FIGURE 2-1. HEADGEAR SHOWING STATUS AND ROLE

its broad sense includes the design and symbols used in housing, utensils, furniture, clothing, and the artifacts of religious worship, as well as painting, sculpture, ceramics, textiles, and architecture.

In contemporary society, art is everything from a bread wrapper to a nonobjective painting, from a teakettle to a skyscraper. The nature of our culture is reflected in the quality of things we use and produce. The level of artistry achieved may range from cheap ornamentation to what is called "great art." The standards of evaluation in art are in part culturally determined, "good" and "bad" art being somewhat relative. But considerable agreement can be found, among people who have developed sensitivity to art forms, in what is superior and what is not.

ART IN EDUCATION. As teachers of art, we are concerned with the use of art as a language. Children can be taught to speak to and listen to others by means of art. They can become aware of the uses of art to themselves as individuals and as members of a larger group. They can understand how the culture is held together by the communication of art. There is a tendency in American culture to be so concerned with the uses of *things* that the art forms surrounding us are largely ignored. Since ours is an industrial society, let us try to picture what would happen to business if its accompanying art forms were removed. Art would be out of advertising—only words would be used. Appearance would not be considered in the design of manufactured goods—only mechanics would be important. We would not need color. Houses would serve mainly as a protection from the weather. Clothing's only function would be to keep us covered as modesty and climate dictate. Try to imagine what such an existence would be like. Think of the kinds of pleasure we derive from good design in clothing, homes, and furniture, as well as from those objects we create for their beauty alone. The anthropologist Hoebel said, ". . . man could survive without art, but to do so he would have to return to an ape level of existence." [3]

Such flights of imagination lead us to take a serious look at the place of art in culture, and to see art as part of the *foundation* of the educational program needed by every child. To help us become objectively aware of the functions of art in our culture, we can observe how art operates in other cultures. By observing how children of other groups learn, we can help our children to learn about their own art.

FUNCTIONS OF ART IN CULTURE

The functions of art in culture are (1) to maintain the concepts of reality, (2) to maintain the culture, its organization and roles, and (3) to enhance the appearance of objects.

MAINTENANCE OF THE CONCEPTS OF "REALITY"

Sand paintings show in visible form the Navahos' concepts of the nature of the world, its beginnings, the origins of man, and the whole complex myth system for maintaining their concepts of what is good and what is not good. The paintings are used as part of their ritual to help communicate the structure of their belief. In the healing ceremony, the medicine man uses the sand painting to create a feeling of direct contact between the patient and the "holy people." Not only does the patient see the visual symbol, he sits on it and is rubbed with sand from it. The ritual is a dramatic art form, the sand painting a visual art form for maintaining their concepts of reality and training their children.[4]

Much art of the Romanesque, Gothic, and Renaissance periods was created to communicate religious concepts to the non-reading population. In our society a wide range of religious artistic symbolism exists. The churches that spread out from the Puritan tradition have had a standard of simple beauty. Often a single un-adorned spire indicates a place of worship. By contrast, religions that use elaborate ceremonies have ornate churches with stained glass windows and altars rich in symbolic communication. With the advent of modern architecture the symbols of religious art have retained their meaning but changed their forms. All religions attempt to explain the nature of the universe—of reality. People have very strong feelings about the concepts they have developed or have learned from their ancestors. Artistic forms, as expressions of these feelings and convictions, can be found everywhere. Power,

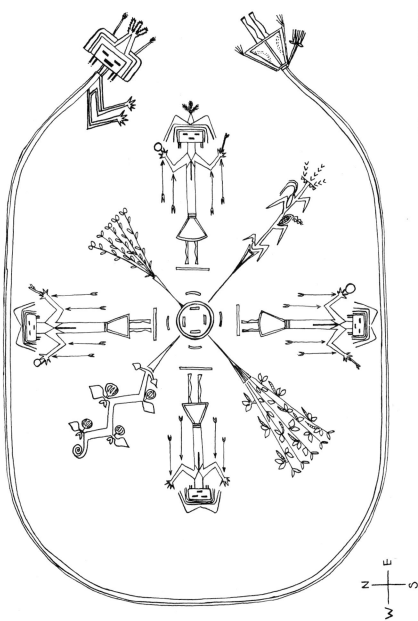

FIGURE 2–2. NAVAHO SANDPAINTING

N
E
W S

strength, permanence, elegance, or purity are some of the concepts communicated through church architecture.

The Kwoma people of New Guinea worship a *Marsalai,* a carved wooden idol. The artist who can make one has a position of prominence. The idol is used in secret societies, which in turn give continuity to the social organization of the group, give boys a means of achieving adult status through membership in the group, and separate the roles of the sexes. The men know that the *Marsalai* is only an idol, but women and small children live in fear of its power, though they never see it. The idol symbolizes an evil power that all the Kwoma fear. The fear holds the group together as a workable society. The abstract power becomes objective reality as an art form.[5]

These examples show how mankind uses art forms to give more meaning to interpretations of the nature of the universe. Language symbols alone are not enough, even for highly literate people.

ART AS CULTURAL MAINTENANCE

As forms of communication and historic record the arts help maintain culture. Even after long periods of time we can learn much about another people by studying its art forms. The Egypt of the Pharoahs seems remote in space and time, yet we can see and touch the tools, the buildings, the jewelry, the calendars, mummies, and religious artifacts that have been so well preserved. Many museums throughout the world have objects from this ancient culture. One can achieve empathic understanding of those remote people by studying the ways they enhanced their lives. He shares in some degree the quality of their experience as he responds to their art forms.

If we can do this with groups remote in time and space, think of the cultural impact of learning and experiencing from one generation to another in the same culture. A small child walking down a city street learns visually about his culture. The kinds of buildings mean different kinds of functions; libraries, post offices, and court houses are impressive in size and in importance to his life. What people wear tells what they are—policemen, big boys, dignified people, undignified people, soldiers and sailors, business-men in tailored suits and grocers in aprons. The three-year-old boy who said, "Ladies wear dresses and mothers wear jeans," was observing that costume defines occupation and role. Displays in windows, billboards, signs on telephone poles, theater marquees, all teach him about his culture.

The homes, the implements, and the decorations children see are constructed in conformity with the social organization, the beliefs and traditions of their groups. Clothing and body decoration indicate status. The manner of dress, nearly always differing between the sexes, may change from childhood to adulthood. Wearing lipstick and nail polish is a sign of "growing up." In another culture, body painting of another kind, or tattooing, may indicate an adult role—social position, occupation (warrior or medicine man), or tribal affiliation.

Another dimension to visual learning has come with movies, television, cartoons, and magazine "art." Much of the play of today's children is in the form of vicarious experience. They observe their culture indirectly, through someone else's interpretation. The cowboy whom they emulate as a cultural hero is interpreted for them. They have little or no real experience with such characters. Even the actors who play the roles seldom have contact with a cowboy who actually lives like the traditional cultural hero. Folk-tales and myths are used in many societies to educate children in the behaviors that are ideal for that culture. In our society, mass media are taking over the function of transmitting the cultural values and attitudes to children.

IMPLICATIONS FOR TEACHERS. Considering the impact of television, motion pictures, and all the other visual means of learning about the culture, it seems important for children to realize that all this visual learning is going on, so that they can learn to be discriminating about what they accept. Discuss with them such questions as these: Does a particular television show give a true picture of life in our society? What do certain kinds of advertising try to make you believe? Show the children a short movie more than once, and ask them to watch the second time for things they did not consciously see the first time. Critical analysis is necessary if a realistic, rather than an exaggerated, version of our culture is to be maintained.

ART AS ENHANCEMENT

Have you ever wondered why we decorate money? Why do we go to the great cost of minting coins and engraving currency? Apparently decoration gives added meaning. From ancient times to the present we have enhanced the value of money by decorating it with symbolic forms. We use images of our cultural heroes, our mottoes of faith, and our national seal to authenticate the worth of a coin. The decoration of baskets and pottery, of tools and implements, indicates a need of mankind to enhance the appearance of things he uses. Where the symbols used are part of the folklore, the enhancement has direct value in maintaining the culture.

The spoon designs in Figure 2–4 have their roots in different periods. In our culture, where we have borrowed the symbols and styles of so many periods, the ideas in our ornamentation have often lost their original meanings. We have collected from all over the world, mixing and adapting decorations as fashions changed, at the same time inventing our own forms, as any culture does. Recently a basic concept of design has come to the fore: *the function of an object determines its appearance.* A covered dish shaped like a chicken on a nest may be prized as part of our cultural history, but we are likely to serve our food from a dish designed to

FIGURE 2–3. ART ENHANCING THE VALUE OF MONEY

FIGURE 2–4. SPOONS REPRESENTING MANY CULTURES

look like a *dish* and nothing else, easy to care for, durable, and with decoration that in no way impedes function. Many artists believe that such design is a more honest expression of our contemporary culture than is the continued use of borrowed symbols.

The kind of decoration used to enhance daily living varies among the cultural groups. In any classroom, there may be pupils

FIGURE 2–5. CONTEMPORARY AND BORROWED STYLES
IN COVERED DISHES

who are so unfamiliar with a given form of decoration that they are unable to respond to it. A perceptive teacher can meet this challenge.

AN EDUCATIONAL MODEL. An art consultant was demonstrating the use of design in table setting to a junior high school home economics class. Various types of pottery, china, linen, crystal, silver, and stainless steel were used to demonstrate informal buffets, family meals, formal teas, and dinner settings. The girls were informed that they could work with these materials themselves at a later session. Three girls in the class appeared uninterested, and the consultant was unable to draw them into the discussion. Conferring with the teacher, she found that they were the children of itinerant fruit pickers. They had lived the last three years in a canvas tent house, even during severe winters. She found herself wondering what she could use that would have meaning for these girls whose subcultural background was so different from that of the rest of the class. Apparently the art forms she was using (crystal, linen, china, and pottery) had little meaning for these students. Already she had included objects from the ten-cent stores that had been selected for both good design and small expense. But apparently in the classroom setting they did not appear familiar to these girls.

A walk through the migrant workers' camp on the river flats gave her some clues about how the girls were used to living. At a later class period, one of the four tables in the room was covered with bright lemon-yellow oil cloth. The table utensils, plates and cups were tin. In a large, cleaned and polished tin can stood a large bouquet of wild daisies from the river's edge. White paper napkins, to match the wild flowers, were carefully folded. The class was invited to work in groups setting the tables. The consultant started working at the yellow table, asking one of the three reticent girls to help. Soon all three became involved. The consultant had begun to establish a bridge between what was familiar to the girls and what she was trying to teach. Had she not recognized the existence of differences in culture, values, and attitudes, and found objects that had meaning to the girls, she might have been unable to bring them into the learning situation.

This situation is a good example of cultural maintenance through decoration. The middle-class girls in the group understood the living pattern represented by linens, glassware, and china. The art forms reinforced the patterns of behavior. An Englishman living in the tropics, who maintains the custom of afternoon tea, has his English china tea service, silver, and linens to help preserve his cultural pattern. A Japanese tea ceremony without the traditional utensils for serving would soon lose its effectiveness in maintaining the aesthetic ideal it embodies. To maintain a culture without art forms would be difficult. To educate children in the cultural pattern without the help of art objects that symbolize ideas and values would be even more difficult.

SEPARATION OF FINE AND APPLIED ARTS

Generally, the term *applied art* means the transfer of the forms and designs discovered in the fine arts to the production of useful objects. The fine arts, in this context, are considered as those art forms that have value for themselves alone.

The separation of the fine and applied arts has not been as marked in all societies as it is in ours today. Irwin Edman, the philosopher, has compared the industrial cities of England and the United States to classical Greek cities. The towns dominated by factories grew rapidly near the end of the nineteenth century, when quantity production of goods was emphasized, machine methods were standardizing the objects of everyday life, and utility rather than grace determined how buildings would look. At the same time, the movement of "art for art's sake" widened the gap between the fine and the applied arts by maintaining that the "arts" were free of any social, moral, or practical obligation. Greek cities, by contrast, were built with strong emphasis on aesthetic relationships among all the art forms. The buildings were designed to be used *and* to give aesthetic satisfaction to the people looking at them.[6]

Both kinds of cities remain with us. People travel thousands of miles to look at the Greek cities. The industrial cities still serve their purposes and are in many ways central to Western culture.

City planning and architectural advancement have helped to improve their appearance. But the emphasis on quantity production and utility, which these cities symbolize, is still strong in our culture. The field of industrial design has contributed to higher standards in the appearance of products. But a large part of our population has not recognized that a refrigerator or a typewriter has aesthetic value and is a form of art. Art education can help to promote continued improvement in aesthetic qualities of the environment by showing the contribution of the fine arts to the applied arts. The influence of the French Cubists on contemporary industrial design is a good example.

SOURCES OF TASTE

A person's taste is shown by his like-dislike behavior. It develops within a given personality growing in a given cultural milieu. The individual's response is related to the personality structure he has developed, affected usually by the values and attitudes of his group. The commonly heard statement, "I know what I like, but I don't know why I like it," usually means that the individual has learned his preferences unconsciously. A person may choose to live in a Cape Cod, ranch, or contemporary functional house without being able to analyze all the factors that determine his preference.

In addition to forming tastes unconsciously, we often listen to other people's statements of what should be liked or disliked and accept their prejudices without questioning them. For example, an art education book published before 1930 made this statement: "The use of blue and green together is not good." No reason was given. The principle was only an expression of an attitude that was current at that time. Now blue and green are used together in profusion. They have always existed side-by-side in nature. Only recently have orange and magenta been accepted as a usable combination.

The teacher is a "taste-maker." He reinforces or opposes the child's acquired attitudes or, by encouraging him to explore the dimensions of design and color, helps him to develop confidence in his own ability to make judgments. The child expands his aesthetic awareness by observing the taste of other people. The like-dislike behavior of individuals of the same local ethnic, religious, social, or economic status will probably be more alike than those of other backgrounds. Russell Lynes suggests that there are three kinds of taste in our society—the highbrow (whose taste has been developed through experience in intellectual pursuits and the fine arts), the lowbrow (who absorbs and maintains without much questioning the "popular arts"—the unrefined folk forms of dress, ornamentation, jazz, language, and calendar art), and the middle-brow who fits anywhere between the two.[7] Max Lerner says of these categories, ". . . the middle class, which has come to dominate the rest of the culture, has found forceful challenges in the realm of taste and feels isolated between the snobbery of the high-brow intellectuals and the vulgar energies of popular culture."[8]

Your tastes are your "own." An exploration of the tastes of your contemporaries will show you which attitudes you have adopted without examination and which have grown as a result of your own observation. The darkened area in Figure 2–6 symbolizes an individual's taste. As a member of a nation, he shares some kinds of experiences with all his fellow citizens. Certain experiences will

FIGURE 2–6. SOURCES OF TASTE

be of importance only to a smaller group—social, economic, or other. The individual is more or less strongly influenced by training and experience within the groups of which he is a part. His personal sensitivity and readiness further determine his taste.

LEARNING ART IN BALINESE CULTURE

In order to evaluate the way children are exposed to and learn about art in our culture, we can observe the learning of art in other cultures. Art is one of the major forms of *enculturation,* the learning by a child of his culture, including (1) the concepts of reality, (2) the cultural heroes, (3) acceptable behavior, (4) history, and (5) sex roles—the whole pattern of behavior of his group.

Balinese culture, despite foreign influences since World War II, is considered to be one of the richest societies in its use of art forms. Theatre, dance, painting, sculpture, and religion are integrated with one another; the same heroes, demons, and symbols appear in each art form. Almost every Balinese participates in some way in the arts. There is no extreme differentiation between the most gifted and the least gifted, between the professional and the amateur artist.[9] Balinese children are considered to be small adults and so participate in most of the ritual and art of the society. Time is considered to be circular, every person being reborn to earth every fourth generation. For this reason the child is held in high esteem and is not a lesser citizen. As a babe in arms he attends solemn rituals. The front rows of theatrical performances are filled with children. They share in the rituals of prayer. Although they may run naked most of the time, they wear elaborate costumes for the ceremonial feasts.[10]

Jane Belo studied a Balinese village where the children had no formal training in painting or creating *wajang* (shadow play) puppets; yet they were able to portray, in great detail, elements of their culture in unfamiliar art media.[11] During a period of three months Belo encouraged the children to come to her house to draw. They came when they wished, apparently impelled by the pennies she gave them for their drawings and by the chance to use the art materials. She gave them neither instructions nor assistance. They did not help each other except by looking at the others' drawings.

FIGURE 2-7. A BARONG DANCING IN THE ROAD*
BY I GANDIR, AGE SEVEN

Only boys agreed to draw. In this culture the woman's role is to dance. The girls refused to draw even when offered money to do so.

In the drawing by I Gandir, age seven, a very complex organization is evident (Figure 2-7).* A *barong* (demon) is dancing in the street; people are striking cymbals and gongs, carrying parasols that are part of the ritual. The face of the demon is drawn in detail showing that the child has learned a great deal about sculpture.

Figure 2-8 is a six-year-old's drawing of a *wajang* scene—a battle between a god and a cultural hero (the shadow plays often show two characters in opposition to each other).[12] This drawing shows awareness of fine detail and of style of expression.

Figure 2-9, by a five-year-old, seems to us more like schematic drawings of children in other cultures, but there is no organization on a base line such as might be made by children learning to put symbols of writing on a line. There is evidence of early perceptual training in learning complex visual detail. Belo says of their visual training, ". . . the children quite early learn to distinguish the finely drawn and delicately noble heroes from the large-mouthed, threatening demon figures and the more robust, crude-featured outlines of the comics."[13]

*Figures 2-7, 2-8, and 2-9 reprinted from *Childhood in Contemporary Cultures,* ed. Margaret Mead and Martha Wolfenstein, by permission of The University of Chicago Press. Copyright 1955 by The University of Chicago. Copyright The University of Chicago 1955. All rights reserved. Copyright 1955 under the International Copyright Union.

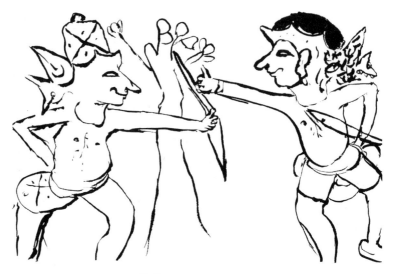

FIGURE 2–8. THE GOD KRESNA FIGHTING WITH THE HERO SALJA*
BY I LANOES, AGE SIX

FIGURE 2–9. A COW LYING DOWN, A MAN, A BIRD, AND WAJANG*
BY I DAPET, AGE FIVE

This study of the drawings of Balinese children showed that the older children were more closely bound by the cultural symbolism than were the younger. Younger children made symbols of realism mixed with adult culture symbols. One scene by a small boy depicts a *wajang* figure, in all his regalia, driving a motor car and being stopped by another demon. Belo found only two children who did not draw in the cultural stereotypes. Both children were deviant in other kinds of behavior as well.

LEARNING ART IN WESTERN CULTURE

The main factor in Balinese culture is the integration of art forms with daily life. Children are exposed to rituals from infancy. Continual perceptual training in the symbols they will use in their own work prepare them for creative activity. Work in art is of high value in the culture.

By contrast, basic value conflicts in American society make it difficult for many children to shift values between home and school. The concept of the artist as an uncommon man, the fact that few can get ahead commercially in the fine arts, the belief that it takes too long to do things skillfully by hand in a machine age—all these factors contribute to the separation of the arts from living in Western society. If such ideas are accepted by adults in the home, a child is not likely to see any connection between an "art class" and his daily life. This attitude is very different from Balinese culture where every child has an artistic role to play.

It is a paradox that man is often least aware of the visual qualities of objects with which he is most familiar—things like dishes, chairs, stairways. In a primitive society he may have made—and designed and decorated—these things. In an industrial society he uses many objects he has not made, and when he is consciously aware of them it is their "uses" that he sees, more than their "art." If he has worked to produce them, his part may have been so small that he has experienced no personal satisfaction in accomplishment.

The elementary teacher in Western culture, who is introducing art activities to children, has many dimensions to consider. One of them is this tendency to be unaware of the art we use all the time,

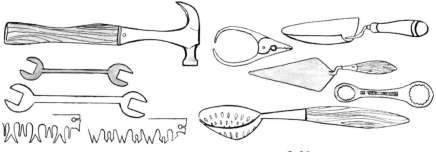

FIGURE 2–10. ART FORMS ALL AROUND US

another, to have basic values that hinder our enjoyment and recognition of art.

In the next chapters we will deal with differences among children in art behavior. This is a psychological study, but the environment in which the individual grows should be considered as we go along. A child, as an individual, develops within a group situation. His culture plays an important part in developing his individuality. His unique response to art will, in part, be influenced by his particular cultural experience.

SUMMARY

Every culture has some form of art. Standards of quality vary from one society to another. The major functions of art are: (1) to maintain the concepts of reality of the culture through ritualistic and religious symbolism, (2) to maintain the organization and roles within the culture through communicating status in clothing, architecture, and ornamentation, and (3) to enhance the appearance of the artifacts of the culture.

Not every culture separates the fine from the applied arts. There is a tendency among industrialized countries to separate the aesthetic from the useful quality of objects. Although the quality of much production is being improved, the general public tends to neglect the aesthetic quality of manufactured goods, even when they are well designed. Fashion rather than aesthetic quality appears to be the basis for judgment.

The taste of an individual develops within him and is affected by the attitudes and values of his own group. The teacher, among other people, is a taste-maker. He is either reinforcing children's preconceived likes and dislikes or encouraging them to question and evaluate their own decisions.

Learning about art varies among cultures. To the Balinese, art is at the very center of existence. Everyone has an artistic role. All the art forms are integrated with one another. Children are encouraged and rewarded for artistic achievement. In Western culture there may be strong discrepancies between the values of art that a child might learn at home and the values a teacher may be encouraging in school.

REFERENCES

1. Ralph L. Beals and Harry Hoijer, *An Introduction to Anthropology* (New York: The Macmillan Company, 1953), p. 538.

2. Melville Herskovits, *Cultural Anthropology* (New York: Alfred A. Knopf, Inc., 1955), p. 235. Reprinted by permission.

3. E. Adamson Hoebel, *Man in the Primitive World* (New York: McGraw-Hill Book Company, Inc., 1949), p. 161. Reprinted by permission.

4. Clyde Kluckhohn and Dorothea Leighton, *The Navaho* (Cambridge: Harvard University Press, 1956), p. 151.

5. John W. M. Whiting, *Becoming a Kwoma* (New Haven: Yale University Press, 1941), pp. 215–216.

6. Irwin Edman, *Arts and the Man* (New York: W. W. Norton and Company, Inc., 1939), pp. 42–43.

7. Russell Lynes, *The Tastemakers* (New York: Harper & Brothers, 1954), pp. 310–333.

8. Max Lerner, *America as a Civilization* (New York: Simon and Schuster, 1957), p. 646. Reprinted by permission.

9. Margaret Mead, "Children and Ritual in Bali," in *Childhood in Contemporary Cultures,* ed. Margaret Mead and Martha Wolfenstein (Chicago: University of Chicago Press, 1955), pp. 47–48.

10. Jane Belo, "Balinese Children's Drawing," in *Childhood in Contemporary Cultures,* ed. Margaret Mead and Martha Wolfenstein (Chicago: University of Chicago Press, 1955), pp. 52–69.

11. *Ibid.,* p. 54.

12. *Ibid.,* pp. 68–69.

13. *Ibid.,* p. 56. Reprinted by permission

3

Children's Individual Differences in Art

Art educators and psychologists have long tried to explain children's art. At different times teachers have accepted particular theories as being "true" and have taught accordingly. Some of these theories resulted from teachers' long experience with children in art. Others, particularly those developed in Europe, were derived from analyses of large numbers of children's drawings, without consideration of environment or past experience. Other observers recorded the development of children, singly or in small groups, over long periods of time and from their findings attempted to generalize about all children. Most of these studies were made in an attempt to find an age-based pattern of growth which the observers believed to exist.[1,2]

Recent research in psychology and anthropology indicates that we must consider many factors to understand the complex process of a child as he responds to his environment and expresses his response in a drawing or painting.* As early as 1936, Anastasi and Foley analyzed the cultural influence on children's art behav-

---

* The author is indebted to Jerome S. Bruner, "Personality Dynamics and the Process of Perceiving" in *Perception: An Approach to Personality,* edited by Blake and Ramsey, used by permission of The Ronald Press Company, for some of the ideas expressed in the following pages.

ior and found that different environments produced different types of art in children of the same age—differences in the amount of detail, subjects, colors, complexity of organization, and the quality of the drawings.[3] Although much further research has been done, it is surprising how little of it has been used in the formulation of new art education theories. The conflicts among existing theories are impressive.

The need for a more inclusive theory of children's art has been shown by an advanced study of psychology and cultural anthropology, as related to the art process. From this study, the author has developed the "perception-delineation" theory, based on an understanding of the nature of children's perceptions, of the way they organize and use information, and the ways in which they communicate their ideas.[4] Specifically "perception-delineation" (P-D) is a broad term used to identify the process in which a child or an adult (I) is prepared to perceive his visual world, (II) is affected by his psychological environment, (III) organizes the information he receives, and (IV) creates or borrows symbols to communicate his responses. The act of producing the symbols is the delineation.

The four points are not separate behaviors within the child, but rather "points" on which to focus our attention. A child who is drawing a puppy is not first "perceiving," then "delineating." He is instead *perceiving-delineating*, that is, performing a complex action involving what he has learned in the past, how he feels, and how he is organizing what he sees. The teacher can better understand the art behavior of children in his class by recognizing that individuals differ in each of the four points.

PERCEPTION AS INFORMATION-HANDLING

We all classify information when we look at anything. The basic processes appear to be common to all people. This action of information-handling takes place at Point III of the P-D process. Because it helps explain the common perceiving process, we will discuss it before we discuss individual differences at Point I.

Perceiving involves handling much more visual information than an individual can think about at any one time. This factor has led researchers to use the concept of "precognitive" sorting processes in perception. Every time we deal with even the simplest visual object we use only part of the information that is reflected on the retina. Pick up a pencil from your desk and put it out of sight. To pick it up you had to look at it. You may have noticed the color and whether it was long or short. But did you consciously notice the color of the printing, the light and shadow made by the shape of the pencil, the color of the metal case for the eraser? Was it a round pencil or six-sided? Unless you were prepared to look for these details, as you might be if you were trying to tell the difference between your pencil and another's, you probably did not consciously think of all the visual details of the pencil. But that information was reflected on the retinas of your eyes. What you responded to cognitively (that is, with awareness) was sorted out *precognitively* (that is, by a process not on a conscious level).

Attneave has introduced some of the concepts of information theory into an analysis of the perceptual process. He deals with perception as an *information-handling process*. Much more visual information is available than we use. Attneave refers to Polyak's estimate that the retina contains not less than 4 million cones, saying, "At any given instant each of these cones may be in either of two states: firing or not firing." [5] The possible kinds of different configurations of visual information that the eyes can handle would reach $2^{4,000,000}$. Attneave has identified three major processes with which we sort out, reject or use, and classify all this information.

1. WE CLASSIFY SIMILAR THINGS AS UNITS. We do not respond cognitively to all the leaves of a tree or to all the blades in a plot of grass. We deal with green trees and grass unless we purposefully look for small details and variations.

2. WE CLASSIFY THE RANDOM BY AVERAGES. When we drive in fast-moving traffic, we do not have time to recognize cognitively each kind of car we pass even though our eyes may be receiving enough visual information for us to do so. We have to average out the visual qualities of all the cars in terms of their movements in relation to our own car. We select and use those averages of movement and direction that are necessary to us in the act of driving, and we constantly change our behavior on the basis of these averages.

3. Finally, WE CLASSIFY ACCORDING TO WHOLES OR COMPLE-
TIONS. If we see part of a face we tend to envisage the rest of the
face; we see part of a circle as belonging to the whole circle.

Arnheim proposes that we see in wholes most of the time,
noting only as much detail as is necessary or as our learning and
experience have prepared us to see.[6] We may see something moving
at a distance and first classify it as a small animal; getting closer
we see enough detail to know whether it is a dog or not. Looking
longer we get enough visual cues to see what kind of a dog it is
and, finally, whether it is our dog. Certain visual cues are enough
to help us decide whether it is ours or not without having to see
all the visual details. In other words, we do not use more visual
cues than necessary to decide how we should behave in terms of
the thing at which we are looking.

In addition to classifying wordlessly, we have another categorizing system—language—which varies from one culture to
another. If your language has only one category for blue and green,
you have a different task in categorizing and using the information
than if you have many words such as yellow-green, green, blue-
green, blue, and blue-violet, to describe this range of hues.[7]

ORGANIZATION OF THE
PERCEPTION-DELINEATION THEORY

Using the P-D theory, we may build an over-all structure
within which to think about differences among children or adults
as they respond to their environment and, in turn, communicate
their ideas in art. This structure consists of what is known about
the process. Within it we can identify the points in which individuals differ. Figure 3–1 shows the relationships between these points.
The research we will examine will help us see the differences among
people at each point in the process.

Point I is over-all *readiness,* the preparation of a person to respond visually to things. This built-in "screen," through which he
selects what he will observe, is made up of his experiences in his
culture and environment, his learning, his personality, and his
over-all growth, each of which we will study in detail.

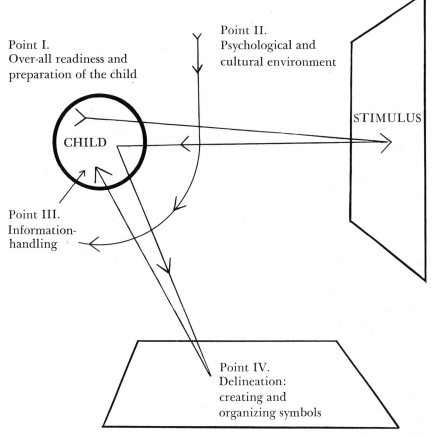

Point I.
Over-all readiness and
preparation of the child

Point II.
Psychological and
cultural environment

CHILD

STIMULUS

Point III.
Information-
handling

Point IV.
Delineation:
creating and
organizing symbols

FIGURE 3–1. PERCEPTION-DELINEATION THEORY

Point II is the *psychological environment* in which the person is perceiving. His feelings, such as anxiety, fear, failure or success, and pleasure, tend to inhibit or encourage his ability to perform perceptually. In Chapter 5 we will see how these environmental factors operate.

Point III refers to how the individual *handles the visual information* he receives. Our attempt to understand this complex process leads us to study the relationship of intelligence (as measured) to ability to handle detail, and the processes of categorizing the tremendous number of visual stimuli a person receives.

Point IV is the *invention or borrowing of symbols* to communicate the responses to one's environment. These responses may be made either to an immediate visual experience or to concepts that are remembered from cumulative visual experience. In other words, a person may delineate a specific person's portrait or, to express a more universal idea, a composite face that expresses his experience with a class of people (such as children, adolescents, peasants) made up of many past perceptions. Sometimes an artist will use a model but will add to his immediate perceptions all his past perceptions of this individual to give depth to the expression in the portrait.

A visual symbol or schema, as it is sometimes called, is any mark or form which has meaning. Railroad crossing signs, stars and stripes, red crosses are examples of well-known visual symbols. Artists and designers use many symbols, often less obvious, to communicate to us. The drawing at the beginning of this chapter, with many forms similar but each one different, symbolizes the likenesses and differences in children we are studying.

The "perception-delineation" theory is divided into "points" for identification of contributing factors. In some degree it is a sequence. Readiness, which includes the child's total preparation, comes before any given perceiving. But readiness also influences the way the child responds to his psychological environment at Point II and the way he organizes or handles this information at Point III. Finally readiness encourages or inhibits his ability to express artistically at Point IV. Each point is related to each other point in the theory.

Our purpose in this and the next chapters of Part One is to identify these points and to describe the individual differences children may have in each of them. We will be primarily concerned with what teachers must recognize in order to teach art more effectively.

READINESS: RESPONSE SETS

Readiness is a term used to describe our over-all preparation for performing a task. Part of total readiness to perceive or perform is the "response sets" we have learned—*the habitual tendencies to re-*

spond in certain ways to things in our environment. The culture we belong to, the ways we have learned to relate to space, our flexibility or rigidity in accepting new things, our past perceptual training, all contribute to our "sets" and readiness to perceive. The over-all physical development and condition of a person also contributes to his readiness.

All of the factors we will study under "readiness" are in operation at Point I of the P-D theory as seen in Figure 3–1. It is the *interaction* of all the variables in preparation, learned "response sets," and physical condition that equal an individual's readiness at any given time. This analysis of readiness applies to adults as well as to children and should help you to understand both your own and their behavior.

PRIOR LEARNING

What we know about a thing operates in some degree as a control over the way we can see it. This body of knowledge has built a response set. The way we perceive the qualities of an object, its usefulness, is affected by the "set" of prior training. Two research studies demonstrate this.

FUNCTIONAL FIXEDNESS. Two groups of students were given training, one group with an electrical switch, the other with a relay. A switch and a relay have practically the same function (to make, break, or change the connections in an electrical circuit) although they look somewhat different. They are about the same size. In this training one group examined a *switch,* learned what it would do, and learned to recognize it as an object having a definite use. The other group did the same with the *relay.* After this initial training the students were tested individually with the two string problem—tying together two strings, hanging from the ceiling, too far apart to be reached at the same time. The purpose was not to see how they would solve the problem, but rather which of the two objects on the table, the switch or the relay, they would use. (The solution is to tie an object on one string and swing it like a pendulum so that both strings can be brought together.) Most of the students used as a weight the piece of equipment they *had not* learned about. If they knew a thing was a switch, it *was* a switch, not a weight. A third group, all engineering students who had used both kinds of equipment, were almost equally divided in their choice of switch or relay. After the test the students were asked why they had chosen one piece or the other. They gave many rationalizations, and some students were vehement about the correctness of their solutions.[8] This type of response set is called "functional fixedness."

In another experiment students were asked to match the colors of cut-out shapes with colors on a color wheel. The subjects watched as the shapes were cut out of the *same sheet of orange paper*. When presented with the paper figure of a banana and then asked to turn away and select the matching color on the wheel, the students tended to choose the yellowish hues. With other objects, including figures of a carrot and a tomato, they selected a color on the wheel near the color of the real object as learned from past experience—even though the task was to match the exact color of the shape which they had seen cut from the same orange paper. In this case the immediate prior learning (that all the paper shapes were the same color) was not as cogent as was the lifelong learning about the objects.[9]

The two studies indicate that, when prior learnings conflict, the stronger habitual learning tends to prevail. With the switch and the relay, all the students had the same visual image of the two instruments reflected in the retinas of their eyes. Point I of the P-D process was in operation in their choice of qualities to respond to. Their preparation for the task was different. Knowledge of the mechanical parts identified (and limited) the uses students could see in one object. Size and weight (qualities needed to construct a pendulum) were easier to identify with the object that was unfamiliar, whose specific qualities and functions were less known.

In the second experiment the well-known shapes of familiar objects appeared to be the most important factor in identifying them, even when the color was the visual quality to be matched. Point III was in operation when the students grouped the visual information into the categories they knew best.

As teachers, we can recognize several major implications from these experiments: (1) children handle differently the visual information they receive in the classroom, (2) since these differences appear to be in large part learned, more adequate means of handling visual information can be taught, and (3) teachers can prepare children for more complex visual tasks by helping them to understand the nature of new things in terms of what they already know.

If a teacher should ask children to respond through art to an object that was new to them, they might respond like those trained to use the switch responded to the relay. They might ignore many of its properties. If they had explored the functions of the object, learned a great deal about it, they would tend to be prepared to look for more details in it. Also, if they learn to look for many possible uses of things, they will not be so likely to experience functional fixedness (being limited to the uses one has learned).

To make an African mask more meaningful to children, so they can respond more fully to its visual qualities, the teacher could read aloud the story of symbolic meaning behind the mask, its functions in the lives of the people who made it—its part in tribal ritualistic life. The class could learn how it was made, the tools used, and the role of the artist who made it. To understand the structure and possible forms of masks they should view it in many lights to see its contours and design, the textures and colors. All of these understandings increase the children's preparation for observing the object. *This is an example of reciprocal action between cognitive understanding and visual perception.* Knowing the nature of the mask increases the number of things one will look for. Being able to look at the mask in terms of its visual qualities enriches the concepts the children are developing about African masks. To give them less restricted learning about the mask, they could be encouraged to improvise on it by making masks of their own. More advanced children might like to design masks for our own culture or for another group of people they are learning about.

Another learned habit is assuming that a certain pattern of lines means a certain shape. At the Hanover Institute there is a wall with three peepholes. People who look through the holes see cubes, and all the cubes look alike. Yet when they go around to the back of the wall they see that they have been looking at (1) a wire cube-shape, (2) a drawing of a cube on a board, and (3) a construction of wires and strings that does not resemble a cube from any viewpoint except that of the peephole.[10] The revelation that their perceptions are not always adequate is disturbing to some of these observers; they have always depended on their perceptions to tell them how to respond or to behave, and here they discover that their perceptions can be unreliable.

Our learned habits of perception are necessary to us in order to deal efficiently with what we see, but they do not tell us the exact nature of our environment. The important concept for teachers to understand is that children, depending on their background of experience, develop different cues for interpreting their environment.

COGNITIVE AND VISUAL LEARNING

Try to imagine a child who lives in an Arctic region and has never seen a tree. His teacher has told him about the jungle. Books have shown him pictures of tropical trees and told him their uses. He has a concept of a tree. This he has learned by a cognitive (conscious thinking) process. His concept of trees is different from that of a child who has experienced trees as something to climb and to build tree houses in. A third child, who has been encouraged to develop an awareness of the visual qualities of trees, their forms, the effects of light and shade on color, and the way they change shape in the wind, will have still another kind of preparation for seeing. Each of these children, introduced to the idea of tropical trees, will utilize his individual past experience as he imagines what the tree is like. These same factors will function in his responses to trees in his own environment. The child who has had all three types

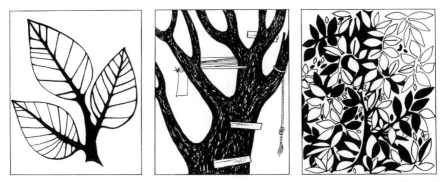

FIGURE 3–2. THREE CONCEPTS OF "TREES"

of training—cognitive, tactile, and visual—has the greatest potential for responding.

There is a tendency for us to identify things by their functions rather than by their visual qualities. For example, a child learns the *thinglike* quality of the ball—its functions, such as rolling and bouncing. Adults teach him about balls through manipulation—learning to roll, catch, and bounce a ball. Rarely are the visual qualities of a ball in light and space introduced to him; nor is he encouraged to respond to a ball visually except for simple recognition of size and color and possible decoration. For this reason he tends to learn to see the ball as being the same size twenty feet away as it is in his hand, the same color in bright light as in shade. Similarly, if he has a building block it does not change in shape or appearance for him when he sees it to the left or right, or above or below his line of vision. These tendencies to depend on what is known are called *constancies*.[11] The constancies are needed to make the cognitive nature of things clear. Man needs to *know* what a thing *is,* regardless of its distance or angle from us. But use of the constancies alone obscures his seeing the *visual* qualities of things. The perceptual constancies are:

1. BRIGHTNESS AND COLOR CONSTANCY—seeing objects as the same color and the same brightness, regardless of the particular color of light or shade they are seen in at a given time. Observe carefully the color you actually see when you place the same brightly colored object in direct sun or in shade. You will find that the light or color in the surrounding area will change the appearance of colored objects. Most of us operate visually without taking this change into consideration. A photographer knows how important a light meter is to find out just how much brightness or light is reflected from an object.

2. SIZE CONSTANCY—seeing objects as the same size or as compromised size rather than as the actual comparative size, depending on the distance between the object and the viewer. When an artist holds up a pencil with his arm outstretched, he is helping himself to overcome what he knows about size relationships by measuring the relationship between something close and something far away, as it appears visually. Try this method of the artist. Stand

at the corner of a building and, holding a pencil vertically, measure the difference in height of the nearest and farthest windows of the same actual size and on the same floor. Although you have been aware that the visual size gets smaller as an object recedes, you may be surprised by how *much* smaller it becomes.

Hilgard indicates that there are three ways we can see perspective: (a) ". . . according to the geometry of perspective, seeing it as smaller the farther away it is. . . . The retinal projection of an object at 20 feet is half the retinal projection at 10 feet"; (b) by the size we know the object to be; (c) by a compromise between what we know and what we see.[12] Most people see distance by some degree of compromise. Teachers have found people who apparently have not considered perspective at all and who appear most dependent on knowledge. Arnheim describes the reaction of a young woman who hid her face in terror the first time she saw that lines converge in space.[13] The author has had drawing students who were quite upset when they learned that they were responding so inadequately to what they saw. Suddenly to see the visual world in perspective when it has always appeared flat is quite a change for some people.

3. SHAPE CONSTANCY—a tendency to see things the same shape regardless of the angle from which they are viewed. For example, those windows you just looked at are all rectangles, and even though you discovered a difference in visual size you may not have recognized a difference in shape. Look again. When you are parallel to the building and the windows right in front of you are at eye level, they are rectangular. As you walk toward one corner they gradually become more trapezoidal and just before you go around the corner they become straight lines. Many of us have not been trained to take these changes into consideration. Some art students and many children draw all windows as rectangles, even when they show two sides of a house in a drawing.

Try another visual experiment. Take a round bottle or glass with a large enough top to see the circle clearly. Hold it with the top above your eye level and gradually lower it. What happens to the circle? Is it always a circle? If you do not have a suitable object, make a circle of your thumb and forefinger and watch it

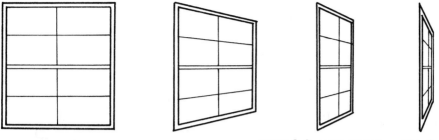

FIGURE 3–3. WHAT SHAPE IS A WINDOW?

change shape as you lower it below your eye level. Study a transparent tube. At any given position are the "circles" at top and bottom identical in shape? Can one be an ellipse and, at the same time, the other be a line? The two circles become the same shape only when the center of the tube is nearest your eye level—half of it above the horizon line and half below it.

Children do not make the same compromises in size or space relations that trained adults do. X-ray drawing, showing the inside and outside of objects, and unusual size relationships often found in children's drawings may be caused by differences between children and adults in the way they adjust *what they see* to *what they know.* Wide individual differences among both children and adults are found because the learning factor is always present; we do not all learn the same things in the same way and to the same degree.

Experiences, such as seeing the way colors change in bright light and shadow, observing things grow "smaller" with distance, watching the way objects change their perceived shapes in space, will help children to develop a keener responsiveness to their world. Encouraging children to explore their visual world is better than introducing them to formal perspective systems before they have learned to *see* perspectively. A child who has developed awareness of forms in space is prepared to learn some of the systems for symbolizing space, such as one-point and two-point perspective. Differences in children do not permit us to say at what age this learning should begin. But any teacher who has found that a child is ready should be able to teach him perspective. We will deal with some of the elements of perspective in a later chapter so that you can help those children who want help.

ORIENTATION TO SPACE

It has been recognized for some time that people differ in their orientation to space. Lowenfeld has described "visual" and "haptic" people as having certain inborn tendencies. He defines the extreme haptic as a person who is ". . . normal-sighted and uses his eyes only when compelled to do so; otherwise he reacts as would a blind person who is entirely dependent upon touch and kinesthesis." A visually-minded person he defines as one who ". . . is entirely lost in the dark and depends completely on his visual experiences of the outside world." [14] Lowenfeld feels that individuals tend to group toward the extremes in distribution of these traits. However, the process of space orientation is much more complicated than just the use of touch versus the use of vision. Recent research indicates that other important influences on space orientation can be found. It must be recognized that Lowenfeld has made a major contribution to thinking in art education but that the haptic-visual concept cannot account for all the variations among people in perceptual orientation behavior.

Considerable research was done for the Air Force on the problem of how people orient themselves to space. Information was needed because pilots in training were often found to be deficient in their ability to bring themselves to a true upright position in the air. The tests were devised to determine whether individuals used postural cues to right themselves or were more dependent on what they saw. "Field" as used here refers to the immediate visual environment.

> ORIENTATION TO SPACE. The subjects were seated in a chair that could be tilted by the use of levers to the left or right. The chair was in a small room that could also be tilted to the left or right, either with the chair or in the opposite direction, and to different degrees. Both chair and room could be manipulated by the subject or the experimenter. Sitting in the chair in a normal position the subjects were blindfolded, then moved to a position where neither the field nor the chair was at the true upright. Then, after removing the blindfold, they were given the task of righting themselves.
> Some of the people who used their bodily feelings of up-

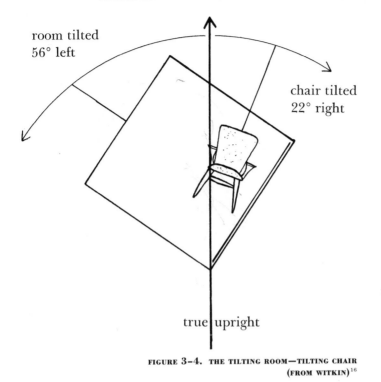

room tilted
56° left

chair tilted
22° right

true upright

FIGURE 3-4. THE TILTING ROOM—TILTING CHAIR
(FROM WITKIN)[16]

rightness were able to right themselves regardless of the slant of the room. They could recognize that the room was not upright, separate themselves from the field—the room around them—and achieve the true upright. At the other extreme were people who would align the chair according to the tilt of the room, sometimes even pulling themselves through the true upright to achieve the alignment. A large majority made a compromise between the cues from the field and the cues of their bodies and said they were right side up when they were at a point between the field and the true upright. People who depend on cues from their bodies are said to be "posturally oriented." Those who depend on cues from the field are "visually oriented." [15]

A cue is a stimulus that gives us information as to how to respond. When we are hungry we get feeling cues that it is time to eat. With our eyes we receive cues from our environment. The kind of information we get depends on which kinds of receptors (senses) we are using. Usually we are using more than one set of receptors. When hungry we usually start looking for something to eat. If we are in a kitchen, we have three sets of receptors working, giving us hunger cues, visual cues, and olfactory cues. If we *hear* someone working in the kitchen as well, even more cues are available to us. In the study of space orientation, researchers are finding that people tend to differ in which sets of receptors they use to get cues about their uprightness and their relation to space.

CHILDREN'S SPACE ORIENTATION. Witkin used the same tests in a study with children, ages eight to seventeen. Although he found wide variation in children at these ages, he found a tendency for the group as a whole to be more visually oriented in their younger years and to become more posturally oriented as they grew older. Averaging the responses of the boys and girls separately, Witkin found significant sex differences appearing by age fifteen. At that age the boys became more posturally oriented and the girls more visually oriented. In each group there were wide differences.[16] Also, he found that even the most visually-oriented people were able to use postural cues very successfully when blindfolded.[17]

Harriet Linton retested much of Witkin's work and found similar results. She further tested the relationship between the ability to use bodily cues and the ability to separate figure from ground in a complex visual task. The embedded figure test surrounds the drawing of an object (the figure) with a number of lines or colors (the ground) that tend to hide the form of the object. She found a strong tendency for posturally-oriented people to find the embedded figure much faster than people who depended on the field.[18]

CHILD-REARING PRACTICE AND SPACE ORIENTATION. Witkin, curious about why people learn different ways of orienting themselves, has begun research that relates child-rearing practice to space orientation. He studied a group of ten-year-old boys. They were given the battery of space orientation tests. Then interviewers, who did not know the boys' test scores, interviewed their mothers. The mothers were evaluated in terms of whether they were "growth-constricting" or "growth-fostering." Those mothers who appeared more fearful for their sons, who restricted their range of activities, and who did more for them than is usual were identified as "growth-constricting." Those mothers who were "growth-fostering" were not especially protective. It was found that those boys whose mothers gave them more freedom were able to separate themselves more from the field and were able to use postural cues in orienting themselves to space. Those whose mothers restricted their growth were more dependent on the field.[19]

INFLUENCE OF AUTHORITIES. Linton identified another factor in perception: the influence of authority figures on people's perceptual skills. Subjects in a darkened room were asked to estimate the distance a moving light traveled. After several trials an average was made of their estimates. Before the second set of trials was made an authority figure (in this case, one recognized to know more about psychology than the subjects) gave his estimate of the distance the light moved. His estimate to each subject was 5 inches longer than that subject's average in the first trials. Most subjects changed their estimates to be like that of the authority figure. Only thirteen per cent of the subjects were uninfluenced by the authority figure and performed in the second set of trials as they had in the first. These same subjects were also most successful in separating figure from ground, and in using postural cues.[20]

This study indicates that ability to resist the visual field is related to ability to resist authority figures as well. It also supports the hypothesis that people's space-orientation tendencies are related to their approach to their environment and experience as a whole. Space-orientation tendencies appear to be in a large part learned and developed at an early age. The sex differences Witkin found at age fifteen may be due to the culturally defined dependency role for women.

IMPLICATIONS. The earlier haptic and visual concept of children needs to be revised to account for learning. If space-orienting tendencies are not largely genetic, then children can be trained to use both kinds of cues. A visually-oriented child can learn to use postural cues through experiences like dancing or taking a running position while blindfolded to encourage him to "feel" the position. These kinesthetic experiences can be used for motivation for drawing or painting.

Visually-oriented children often lack independence. Encouraging a child to make his own decisions and to evaluate his own work, and giving him confidence by helping him succeed will help the effectiveness of his learning postural cues. If both the teacher and the parents continue to support his dependence by making his decisions for him and giving him little free choice, the perceptual training alone will probably be quite ineffective.

The posturally-oriented child, who according to this research can use his bodily feelings as cues to his environment, can resist the field. Unlike the haptic or the totally nonseeing child, he can separate out figure from ground and handle more detail. Because he has these special abilities, he can probably be trained to become more observant of the field without becoming dependent upon it. Many children apparently learn to use both kinds of cues.

NOTE. The word *visual* has been used in two ways in the preceding discussion because the material was taken from two bodies of research. In the study of space orientation, *visual* was used to refer to the cues an individual took from his visual environment or field, as opposed to those cues he took from the receptors of his body, which were labeled *postural*. In the study of cognitive vs. visual perception, *visual concepts* were derived from form and surface elements of objects as seen in space and light, as opposed to *cognitive concepts* of objects derived from past learning.

We have suggested that people need all four kinds of ability in handling information to deal adequately with experience—cognitive understanding, awareness of visual details, use of both postural and visual receptors for getting information from the environment.

The habits of depending on one type of response or the other, or using both, operate at Point I of the P-D theory. They are part of the "screen" through which an individual views the world. Dependence on one or the other means that different kinds of information are available for organization at Point III.

RIGIDITY-FLEXIBILITY

Some people are very closely bound to their past experience and rarely change the response sets they have learned. These people are called "rigid." It is difficult for them to respond adequately in new situations, to solve problems in other than their habitual ways. They often are very intolerant of ambiguity. This means that they tend to reject situations where clear black and white decisions are not possible, or where they don't understand what is going on. Flexible people, by contrast, can move easily into new situations. They are not troubled if they cannot see the immediate solution to problems. They can deal with the gray world between black and white solutions to problems where many variables are involved.

Being rigid or flexible is not now considered to be an over-all factor in personality. Often a person will be flexible in some things and rigid in others, because of some past anxieties about them. But some people do tend to be more rigid or more flexible in their general approach to novelty and to problem-solving. These tendencies operate in perceptual tasks.

> PERCEPTUAL RIGIDITY. When wearing glasses with aniseikonic lenses (glasses that make objects appear tilted to the observer), people who were more rigid tended to take longer to see the tilt, and to see less tilt, than did people who were more flexible. Both types of people were then given a test with blocks with nonsense symbols on them. They were told to figure out what to do with the blocks and then to proceed to do it. Actually, there was no "right" solution. Flexible people were more willing to try solutions, while rigid people made few attempts and asked for many directions from the experimenter.[21]

In Chapter 6 on creativity, we will discuss flexibility-rigidity in detail. It operates at Point I of the P-D process when a person depends on his response sets and past experience, which can limit what he will look for, at Point III when he organizes the visual information he receives, and again at Point IV when he creates symbols to express the concepts he has derived from his visual experience.

Traits usually appear as closely related clusters of behaviors, or as parts of or contributors to other traits. Functional fixedness (limitation, by past training, of the possible uses of tools and materials) is a form of rigidity.

IMPLICATIONS FOR PRACTICE

Characteristics developed through previous training operate as response sets in the perception-delineation process. They are found at Point I in Figure 3–1. In some degree they are also in operation at all the points in the process. Keep in mind that it is not the *sum total of these factors* in a given personality, but the *interaction of these factors* that is in operation in the behavior of a child at any given time.

PRIOR LEARNING

If we assume that we all see the same things in the same way, perceptual training does not seem so important. The evidence that past learning prepares us to see *with bias* makes the great importance of perceptual training more apparent. When we consider how constantly we depend on visual cues to determine behavior, the visual act takes on far greater significance, not only in art education but in other forms of education.

Children can be encouraged to respond *both* cognitively and visually with more adequate use of cues in interpreting the nature of things. For example, if the subjects in the orange-paper test had had enough learning experience and opportunity to observe the nature of color and its subtle transitions, they might not have been so strongly influenced by what they "knew" about the color of the objects.

Research on the influence of authority figures on the way people see things indicates that pressure to conform, pressure to respond "correctly," as others respond, can influence the way children respond.[22] The role of the teacher in helping children increase the range of their perceptual awareness should be that of a catalyst, one who encourages exploration of ways to see rather than one who directs learning to see.

The functions and qualities of objects can be enriched if children learn how to perceive tools and materials in a flexible manner, rather than developing functional fixedness. Children who learn a "right" way to use crayons, such as using them like pencils and staying within the lines in color books, may have trouble using crayons in other ways. The child who has been introduced to crayons as a tool that can be used in many ways has a better chance to become flexible and inventive in their use. This does not mean that specific art skills should not be taught. When a pupil's eye-hand coordination and small muscle development as well as perceptual skills warrant it, a specific technique can be taught. But even in this case the pupil can learn that the method is one of several that are useful with a given medium. A case study and group studies will illustrate this.

A CASE STUDY. A serious art student was very inventive with water color and mixed media such as ink and tempera, crayon, water color and ink, but with oil paints he was rigid. He had had considerable training under master teachers in *the correct* way, *the correct* techniques for using oil paint. Try as he might he was unable, through his own efforts, to be as inventive in oil as in other media in which he had not had such training. It was only after considerable encouragement, including discussion of reasons for rigidity, that new, more flexible uses of oil paint were developed. He was easily discouraged, so he needed to be continually reminded of the strengths he did have. Each small breakthrough to new methods was rewarded by praise. At the end of the term both the instructor and the student felt that he had made enough progress and had enough understanding of the effects of prior training to work freely by himself. His was an example of functional fixedness, as we saw in the experiment with the switch and the relay.

A GROUP STUDY. In an art education class for elementary teachers, extremely varied responses were found to the task of making something with "junk" (clothespins, coat hangers, wire, yarn, buttons). A questionnaire about responses to the assignment was given at the end of the period. The key question was "Did you feel comfortable doing this?" Of the nineteen students, seven said they had been frustrated at first but gradually gained confidence and began to enjoy the process. Ten students said that they enjoyed the whole process and had no feelings of frustration. Two students reported that they disliked the process altogether.

Analysis of the background of the students indicated that

these two were the only ones in the class who had had traditional art training (learning *the* "right" techniques rather than exploring many possible techniques) with water color and oil painting. They reported in an interview that they found it very difficult to *see* any artistic use for junk. Their prior training, like that of the subjects with a switch and a relay, inhibited their use of familiar materials for a new purpose; in addition, they were unable to see unconventional materials as suitable for a conventional activity.

Interestingly, one of the students who reported that she enjoyed the junk construction very much had had a great deal of trouble working with traditional art materials. She reported that the junk was "real" to her and easier for her to make something out of. But paint was too remote from "real" things and she could not get ideas while using it.

The objective in encouraging teachers and children to use materials in an unaccustomed way, as in junk construction, is to

FIGURE 3–5. A REPRESENTATION OF THE UNITED NATIONS

FIGURE 3-6. THE DYNAMICS OF THE UNITED NATIONS

help them develop habits of exploration with tools and materials. The final object may not be a "work of art" but the experience can contribute to the over-all habits and attitudes needed by artistic and scientific people—in this case flexibility in "seeing" the possibilities of diverse objects.

AN ELEMENTARY CLASSROOM STUDY. One kind of prior learning children may have is that *picture-making means illustration.* Textbooks and story books are a main source of children's learning about pictures. The realism of the illustrations may account for the importance many children begin to give to realism in their drawings at about fourth grade.

A sixth grade teacher had a highly motivated study of the United Nations. The children actually held a meeting, having done considerable research on the key issues. Children took the parts of U.N. members. They became quite involved in their role-playing and the session became very intense as issues were argued, indicating that the children had become emotionally as well as intellectually involved in their study. In a culminating art experience the children drew pictures of the United Nations Building. Some were very handsome and bold representations, as in Figure 3–5, but one child (Figure 3–6) symbolized the dynamics of the United Nations by abstractly showing through color the dynamic forces of the different racial and political groups on each other. The latter painting represented the function of the organization rather than appearance of the building.

The effects of prior learning can be seen in both kinds of painting. The children who depended on realism to express their response may not have had encouragement to create abstract symbols. The child who was able to express his response independent of realism may have been limited in visual awareness.

COGNITIVE AND VISUAL LEARNING

Learning to look at objects in space as they move from area to area will give pupils better cues for identifying and responding to objects in terms of their surroundings. There is some indication that children often have better understanding of things in space when they draw the inside and outside of things than they do later when their cognitive learning tells them they cannot see inside and outside at the same time. The use of the base line for organizing objects in space has been considered a developmental pattern in art. This use usually appears in children during their first and second years of school, at the same time they are learning to organize letter and number symbols on a line. It does not seem surprising that they learn to put picture symbols on a line.

Children who are aware of the existence of the constancies—color, size, and shape—can reduce their limiting effects by learning to observe visually as well as cognitively.

ORIENTATION TO SPACE

Children in elementary school have already learned a pattern for orienting themselves to space. A part of the pattern is the degree of independence from the influence of the immediate environment (especially the visual environment). Some perceptual manifestations of independence are the abilities to separate out details, to find the figure in a ground, and to rely on bodily feelings in responding to the visual world.

Differences in space orientation influence the way children see relationships between things, the way they organize objects, and the degree to which a painting involves their own position as an observer or as a participant. The child's postural or visual orientation is related to his habitual means of responding. It is part of his readiness at Point I of the P-D theory. It influences whether he gives attention to cues from his environment or to cues from his own bodily response. We might say it is his means of getting visual information, which in turn influences the kind of visual information he will get.

The drawings in Figures 3–7 and 3–8 are both of the same event. Both children were involved in the same heavy rain and flood. They got different information from similar experiences, in part because they were using different means for obtaining the information. Figure 3–7 is an inventive symbolization of the visual impression of rain, rising water, and two children. Figure 3–8 is a powerful expression of the force of and perhaps the bodily reaction of fear the child felt about the same experience, as if he were in the middle of it experiencing the force of the waters.

If children have had many art experiences and are confident in using them, the teacher can encourage them to use a new means of getting ideas to express. The girl who drew Figure 3–7 could be encouraged to paint how she felt during the storm, and the boy who drew Figure 3–8 could be encouraged to draw what it looked like. Neither kind of response is better than the other, but children who can respond both ways have more understanding and capacity for interpreting their environment.

It is not wise to try to do too many things at one time. When a child is learning a new task or working with an unfamiliar material, help him to achieve success more easily by using his habitual cues. Then later when he is familiar with the materials he can be encouraged to learn to broaden his means of getting information.

Differences in past experience, specific kinds of personality patterns of rigidity or flexibility, and habits of space orientation

FIGURE 3-7. STORM AND FLOOD

all contribute to the individual differences of children in the classroom. There are many personality factors and traits that are
related to children's art that are not yet identified. There is increasing evidence that traits of independence and postural orientation
are often combined with flexibility. As more research is done in
personality and perception, we will be able to understand children's
art expression more fully.

If the teacher realizes that the children are not all starting
from the same point in developing their visual sensitivity, and if
he provides a variety of types of tasks and motivation, he will have
more success in developing perceptual capacities. Continued reward and encouragement for participating in the exciting adventure
of exploring our visual world is a vital contribution to the children's
progress.

FIGURE 3–8. STORM AND FLOOD

A CONTROVERSIAL QUESTION

The emphasis made on the need for perceptual training of children and students may cause some cries of "If you do this you will stifle creativity! Artists today do not just copy nature." This criticism usually comes from people who are not aware of the complexity of the visual process. Visual training increases the wealth of material the children have to work with. If visual training becomes rigid and authoritarian it may inhibit creative activity, but if it is used to motivate visual curiosity and exploration it should widen the range of creativity of students. Much more effect of light and color, of form and line will become available for children to use. They will go beyond *cognitive* categorizing and see many more details and significant relationships as they respond to their environment, both visually and cognitively.

Skill and sensitivity in visual observation are needed for many life activities not directly related to aesthetics. Guidance in making decisions is a major use of our visual information. It seems strange that we do so little training of children in this respect. One reason for this lag in education has been the long-sustained belief that individuals perceive the same things in exactly the same ways. The effect of training and learning in perception has been unnoticed to a large extent. In a scientific age observation is an essential activity. It is the individual scientist who makes the final observation from his instruments. It is he who selects the area upon which his instruments are focused. Part of the basis of his selection is his own personal perceptual experience—what he has learned to see and to look for.

Man is said to live half way between microcosmos and macrocosmos, the very small and the very large. We make new instruments to see great distances, but many of us have yet to explore with the instrument we all have—our own eyes. After children have learned the joys of seeing without mechanical instruments, they can find source material for their art under microscopes and colored lights.

Select three very familiar objects, and either in writing or speaking describe each as you usually deal with it—its cognitive value—and then see how much description you can give about its visual qualities. You may have to turn it upside down to get away from what you know about its usefulness and its "thinglike" quality.

SUMMARY

Perception-delineation is a theory that covers a child's readiness, the influence of his environment, his information-handling ability, and his creative expression in art.

Perception is a complex process of handling a multitude of visual bits of information or cues, so that a response to the information can be made.

Readiness includes physical development plus all the prior

training that determines habits of responding (response sets), including cognitive and visual learning, rigidity-flexibility and orientation to space.

Prior learning can restrict the functions a child can see in an object, if the teaching has taught him that one function is "right." Prior learning can also prepare a child to look for more detail in one object than in another.

People develop habits of depending on bodily cues or on cues from the visual field in orienting themselves to space. Habits are related to how people were reared as children—the more posturally-oriented and field-independent had fewer restrictions as small children. The habits are in large part learned. A majority of people can use both types of receptors, bodily and visual, to get cues to their uprightness.

Traits of rigidity or flexibility, usually operating in some but not all of a person's behaviors, influence the ways he will accept new things and deal with ambiguity.

Information-handling ability can be increased if children learn both cognitive and visual means of perceiving and learn both body and field cues in relating themselves to their environment.

Learning to use new tools and materials should be more an exploration of their possible uses, rather than an exact learning, to help prevent "functional fixedness" (being unable to use a thing except in the way one has learned it).

The perceptual constancies are necessary for cognitive perception. Children who are not aware of how much they are affected by the constancies may disregard visual qualities of objects in space. Training will help children to overcome the limitations of extreme dependency on constancies.

Children can be encouraged to learn about and accept new things by relating them to what they already know.

RELATED ACTIVITIES

Throughout the section on the constancies, experiments were suggested. If you have not done these, take time now to observe how color changes in light and shade. Observe how forms change, depending on the point from which you observe them.

Closing one eye, measure with a pencil at arm's length the size of windows or the near and far corners of a building. How much smaller is the far corner than the near? Observe a railroad track or a long road, noticing how the lines converge; the railroad ties become closer together and the neighboring buildings and telephone poles become increasingly smaller the farther away they are from you.

Begin a collection of interesting textures that you could use in your classroom. If you are taking a course in science for the elementary school, you will find many interesting samples there. Perishable things like sea vegetation can be preserved by being cast in wet plaster of Paris. Plastics are now available for preserving vegetable and animal life. Many inanimate objects have varied and interesting textures that do not need a preservative.

Try to spend time as you are walking between classes or on the way home looking at textures. Textures, affected by the light on them, are around us all the time. Many of them are very beautiful, but we rarely have time to look closely and respond to them. The picture in Figure 3–9 might be of a landscape. Actually, it was taken by a photographer pointing the camera toward his feet while standing among tide pools of an ocean ledge.

FIGURE 3–9. TEXTURES IN NATURE

REFERENCES

1. Florence Goodenough, "The Intellectual Factor in Children's Drawings" (doctoral dissertation, Stanford University, 1924).

2. Anne Anastasi and John P. Foley, Jr., *Differential Psychology: Individual and Group Differences in Behavior,* rev. ed. (New York: The Macmillan Company, 1949), pp. 851–855.

3. Anne Anastasi and John P. Foley, Jr., "An Analysis of Spontaneous Drawings by Children in Different Cultures," *Journal of Applied Psychology,* XX (1936), 689–726.

4. June King McFee, "Visual Arts: Psychological Implications of Individual Differences in the 'Perception-Delineation' Process" (doctoral dissertation, Stanford University, 1957).

5. Fred Attneave, "Some Informational Aspects of Visual Perception," *Psychological Review,* LXI (1954), 183.

6. Rudolph Arnheim, *Art and Visual Perception* (Berkeley: University of California Press, 1954), p. 130.

7. Benjamin Lee Whorf, *Four Articles on Metalinguistics* (Washington, D.C.: Department of State, Foreign Service Institute, 1950), p. 5.

8. Herbert G. Birch and Herbert S. Rabinowitz, "The Negative Effect of Previous Experience on Productive Thinking," *Journal of Experimental Psychology,* XLI (1951), 121–125.

9. J. S. Bruner, L. J. Postman, and J. Rodrigues, "Expectation and the Perception of Color," *American Journal of Psychology,* LXIV (1951), 216–227.

10. Merle Lawrence, *Studies in Human Behavior* (Princeton: Princeton University Press, 1949), pp. 67–69.

11. Ernest R. Hilgard, *Introduction to Psychology,* 2nd ed. (New York: Harcourt, Brace and Company, Inc., 1957), pp. 363–370.

12. *Ibid.,* p. 368.

13. Rudolph Arnheim, *Art and Visual Perception* (Berkeley: University of California Press, 1954), p. 131.

14. Viktor Lowenfeld, *Creative and Mental Growth,* 3rd ed. (New York: The Macmillan Company, 1957), pp. 262–263. Reprinted by permission of The Macmillan Company.

15. H. A. Witkin, H. B. Lewis, M. Hertzman, K. Machover, P. Bretnall Meissner, and S. Wapner, *Personality Through Perception: An Experimental and Clinical Study* (New York: Harper & Brothers, 1954), ch. 2–8.

16. *Ibid.,* p. 52.

17. *Ibid.,* pp. 120–152.

18. Harriet B. Linton, "Dependence on External Influence: Correlates in Perception, Attitudes, and Judgment," *Journal of Abnormal and Social Psychology,* LI, No. 3 (1955), 502–507.

19. Herman A. Witkin, "Perception of the Upright," *Scientific American*, CC (February 1959), 50–56.

20. Harriet B. Linton, "Autokinetic Judgments as a Measure of Influence," *Journal of Abnormal and Social Psychology*, XLIX (1954), 464–466.

21. Wesley C. Becker, "Perceptual Rigidity as Measured by Aniseikonic Lenses," *Journal of Abnormal and Social Psychology*, XLIX (1954), 419–422.

22. Harriet B. Linton, "Autokinetic Judgments as a Measure of Influence," *Journal of Abnormal and Social Psychology*, XLIX (1954), 464–466.

4

Individual Differences in Development in Art

Art is a language with which the child communicates his experience. His behavior in art is not a separate activity unrelated to all his other behavior. He uses his intellect, his perceptions, his creativity in order to organize what he is learning from his expanding activities. In order to understand more fully children's behavior in art, we must be aware of developments in the field of child psychology. As this field grows and as new research is completed, we should get new directives for our study of child growth in art.

We will consider some of the most important child growth studies that have particular implications for art education. In terms of the perception-delineation theory we will study how individual differences in rates of growth can influence children's overall *readiness* at Point I, their reaction to the *psychological and cultural environment* at Point II, their ability to *handle visual information* at Point III, and the relationships of motivations from the culture in their *creative work* at Point IV (see Figure 3–1, page 41).

71

GROWTH AND DEVELOPMENT

The study of child development has undergone major changes in the last ten years. Growth is now seen, not as something that happens in isolation, but as an interaction with the environment. Cross-cultural studies compare child-rearing practices and growth in different segments of our society and in quite different cultures. The purpose of these studies is to understand more about the influence of culture and training on children's patterns of growth.

A second major shift in research has been from efforts to find age-based patterns of growth (to ascertain what is "normal") to a study of individual variation in growth. Before this shift in emphasis was made, large numbers of children for each age would be studied to see how the average six- or ten-year-old would perform in many kinds of tasks. Tests were given to measure vocabulary, reasoning, computation, memory, eye-hand coordination, and other variables. Height, weight, and skeletal and muscle growth were measured. Often the concept "average" was interpreted to mean "best," and a child too far from average, especially *below* average, was considered to have a disadvantage that would stay with him (his rate of change was not expected to vary). Averages for large numbers of children obscured the changes in rate of growth for any one child. This method of study did not give information about the interrelatedness of all the factors of growth in any one child.

The longitudinal study was developed to overcome the limitations of research that recorded averages alone. The observers in a longitudinal study record growth patterns of many children over a long period of time. Although some of these studies began over thirty years ago, their findings are just now becoming available.

VARIATIONS IN GROWTH PATTERNS. The Berkeley Growth Research, at the University of California, was a study of children from birth through age twenty-one. Nancy Bayley, later director of Child Development at the National Institute of Mental Health, worked on the project throughout the years. Her summary of the findings is very important to the understanding of current thinking in child development.

In this study records were kept of forty children. I.Q. and physical development were measured consistently. After analyzing the patterns of change through these years, Bayley gives us these insights into the nature of development:

    1. Few children follow consistent growth patterns with each factor developing at its same rate throughout the child's development.

    2. Few children actually follow the age-based norms. A norm or average of height is found by adding all the heights for an age group and dividing by the number of children measured. Few of the children are actually at the norm. (Unless we know the deviation of the scores from the norm, we do not know whether the heights were clustered closely around the norm or whether many of the children had heights quite far from the norm.)

    3. To think of a child's development as the sum of intellectual, psychological, and physical growth is inadequate. Each of these is in part dependent on all the others. Each is developing at a different and often fluctuating rate.[1]

A child with high verbal skills but with slowly developing motor skills is a good example. A teacher who does not recognize differences in growth patterns and their influence on each other may misinterpret his behavior. If the child's writing ability develops slowly but he reacts well orally, an uninformed teacher might assume he just is not working at writing and may punish him for his lack of effort. The child, unable to understand his difficulty, may react by being rebellious, by switching to a task in which he is more sure of success, or by retreating from the situation—refusing to try at all.

To understand such problems we need as much information as possible about each child. *By acting without knowing, we may be increasing a child's problems rather than helping him overcome them.* On the basis of the Bayley report we need to remember that a pattern of growth for a child at age seven *may not be his pattern at age ten.*

This newer approach to child psychology has been called "organismic." This term, borrowed from biology, means that the parts of the whole organism are in a sense independent and at the same time interdependent. Although growth or function of any part can be measured by itself, it can never be considered as truly separable from the other parts. The activity of the whole organism is the interaction of parts and is thus dependent on each part's stage of development. To assess adequately a child's development, a teacher should consider all the individual and environmental factors that may have influenced him, as well as the varying rates of his physical and psychological growth.

INTELLIGENCE AND PERSONALITY DEVELOPMENT. Another longitudinal study by Sontag at the Fels Research Institute on Human Development at Antioch College was concerned with relationships between I.Q., personality development, and physical growth. One hundred and forty children from various socioeconomic levels were measured in their degree of dependency or independency, their need to achieve and enter competition, their I.Q., and their physical development.

Dependency-independency measurements of children came from interviews with parents and observation of the children. Questions like these were asked: "How much help does the child need in caring for himself?" "Does he dislike being left with other adults?" "How early did he dress himself?" "How far away from home is he allowed to go?" Observations of the children with their parents gave cues about the dependency of the child on his parents. His need to achieve and his competiveness with other children were observed in his activities with other children. Independence of his peers was observable in the degree to which the child was anxious to compete with other children, was self-reliant and not afraid of new situations.

These measurements were made every six months from age 2½ to 10. The rates of I.Q. change and physical development were measured in the same sequence. In analyzing the individual children's patterns of growth the following general tendencies were found:

1. Children's rate of intellectual development is not the same through childhood.

2. Deceleration in their rate of intellectual growth is often found during periods of stress and anxiety in the home when children tend to become more dependent.

3. Acceleration in intellectual growth is related to periods of more independence and need to achieve.[2]

This study supports the organismic concept of child development, with environmental factors being shown as related to changes in the rate of intellectual development. It further points out that a

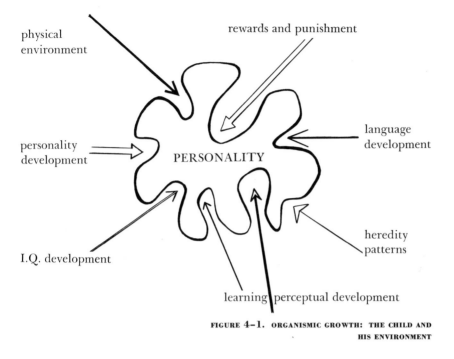

physical environment

rewards and punishment

language development

personality development

PERSONALITY

I.Q. development

heredity patterns

learning perceptual development

FIGURE 4–1. ORGANISMIC GROWTH: THE CHILD AND HIS ENVIRONMENT

consideration of a child, without awareness of the environment within which he is interacting, gives us an incomplete picture of his development.

A CASE STUDY. Joan, in the sixth grade, was considered by her teachers to be superior in art. An art consultant, seeing an exhibition of the class's work, judged Joan's work in design as far superior to the rest of the class. This group was very unusual—the I.Q. range was from 100 to 180, with a median of 140 (i.e., one-half the class had I.Q.'s of 140 or higher). Because Joan's outstanding art skill was an ability to organize abstract forms into an integrated design (see Figure 4–2), the consultant assumed that her intelligence rating was one of the highest. Investigation proved the assumption unfounded—the child had the lowest I.Q. score in the class.

A study of the anecdotal records (teachers' written evaluations of pupils' behavior) showed that several of them felt that Joan had abilities that the tests did not measure. For this reason, the

FIGURE 4–2. DESIGNS OF A SIXTH GRADE GIRL

school psychologist gave her the Children's Wechsler (an individual test in which the examiner speaks with and observes the performance of the child). The psychologist reported that Joan seemed at ease and sure of herself during some parts of the test and anxious during other parts. In the nonverbal half of the test she was highly capable in discriminating between essential and unessential detail (finding the missing parts to pictures). She was also capable in the perception of part-whole relationships (the subject is given the parts to three puzzles and is asked to put them together one at a time). Her highest score was in practical reasoning ability. Here she could make reasonable answers to rather general questions such as, "Why are clothes made of cloth?"

In those areas where her scores were high she had shown no anxiety. In other areas, arithmetic reasoning and digit span (remembering up to 9 digit numbers forwards and backwards) she gave several signs of anxiety—making many hesitant trials, looking to the experimenter for the right answers, and flushing of her face. In these areas her scores were much lower, bringing her average or total score down much more than the scores in the other areas might lead one to expect.

The anecdotal records indicated that the child showed these same anxieties in the classroom during arithmetic. A conference with the mother indicated that the parents felt the child should not be pushed, and that as long as she was doing well in art they were not concerned.

This evidence leads us to ask several questions. Was the I.Q. test an adequate measure of this child's ability? What might be causing the anxiety about arithmetic? Has encouraging the child in art above all other things meant that she has used this means of attaining success without trying in other areas? What effect does the high I.Q. range of the class have on this child? Some of these questions should be explored by a psychologist, but there are some things the teacher can do. He should not categorize this child according to her I.Q. scores alone when there is much evidence that anxiety and lack of earlier success may be influencing her performance. He can try to increase her interest and success in other subjects by integrating them with art. He could ask a mathematics specialist for simple geometry problems that could be related to this child's organizing ability in art. When she sees a real need for arithmetic in solving her geometry-art problems, it may have more meaning for her.

In terms of our study of child growth and development, this case shows how different factors may influence the development of other factors. There is some reason to believe that this child's art ability was developed to such a high level because it was her main avenue for achieving success—she had practiced and had been praised for it over and over. Her experiences in the other parts of the curriculum had been much less rewarding. We are fairly sure that individuals do not work up to their highest level if anxiety also is high. Since this child's anxiety was reported year after year in school, it appears to have been a strong influence on her behavior.

In terms of the P-D theory, a child's over-all development, which includes all the interacting variables of his individual growth pattern, is involved in his "readiness." The teacher needs to be on the lookout for those factors that may be slowing up the whole process. Where it is possible, the teacher can help a child become more secure and less anxious, by being patient when a child's pattern of motor skill development is slow or by finding tasks where success is possible.

PERCEPTUAL DEVELOPMENT

Perceptual growth is the increase in ability to use the visual information that is available, to organize and synthesize it so that we can respond. In Chapter 3 we discussed Attneave's theory of the intellectual-like process that he describes as taking place precognitively—meaning that we are not consciously aware of all the sorting we do. Some research has been made that indicates that children differ from adults in these organizing, synthesizing processes of handling visual information.

DIFFERENCES IN CHILDREN'S ORGANIZING ABILITY. Similarities and differences in perceptual organization were studied with children ages five to eight. Girls and boys in each age group were divided into "bright" or "backward" on the basis of group intelligence tests and school success. In the first test on perceptual organization the children were asked to sort twenty-four cards that were all the same rectangular shape and the same color with four variations in height and width. A perfect score would mean division of the twenty-four cards into four piles of six each. All of the bright eight-year-old children could do this immediately. Only 46 per cent of the bright five-year-old boys and 37.5 per cent of the bright five-year-old girls made a perfect score. The scores of the backward children were lower at every age than those of the bright children, except for the backward eight-year-old girls who also made a perfect score. The number of children used in this test is too small to generalize about specific age level or mental age development in terms of perception, but it does suggest a pattern of greater organizing ability with increasing age and mental ability.

A second test required the children to find a pattern of dots placed among other small figures. Three such designs were shown the child; then he was given, one at a time, line drawings that followed the patterns of the dots in the three designs. His task was to find which design each line drawing came from. Of the eight-year-olds, 87.5 per cent of the bright boys and 66.6 per cent of the bright girls identified the three correct designs, but only 37.5 per cent of the backward boys and 33.3 per cent of the backward girls succeeded. At age five, differences between the groups were not apparent.[3]

This study suggests that in ability to organize visual perceptions and separate out details older, brighter children do better than younger and more backward children. It is hoped that more specific research into the relationship of different factors of intelligence and different perceptual tasks will be developed.

Longitudinal studies of one or two children have supported this view—that generally children see wholes before parts; but wide differences in ability to handle visual information probably are apparent at any age.

RORSCHACH INKBLOTS AS A STIMULUS. The test was not used in this case to study the child's personality, but rather his perceptual behavior in the kinds of detail he gave attention to. To study the changes that might come through age, a more homogeneous group of children was used. Fifty children of superior intelligence of upper middle-class status were observed each six months from ages two through six, and annually from ages six through ten.

The Rorschach test consists of a set of cards, each with a design of an equilibrated inkblot. The test is given to children individually. Records are kept of their responses to questions, "What is this a picture of?" or "What do you see here?" In the standardization of the test are categories for identifying "whole" responses, "large detail" responses, "small," and "tiny" responses. In this study only those responses that indicated whether a child was making a whole, a large detail, a small or a tiny response was recorded. The following results were found:

1. The same inkblot presented to the same child evokes different responses at different age levels.

2. Children are influenced most by the whole blot. (Fifty per cent or more of all the children's responses were to the whole blot except at age nine.)

3. At age nine the children showed an increase in interest in the large details.

4. Responses to small details started at 4 per cent with the younger children and had increased to only 15 per cent with the oldest children.

5. With increase in age, a slight trend toward identification of the parts was seen.

6. With increase in age, a stronger trend toward identification of the parts in terms of color and form was seen.[4]

In comparison with normal adults in Western culture, the children's responses were much more often based on the whole design. Adults usually give from 25 to 30 per cent whole answers.[5]

There are two very important things for teachers to remember from this study: (1) children generally respond to the whole of a stimulus, but develop more ability to deal with the larger parts in middle childhood; (2) even at age five some of these children were giving attention to the smaller details—indicating wide individual differences in ability at any age. Knowing that some of the factors in intelligence are probably related to abilities in perception, we would expect to find a wider range of individual differences in most classrooms than was found among these higher-I.Q. children.

LEARNING OF THE PERCEPTUAL CONSTANCIES. The achievement of perfect constancy means the seeing of size, shape, and color the way the observer knows they are, regardless of distance, viewing angle, or kind of light. If we did not develop the constancies, we would be unable to compensate cognitively for visual changes. We would be like the small child who saw a train a long distance away and wanted the toy train. This child had not learned to react to visual cues in terms of distance; he assumed that the train was in actuality the size it appeared to be in the distance.

Studies of children's development of the constancies show that in our culture, size constancy develops first, with the average ten-year-old achieving ability like that of the average adult. Shape and color constancy develop much more slowly. The average ten-year-old has achieved only 50 per cent of an average adult's capacity.[6] The studies have not considered the effects of perceptual training. We do know that some people trained to see objects as they are in space do not lose their ability to compensate for changes in distance, shape, and color in making perceptual decisions.

Learning to handle information both ways, through what we know of it and through careful analysis of the visual information, gives us more accuracy in our observations. Further, it gives us the capacity to achieve a much richer aesthetic experience, because we get so much information from our environment. In working with children we should use care not to force children to try to learn one way over the other, but should call attention to both the cognitive and visual aspects of things they are observing in many of their activities in science, social studies, and art. In this way they can learn both ways of handling information as they become ready.

The value of learning to handle information both ways is shown in the following situation. One of the large aircraft manufacturers found it necessary to train artists to work with engineers. Artists could conceptualize forms and shapes in space in relation to each other better than some engineers could. The kind of problem that led to the need for artists was shown when a plane design reached the mockup stage (a full-scale model). The crawl-through passage from one compartment to another was too small for a man to move enough to propel himself forward. To overcome such expensive mistakes the artists were trained to draw the objects and assemblies in three dimensions from the blueprints. Their ability to conceptualize objects in three dimensions and in space pointed up limitations in the designs.

PERCEPTUAL DEVELOPMENT IN RESPONSE TO ART. John French, an art educator, constructed a test consisting of 13 pairs of drawings, the same in subject and in organization but markedly different in the amount of detail. The subjects' task was to select which of the two drawings in each pair they preferred. In the first test the subjects were 88 elementary teachers and 142 first grade children. Most of the teachers (89 per cent) preferred the complex pictures. Most of the children (83 per cent) preferred the simple.[7] Using his figures, a comparison was made of the percentages of teachers and of children who preferred four or more pairs opposite to the trend of their group (that is, four simple for the teachers and four complex for the children). Of the children, 27.4 per cent fell within this group, but only 18 per cent of the teachers, indicating wider ranges of individual differences among the children. Also the extremes were greater for the teachers, 62.5 per cent preferring the complex in every case. Only 30.3 per cent of the children chose the simple drawings exclusively.[8]

A second test, given to 554 children from low kindergarten to high fifth grade, showed an interesting transition. The highest peak of preference for the simple came at the first semester of the second grade, with 85 per cent of the choices for the simple drawing. This dropped gradually to 62 per cent at the high third, then radically to 31 per cent in the low fourth. This sudden drop at the fourth grade indicates that more than a developmental pattern is in operation. Children develop at such varying rates that such a sudden change would not occur unless all of them were being exposed to some new influence. At present we do not know what it is. One possible influence might be the shift from the more child-centered primary grades to the specific learning of skills that often is begun in the fourth grade. Some writers believe that the fourth grade is a time when many children are breaking away from home ties and becoming part of the peer group. Whatever the reason, we need to watch the phenomenon and seek more evidence to direct us in teaching.

This study supports the generalization that perceptual development, as shown by the children's preferences in this case, moves from *wholes to parts,* but with wide individual differences at every age. While the majority of first, second, and third graders prefer the simple to the complex, there are children who can handle the more complex visual material.

Rudolph Arnheim, a psychologist who has devoted much time and thought to the relationship of psychology to art, supports the whole-to-parts direction in perceptual growth, but he points out that this is ". . . only one factor [in development and that it is] overlaid and modified by . . . the personality of the child and the influences of the environment." [9]

INTELLECTUAL GROWTH AS A VARIABLE IN PERCEPTUAL DEVELOPMENT

One of the major variables in the perceptual development of a child may be his intellectual development. We have seen in the Sontag study that environment plays a role in the acceleration or deceleration rates of I.Q. increase in children (see p. 74). In any large sample of children at any given age a normal curve of scores on a Stanford-Binet or other intelligence test will usually be found. This means that, in an ungrouped classroom, scores are likely to be clustered around 100 with deviations in both directions. The mean I.Q. will vary from one classroom to another. The variation may be due to a real difference in average intellectual ability. It may also be due to differences in ability to respond to verbal tests. In some communities, such as those where professional people live, the de-

velopment of language skills is necessary for a child to get recognition of his achievement. In other communities there may be a high
proportion of children whose families do not stress reading and
quality in verbal expression.

INTELLIGENCE AND ABILITY TO HANDLE DETAIL. A study was
made of college students to discover the relationship between intelligence (as measured by the Wechsler vocabulary test) and the
ability to handle visual patterns. In the visual test the students
were shown forty patterns of white dots arranged within the possibilities of a square subdivided into twenty-five squares. Half the
patterns were symmetrical as in Figure 4–3, half were asymmetrical as in Figure 4–4. Each pattern was projected by a tachistoscope on a screen for ⅕ second. The students attempted to
reproduce the pattern on a grid sheet. The number of misplaced
dots was recorded by the tester. It was found that the highest-
I.Q. students made the fewest mistakes. The correlation between
I.Q. and ability to reproduce the asymmetrical patterns was
significantly high, indicating that the higher the intelligence the
greater the probability that the person can handle less well-
ordered (in this case asymmetrical) visual information.[10]

LEARNING AS A VARIABLE IN PERCEPTUAL DEVELOPMENT

The education of an artist includes a great deal of perceptual
training, careful analysis of visual details, study of subtle relationships between things, and discovery of ways to interpret details in

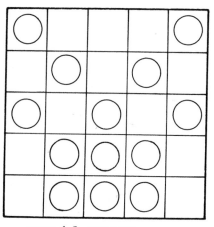

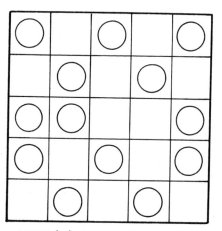

FIGURE 4–3. SYMMETRICAL ARRANGEMENT   FIGURE 4–4. ASYMMETRICAL ARRANGEMENT

his work. Drawing and painting require careful observation of one's own work as one creates details.

THE VISUAL HABITS OF ARTISTS AND NON-ARTISTS. A bi-dimensional camera was used to measure the way a person's eyes focus on simple and complex patterns. Artists tend to make their original fixations on the complicated pattern; non-artists, including a sample of engineers, tended to fixate initially on the simple designs and to spend most of their time observing them.[11] Other researchers found that non-artists tended to prefer simple symmetrical drawings while those trained in the arts tended to prefer complex, asymmetrical drawings.[12] These studies reflect in part the differences in perceptual training of the two groups.

CULTURE AS A FACTOR IN CHILDREN'S PERCEPTUAL GROWTH

In the anthropological sense, culture means the attitudes, values, the patterns of roles and acceptable behavior, and the concepts of reality shared by a group of people. The particular culture that a child lives in affects his perceptual development and the nature of his art. The culture influences the direction of his perceptual training by giving him many more opportunities and rewards for observing the things important to his group than for observing those that are not stressed. In order to see the differences among children who have experienced different cultures, we will examine nonliterate cultures. The purpose here is to give us better insight into our own culture and its many subcultures.

THE ZIA INDIANS. Among the Zia Indians of New Mexico a marked difference in the drawing ability of boys and girls has been observed. The differences become apparent in the first grade and continue throughout life. In this culture boys are expected to be able to paint animal pictures on the walls to encourage animal fertility. A requirement for attaining manhood is the ability to paint the ceremonial masks and other religious objects. Parents and siblings encourage the boys and praise their progress. Girls, on the other hand, are not given representational art goals to work toward; their art work is limited to geometric designs on pottery. Boys, who are encouraged to observe and draw many things, draw pictures that show greater detail than do the girls' pictures. The difference in sex roles in this culture has a strong relationship to the perceiving and drawing behavior of the children.[13]

THE OROTCHEN CHILDREN. The Orotchens are a nomadic tribe of Northern Siberia who live by herding reindeer. In a climate of long winters, short springs, and rainy colorless summers, the Orotchen is dependent on reindeer for his food, clothing, and shelter. At the time of this study the only apparatus these people had from the outside world consisted of a few pots and sewing equipment. The group had little visible art form. Their tents were undecorated; clothing and shelter were their major productions. A few members of the group had been in the outside world, and some of these had learned to read and write. Literacy was estimated at 2 or 3 per cent. The children had never been to school and, except for a few wrappers on packages, were not familiar with symbols that have meaning on a page.

An anthropologist, studying the tribe for a summer, ran a school for the children. There were a few primers that included simple pictures. The teacher also provided sketch pads and pencils. Not being an artist himself, he did not attempt to teach the children to draw. These children had received no drawing training, but all their drawings showed the influence of sharpened visual perception and keen observation. One drawing of a reindeer by a ten-year-old boy has foreshortening in the antlers and legs indicating the forward motion of the animal (Figure 4–5A). The general size and proportion are lifelike. The eyes and the antlers show fine detail. (A man in the same picture is a stick figure with little attention to detail except that he has a head, a

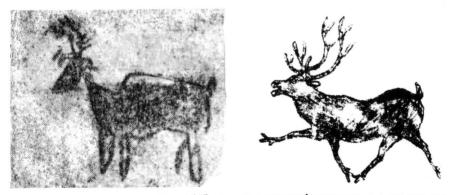

FIGURE 4–5. OROTCHEN CHILDREN'S DRAWINGS. A. A TEN-YEAR-OLD
B. A THIRTEEN-YEAR-OLD (FROM A. SCHUBERT)

body, two arms and two legs.) A drawing by a thirteen-year-old (Figure 4–5B) shows sensitivity to the essence and feeling of the reindeer through the use of beautiful line and form.[14]

What is important to the child, the values he has learned, directs him to observe some things more closely than others. The importance of value as a director of perceptual training is clearly evident. Among the Orotchens the reindeer is the central factor in the culture, and observations of the reindeer are reinforced again and again throughout the life of the child.

> THE CHAMORROS AND THE CAROLINIANS. A study of the perceptual tendencies of children on Saipan was made by two psychiatrists who are highly skilled in the use of the Rorschach Inkblot Test. Part of their purpose was to determine whether these children responded to fine or to large detail in responding to the ink blots. Fifty boys and fifty girls in each of the two tribes, the Chamorros and the Carolinians, were selected. They ranged in age from five to seventeen. The researchers found that whole responses and large detail responses occurred twice as frequently in the records of the Carolinian children as in the records of the Chamorros. This is an example of an island having two cultures which differ to the point that their children's perceptual responses are measurably different.[15]

In each of these groups, differences in culture roles or in values tend to vary the perceptual experience, practice, and in some cases the art activity of the children. We can assume that such differences would be found among children in Western cultures as well. Anastasi and Foley, differential psychologists, carefully analyzed the drawings at an international exhibition of children's drawings, held at Rockefeller Center in 1934. Children between six and twelve from forty-one countries were represented. Differences in emphasis in detail in the same painting, comparable to those of the Orotchen children's, were found. Wide differences in the amount of detail and in the kind of subject matter appeared among the children of the same age in Western culture countries.[16] In the drawing of vegetation, European children tended to show only the general features while children in tropical areas drew plants in such detail that varieties could be identified. Children in societies where ceremonial dress is elaborate, such as Hungarian, Czecho-

Slovakian, Balinese, and American Indian, often showed the costumes in great detail but neglected detail in other objects.

CULTURE AS A DIRECTOR OF DRAWING DEVELOPMENT

In cultures where a strong system of symbolic communication has been developed (such as the Kwakiutl) the children's drawings tend to approach the "symbolic realism" of the culture. In the case of the Orotchen tribe, there was no apparent system of communicating through symbols in the culture. Yet the children's perceptions of the highly-valued reindeer were so acute that they were able, without instruction, to draw them in detail. In drawing objects like the human figure they tended to use the crudest form of symbolism. The cultural values acted as directors that accelerated their drawing ability of some objects and neglected it in others. By contrast, in those cultures where a strong pictorial art form exists, the children tend to develop their drawings in terms of the accepted culture symbols.

BRITISH COLUMBIA INDIANS.   Psychologists Anastasi and Foley studied the drawings of children of the Indian cultures from the Kwakiutl, Nass River, Bella Bella, Haida, Tsimshian, and Bella Coola tribes. The children, 90 boys and 69 girls attending a government school at Alert Bay, ranged in age from five to eighteen.[17]

The drawings had been collected in 1931 by anthropologist Franz Boas, who had asked each child to draw an animal. These children had been affected by Western culture to some degree at the school, but the influence of their own culture and experience was clearly evident. Individual differences were found at all age levels. The psychologists found that many of the children from age nine up were drawing "stylized" symbols of animals as found in adult art of their own tribes. These included the culture symbols of the killer whale, the sea lion, the mythical thunderbird and double-headed serpent. The drawings were similar to those of adults, not only in subject matter but in technique. Another group of drawings by children in both the younger and older groups were outline symbols but had little detail. Some of the children made realistic drawings of animals in their immediate environment, the boys of animals to be hunted and the girls

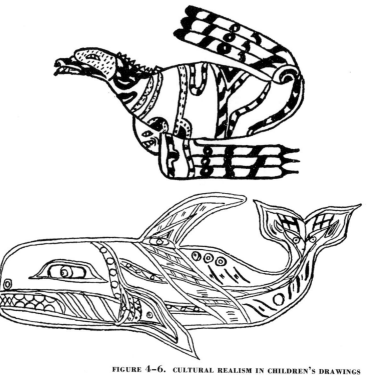

FIGURE 4-6. CULTURAL REALISM IN CHILDREN'S DRAWINGS
(FROM ANASTASI AND FOLEY)

of the smaller domestic animals.[18] Anastasi and Foley summarize their analysis of these drawings:

> Both the subject matter and the technique of the drawings reflect specific cultural and experimental factors rather than age differences or developmental stages. Any attempt to employ specific features of the child's drawing as an index of developmental level independently of the child's experiential background is doomed to failure. An Indian child of the north Pacific coast . . . may produce a symbolic representation rich in stylized details that it would be futile to evaluate in terms of norms established elsewhere.[19]

WESTERN CULTURE AS A DIRECTOR OF PERCEPTUAL TRAINING AND OF DRAWING GOALS

The characteristics of perceptual training in our culture depend in part on the environment children grow up in. If they live in urban communities or in clusters of suburban communities around a large metropolitan center, they will spend a great deal of their lives responding to man-made symbols and constructions. Television, billboard advertising, packages, and movies use forms of visual symbolism to catch both children's and adults' attention. At present we have not been able to evaluate the effect of all of this concentrated visual training. Much of our advertising is made to appeal to needs and to create new needs and values in individuals. The perceptual training that people experience as their attention is directed to all the visual mass media of communication probably is having a far greater effect than we realize.

The artistic symbolism that is most familiar to the majority of children is not present in works of fine art. It is probably a composite of magazine covers, comic books and papers, animated drawings, descriptive illustrations in books, and the less sophisticated advertising art. While the Hopi child has as a goal the drawing of a Kachina, and the north coast Indian child the symbol of the killer whale, a large majority of children in American culture will be trying to find symbols for photographic "realism."

Part of your role as a teacher is to expand children's understanding of the art symbols of Western culture. The concept of art as a means of communication can be explored; and examples can be studied of art that express feelings or that tell a story, from a simple illustration to a mural that is equal in information to a book. Even small children can respond to the relationship between the rhythm and pattern in music to that in abstract art—this, too, is a means of communicating beauty in form. Almost every society has some form of rhythmic pattern in music and decoration on the objects they make. Through art forms you can help children have more immediate understandings of their culture and that of others.

CULTURAL VARIATION IN PERCEPTUAL TRAINING. As we have looked at each culture, we see that the patterns within it are a unifying influence on behavior generally and perception in particular. Children in the same culture are trained in much the same way, the children in one culture being more like each other in their perceptual behavior than like children raised in another culture. Cultural training can also be a differentiating factor—it can create differences among people. In a complex culture such as the United

States, the variation among subcultures is very great. In any given classroom many different subcultures may be represented. The American Indians, among others, are a good example. Many Indian groups, still living on reservations, have shown a greater retention of old culture patterns. The Indians who have migrated from the reservations may exhibit behavior patterns of one or several subcultures—those who have formed small ethnic-living groups retain more Indian culture characteristics, while others have made greater adaptation to their new environment. The result is that many more children of Indian heritage, with varying degrees of acculturation (learning the acceptable patterns of behavior in a new culture) to their new environment, will be in school.

The mainstream of American culture, a branch of Western culture (western European), has its roots in Greco-Roman democracy and Judaeo-Christian ideology. It had a new birth in the Renaissance, when the rights of man were defended and reformulated in English history and replanted and dedicated anew in the Americas. The mainstream has had many cultures flowing into it, other variations of Western culture from Europe, as well as quite different cultural influences from Asia, Africa, Polynesia, and from the native American Indians. Most groups, to some degree, maintain their own identities, and to some degree merge into the mainstream. Each individual represents one or more variations of this whole. A Hopi child may have more problems of acculturation (learning the culture of another group) in going to a public school near his ancient homeland, than would a European child whose home culture grew from the same roots as did the culture of his American schoolmates.

THE CLASSROOM AS A SUBCULTURE

One form of subculture is the self-contained classroom in which teacher and pupils live for several hours a day. For a classroom to operate smoothly the children and the teacher need some shared values and attitudes. The teacher can do a great deal to help children develop a higher value for creative work in art if he has (1) an enthusiastic and appreciative attitude toward art and

(2) a classroom subculture where new and interesting things and ways of performing have high value. The teacher can introduce appreciation of many fine-arts symbols and expressions, can help pupils to become aware of the aesthetic values in nature, in the school building, in the community, and in the tools and materials of everyday living. A teacher who is uninterested or uninformed about art, who teaches in repetitive, inflexible, overly-structured ways, will probably be creating a classroom subculture in which little value is developed for new art experiences.

The teacher may feel that he cannot develop a subculture in the classroom because the children have somewhat different cultures at home. However, most children by the time they come to school have already been exposed to more than one subculture. Parents are often from different groups. Often the family culture changes on Sunday from what it is on other days. With the tremendous increase in mobility, many first graders have already lived in three or more quite different communities.

IMPLICATIONS FOR PRACTICE

Perceptual development evolves from the interaction of several factors of readiness at Point I of the P-D process. We have seen that a child's perceptual development is in part his stage of growth in information-handling. The degree to which he has learned the perceptual constancies, the direction and intensity of his culture's perceptual training, and his intellectual ability and development all contribute to his preparation for any perceptual task. These contribute to his "set," with which he approaches a perceptual experience. They also influence his information-handling ability at Point III, and finally influence the flow of information with which he can be creative at Point IV—delineation of the final art product. His culture also creates the psychological environment (Point II) in which he works, praising him as in the Zia group, encouraging him through the necessity of keen perception for survival as in the Orotchen group.

Far wider individual differences in patterns of growth in art exist in a classroom than some educators have realized. Because of all the cultural influences and the varying perceptual learnings involved, a flexible program in art activities is necessary to allow for differences. But a situation that allows extreme freedom for children does not give them the specific kind of encouragement and motivation that each needs. *Differences must be planned for, not just allowed for.* Any single art activity, if participated in by the whole class, will be limiting for some children. To help you see this, we will take an activity that was presented to fifth grade children by an art consultant in the schools of the same district, and analyze it in terms of what we know about individual differences and the results of the children's work.[20]

The objective of this assignment was to motivate the children to draw from their imagination, to see if some were more creative than others. A simple medium was selected that all the children were familiar with. The teacher distributed large sheets of manila paper and crayons, asking them all to wait for the work to begin. Then he told them that they were going to hear a poem and afterward draw a picture of what they heard. He read to them an Edward Lear nonsense poem.

THE QUANGLE WANGLE'S HAT

On the top of the Crumpetty Tree
  The Quangle Wangle sat,
But his face you could not see,
  On account of his Beaver Hat.
For his Hat was a hundred and two feet wide,
With ribbons and bibbons on every side,
And bells, and buttons, and loops, and lace,
So that nobody ever could see the face
  Of the Quangle Wangle Quee.

EDWARD LEAR (1812–1888)[21]

The children's drawings were kept and analyzed. Wide differences were found in development in art expression.

1. The amount of detail used varied from very simple to very complex drawings.

2. Evidence of ability to conceptualize and draw an idea from the stimulus of the poem ranged from very meager simple line symbols to complex figures with many parts.

3. Evidence of ability to organize parts into a whole ranged from drawing disjointed fragments to organizing the whole idea of the poem.

4. The number of ideas responded to, remembered, and symbolized, ranged from one or two simple objects to most of the ideas presented in the poem.

5. The symbols ranged from stereotypes (such as representing the beaver hat with "Davy Crockett" figures) to the invention of novel forms.

Analyze the drawings in Figure 4–7 to see how much range was found among fifth grade children. Some factors that we must consider in evaluating the children's work are cultural values and attitudes, personality, and prior experience with this type of task. Since this was a somewhat ambiguous poem, the children's responses may have been influenced by their flexibility in accepting new or ambiguous things. The art materials used were familiar, but even crayons may have had negative connotations for some children, depending on their past experience with them.

The task of responding imaginatively to poetry, whether it is clearly descriptive or not, is more difficult for some children than for others. This same art lesson was presented to fifth grades in schools in several different socio-economic neighborhoods. As groups, the children in a neighborhood with many professional people responded in more detail and with more imagination to the poem than did the children in a less fortunate neighborhood. Probably the difference was caused in part by subcultural values and past experience.

The children in the professional and in the low-income neighborhoods had the same range of general ability. How can an outside observer account for the wide difference in response to the poem-centered art session? Possibly the professional people placed a high value on books and read to the children more often. By listening, the children may have learned to deal with imagined scenes derived from the words. In a neighborhood where there is less leisure, or where both parents are employed, adults have less time to read aloud, and they may not be interested in reading. The children will have had little opportunity to respond to poetry.

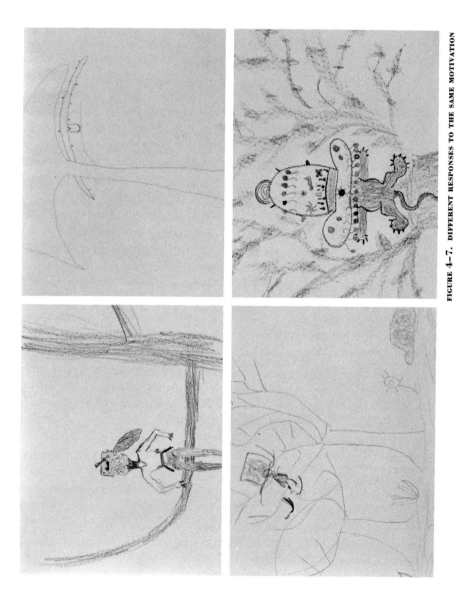

FIGURE 4–7. DIFFERENT RESPONSES TO THE SAME MOTIVATION

Most classrooms have children from both kinds of groups. The differences in value and in past experience of the two groups can be compared to the differences among Zia Indian children, whose sex roles, not social class, separate the experiences and goal-directing values.

A teacher cannot evaluate a child's artistic ability on the basis of one drawing. A poor drawing does not necessarily mean that the child cannot draw or express ideas, or that he does not have a potential for becoming artistic. He may have rejected the poetic type of motivation, or, liking poetry, he may have rejected the nonsense rhyme. Or, liking both, he may have had little opportunity to develop visual impressions and may not have a facility in inventing visual symbols for ideas. His ability to handle detail may be developing slowly. He may have other art interests for which symbols are, *for him,* more easily drawn—such as pictures of rockets or animals or responses to familiar music.

By understanding the child's background and by carefully selecting the means of motivation and the appropriate tasks, the teacher can help the child relate himself to his new experiences. If the teacher doesn't try to relate the child's present activities with his background and over-all development, the child may learn that he is not "artistic." Through understanding as much about the children as possible, their backgrounds, interests, and abilities, and then by introducing a wide range of motivations and tasks, the teacher has a chance to help many children find success in art.

There has been a tendency in art education to use a wide variety of media and activities, but not to experiment with motivation. A single medium can be used with many different kinds of motivation to find meaningful experiences for individual children.

SUMMARY

Longitudinal studies of child development point out the importance of considering *all* the factors of development of a child at a given time. Patterns of development are individualistic. It is the total interaction of the different factors that is in operation at any given time rather than the sum of the parts.

Perceptual development proceeds generally from the ability to handle undifferentiated wholes to the handling of smaller details, but wide individual differences occur at any given age level. The environment of the child, his intellectual capacities, and his opportunities to learn all operate as variables when his development is compared to other children in his own and in other social groups.

A positive relationship has been found between intelligence and ability to handle detail, but both characteristics are influenced by training, reward, and other personality variables.

The wide range of I.Q. in an ungrouped elementary classroom probably accounts, in part, for wide differences in ability to handle detail and to organize responses.

The values and emphasis on certain things in the environment in some cultures serve as directives for perceptual training. The motivation and rewards and the role of the individual in the culture contribute to the amount of detail, type of art form, and kind of symbolism he can respond to and use.

The illustrative and advertising arts are probably the cultural "ideal art" form for a large majority of Americans, but the teacher can help students to increase the range of art forms which they can understand and use.

The differences between children of the same age in the same classroom are overlapping with children in the grades below and above. Most of the differences we have identified are based not on age, but on opportunity, reward, values, and individual patterns of development.

RELATED ACTIVITIES

Handling visual detail is important both in appreciating art forms and in creating them. Here are some tests of your own visual responses. Picasso's "The Three Musicians" (Plate IV) has much detail. The first time you see it you are not able to respond to all that is going on in the picture, although you may have an immediate like or dislike for the whole. You can develop your capacity to respond to a painting by two kinds of visual training—familiarity with the painting and awareness of the visual functions of design. If you have seen many paintings of this artist's style, you already have a head start on becoming familiar with this picture. (As you may have observed, some people are violently opposed to a style of painting they have never seen before.) Write in your notebook or on the endpaper of this book a description of your first response. Then, in the following weeks, as you see it again and again, write down your further responses.

After you have studied the chapter on design you will be able to respond to the painting with more understanding. But to help you in your initial familiarization process let's compare the Picasso with Motherwell's "The Voyage" (Plate III). The Picasso is made up of many parts that can be appreciated as designs in themselves. Motherwell uses a more direct means of communication with fewer subthemes to the major parts. One painting is not better than the other because of the difference in structure, but the impact upon us as observers is different.

If your art library has prints that can be borrowed, select one that seems very difficult for you to understand and keep it in your room so that you see it often. Notice any changes in your feeling about it and try to keep from developing a "set" about it too soon. If your print is from a period in history or from a culture with which you are not familiar, you can increase your appreciation of it by looking up the history of the period and the cultural values and attitudes that contributed to it. Your growth in art appreciation will accelerate tremendously if you (1) understand the cultural background of the art forms, (2) are sensitive to differences among artists in selections and interpretations, (3) are aware of the total impact of each work on you, and (4) have frequent opportunity to respond to art.

As you experience the development of your own capacity to see and understand detail, remember that your pupils can learn by similar methods. Children must have (1) exposure to a work or style until it is familiar, (2) encouragement to give themselves time to get used to a painting before making the decision to accept or reject it, (3) opportunity to relate the new work to something similar that is already understood, and (4) understanding of design, form, line, color, and texture and their interaction with each other.

REFERENCES

1. Nancy Bayley, "Individual Patterns of Development," *Child Development,* XXVII (1956), 45–74.

2. Lester W. Sontag, Charles T. Baker, and Virginia L. Nelson, *Mental Growth and Personality Development: A Longitudinal Study,* Monograph for the Society for Research in Child Development, Inc., Vol. XXIII, Ser. 68, No. 2 (1958).

3. Sylvia Honkavaara, "Organization Process in Perception as a Measure of Intelligence," *Journal of Psychology,* XLVI (1958), 3–12.

4. Louise B. Ames, Janet Learned, Ruth Metreaux, and Richard Walker, "Development of Perception in the Young Child as Observed in Response to the Rorschach Ink Blots," *Journal of Genetic Psychology,* LXXXII (1953), 183–204.

5. J. S. Slotkin, *Personality Development* (New York: Harper & Brothers, 1952), pp. 175–179.

6. Egon Brunswik, *Perception and the Representative Design of Psychological Experiments* (Berkeley: University of California Press, 1956), pp. 82–85.

7. John E. French, "Children's Preferences for Pictures of Varied Complexity of Pictorial Pattern," *Elementary School Journal,* LIII (1952), 90–95.

8. June King McFee, "Visual Arts: Psychological Implications of Individual Differences in the 'Perception-Delineation' Process" (Ed.D. dissertation, Stanford University, 1957), p. 147.

9. Rudolph Arnheim, *Art and Visual Perception* (Berkeley: University of California Press, 1954), p. 143. Reprinted by permission.

10. Norman Livson and David Krech, "Dynamic Systems, Perceptual Differentiation and Intelligence," *Journal of Personality,* XXV (1956), 46–68.

11. Walter A. Woods and James C. Boudreau, "Design Complexity as a Determiner of Visual Attention Among Artists and Non-Artists," *Journal of Applied Psychology,* XXXIV (1950), 355–366.

12. F. Barron and G. S. Welsh, "Artistic Perception as a Factor in Personality Style: Its Measurement by a Figure Preference Test," *Journal of Psychology,* XXXIII (1952), 199–203.

13. Robert J. Havighurst and Bernice L. Neugarten, *American Indian and White Children* (Chicago: University of Chicago Press, 1955), p. 171.

14. Anna Schubert, "Drawings of Orotchen Children and Young People," *Journal of Genetic Psychology,* XXXVII (1930), 232–234. Used with permission.

15. Alice Joseph and Veronica G. Murray, *Chamorros and Carolinians of Saipan* (Cambridge: Harvard University Press, 1951).

16. Anne Anastasi and John P. Foley, Jr., "An Analysis of Spontaneous Drawings by Children in Different Cultures," *Journal of Applied Psychology,* XX (1936), 689–726.

17. Anne Anastasi and John P. Foley, Jr., "A Study of Animal Drawings of Indian Children of the North Pacific Coast," *Journal of Social Psychology,* IX (1938), 363–374.

18. *Loc. cit.*

19. *Ibid.,* p. 374. Reprinted with permission.

20. Arthur P. Newcomb, Jr., unpublished materials used with permission.

21. Edward Lear, *The Complete Nonsense Book* (New York: Dodd, Mead & Company, 1958), p. 388, verse I. Reprinted by permission of Dodd, Mead & Company.

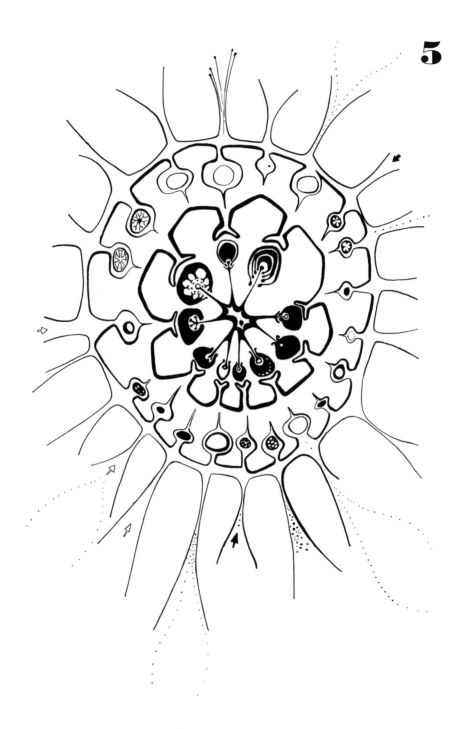

5

Environmental Factors in Children's Work

There are several ways of discussing a child's environment. At all times he is living in a cultural environment, an aggregate of things, people, ideas, values. At the same time he has an environment that is peculiarly his. Each child is interacting with his cultural environment in a different way because of his feelings of threat and non-threat, his past experience with success and failure, the pattern of rewards or punishments he is accustomed to, and his motivation.

According to the P-D theory, the child is in an ever-changing state of readiness (Point I). Many things, including his culture, prior training, and physical condition contribute to his readiness to interpret what he sees in his immediate situation. His interaction with the situation is Point II, the psychological environment. To further our understanding of why children respond in different ways in school, we can temporarily isolate some of the influences on their behavior at Point II.

MOTIVATION

Motivation is that which changes behavior. Some of our motivation comes from basic needs for the goals of food, comfort, and survival. Some motivation comes from secondary or learned needs, which depend on goals established by experience and training. We often use the term *motivation* to refer to the teacher's process of setting up goals that have enough meaning to children that they will strive to reach them. Much of the teacher's work is to recognize the goals that a child already has and to give him experiences that will lead him into changing his goals to some degree. Thus we can say the teacher "motivates"—directs goal-seeking behavior.

It is particularly important that teachers try to help children understand the meaning of rewards in various situations. To illustrate, a teacher solved a serious discipline problem with a boy by finding a way to reward him for behavior that would usually bring punishment. After class one day she found that the boy had made an excellent, original cartoon of her. Though the cartoon was not flattering to the teacher, she carefully matted it and hung it on the classroom bulletin board. The next day she discussed the creative way the boy had made the cartoon. She commented on the interesting art qualities of the drawing, the use of line and design, and she laughed about the humor of the cartoon. She was never again bothered by discipline problems with the boy. This reward helped the boy find a new goal to work toward. Furthermore, she was able to encourage creative ability by rewarding him for divergent inventive behavior.

THREAT AND NON-THREAT

In a classroom where all the children are in somewhat different psychological environments, the same situation may frighten one child, excite another, and cause another to become defiant, depending on how each interprets the situation. One child may find the environment entirely threatening, another may feel no threat at all. A threat to a child may be a fear that the teacher will punish him if he makes a mistake or if he has no talent. A fear of being laughed at by other children is a threat. Another threat is a feeling that the activity is going to make him dirty. Some threats are undefined. The child cannot relate them to a specific fear, nor can the teacher determine why the child is timid or indecisive in the classroom situation.

A threat in the environment may determine how the child behaves in a classroom activity.[1] There is some evidence that a threat can actually limit a person's visual ability.

THE EFFECT OF THREAT ON VISUAL ABILITY. The Kohn study used three similar groups of college students who were shown a picture and then were tested on the details they could remember. The first group was then separated from the others and strongly threatened. Each was asked to sit in a chair equipped with ankle and wrist attachments for giving mild electrical shocks. Also present in the room was other electrical equipment with switches and lights that went off and on. Each student was told he was going to be given intermittent shocks; then he was questioned about his health; and finally, after his anxiety was aroused, he was given one small shock. After this threat experience, the group was shown another picture and given a test on details.

The second group was put into the same threatening room, but they were assured that they would not actually be given shocks. The purpose was to put them in a mild anxiety-producing situation. They, too, were shown a new picture and tested on details.

The third or control group had no threat experience. The electrical equipment was hidden from them, and they were simply given another picture test.

The first group performed significantly poorer after the threat. The second group gained significantly; apparently the slight threat aroused their level of concentration. The control group improved in the second trial, but not as much as did the second group.[2]

This study suggests that, while we do not give electric shock to school children, strong anxiety may reduce their ability to respond to things visually, and inability to remember details may cause them difficulty in organizing their responses in an art expression. Another implication is that tests that use children's drawings as measures of intelligence (such as Draw a Man Test of Goodenough[3] and the Easel Age Scale of Lantz)[4] do not take into consideration the effects of threat and anxiety on a child's ability to remember his visual experience and to organize it into a drawing.

SUCCESS AND FAILURE EXPERIENCE

Young children measure their success and failure by two criteria: (1) their ability to master a new task, such as learning to walk, to reach, or to manipulate; and (2) rewards or punishments received from adults. At a very early age, children begin to develop feelings of self-confidence or of failure. Confidence apparently allows them to evaluate realistically their abilities for future tasks, while a sense of failure prevents an adequate appraisal of their abilities.

LEVELS OF ASPIRATION. Pauline Sears made a study of the goals fourth through sixth grade children set for themselves. The children were timed on word and arithmetic tests. After the first trial they were told their time and were then asked to estimate the time they would take on their next trial. The children who knew they had been successful in previous school work set realistic goals for themselves. Those who had a history of failure set a wide range of goals. Those who had earlier succeeded in reading but had failed in arithmetic set realistic goals in word tests, but were inconsistent in setting arithmetic goals.[5]

In another Sears study, preschool children were asked to choose among six tasks of varying difficulty. Three of the tasks were visual: one required the child to copy designs, another to compare color arrangements and geometric shapes, and another to remember objects after a brief look at them in a box. The results indicated that those children who succeeded in the activities they had selected were consistent in selecting further tasks in which they could succeed. Those children who failed did not have a consistent pattern in selecting future tasks.[6]

These studies suggest that a child who has experienced success becomes more proficient in determining how successful he can be in the future. The teacher can help the child by making certain that he has some kind of success on which to build further successes.

In art, having simple materials to work with should prepare the child for more difficult activities later. At every step, rewards for his efforts will help to build his confidence. The teacher should be cautious in giving his approval. His words, his facial expression and his treatment of the child are the cues the child has to interpret. An unrealistic evaluation of the art work will confuse him. The child can learn to see that everything he does is not necessarily his best; but, if he is making progress in some way, the teacher should point the way for further progress.

A teacher might say, "Mary, you are telling us so many things in your pictures. Look at this one you did last month; see how much more interesting this new drawing is." "Henry, yesterday you did a beautiful drawing in crayon, but you've been using crayon a long time. There are other things to draw with on the table. Would you like to try some of them? See if you don't find you like using them just as much as you do crayon." "Tom, the stories you tell us during sharing periods are so much fun. Do you think you could tell us one of them in art? What kinds of art materials do you like to use best?"

PERCEPTUAL ABILITY. Another study shows that immediate perceptions are affected by past experiences of success and failure. Three groups of college students were given a test of their ability to recognize symbols flashed on a screen by a tachistoscope for $\frac{1}{100}$ of a second. The average number of correct responses was 50 per cent for all groups. The students were then asked to estimate the number of correct responses they could make in the next test. After the second test the subjects of group one were told that they had surpassed their estimate. Group two was told that they had not surpassed their estimate (regardless of actual performance). Group three was told nothing. Further tests were given. Group one, which believed itself successful, improved, increasing the average from 50 per cent to 84.8 per cent correct responses. The "failures," group two, dropped to a low of 30.8 per cent. The control group made a slight improvement. Furthermore, the failure group gave a somewhat larger number of responses, but a larger percentage of them were wrong.[7]

The results of this study indicate that the ability to respond to visual stimuli is affected by failure experience. Failure, like the other forms of threat, tends to reduce the efficiency of children and adults in handling visual information. In all classroom activities the teacher must plan for those children who, because of earlier failure experiences, cannot respond to a large amount of information. In art activities, children who have failed and expect to fail again are not able to respond to motivation in the same way as do those who have been successful.

DISCONTINUITY

Each culture develops a system of right and wrong behavior. Much of this conventional behavior is known by all, and adhered to by most people, because a system of rewards and punishments has been set up to compel people to conform. In Western culture, if people do "right," they are rewarded with money, praise, security, and various pleasures. If they do "wrong," they are punished with ridicule, imprisonment, fines, or even death. While the rules are not always clearly defined, nor the rewards and punishments always consistent, most adults have a fairly good idea of what is expected of them and can take responsibility for their degree of conformity.

Not so the child. He is not born with the knowledge that to say "thank you" is right and to break windows is wrong. He learns item by item what behavior is expected of him. Adults reward and punish him according to *their* values. Not all adults have the same values. The two parents may differ; and when the child goes to school and is in a new subculture, he may find a still different value system, a system that he must learn to conform to by experience. He may find that what he was rewarded for at home brings no reward here, and that what he was punished for at home is not punished here. He is experiencing a *discontinuity*.[8]

DISCONTINUITY AND CULTURE CHANGE

The child must continually deal with discontinuities, because not only is he moving about in several subcultures, he is also living in a rapidly changing larger culture. The core culture and the subcultures are never static. They are acted upon by various forces.

Cultural *maintenance* is the force that, to some degree, attempts to perpetuate the customs and values that are accepted by the group. Parents and schools and other institutions give each succeeding generation the means by which they can maintain the culture.

Cultural reaction is the force of those groups who want to return to earlier ways of life, generally resisting all other kinds of change. In a school this force may appear as suggestions to bring back the "old hickory stick."

Culture change is affected by happenings within the group and throughout the world. Basic inventions that lead to many new inventions influence the whole world. They result in *innovations*. Whenever people of different cultures have contact with each other, *cultural confluence* takes place. People who meet change each other. Cultural confluence has been accelerated by the ease of travel and the widespread distribution of books, art forms, and other means of communication. Wars, threats of war, and catastrophes also change the way of life of a people.

Each child in school represents a particular family variation of the core of a subculture group within the larger society. He is influenced by cultural reaction, cultural maintenance, and culture

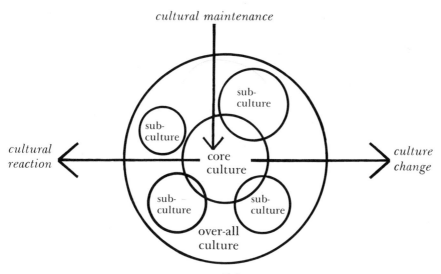

FIGURE 5-1. CULTURAL DYNAMICS IN A COMPLEX SOCIETY

change as the group is influenced. Also the child, being unique, has received his family's culture in a way somewhat different from other children in the same family.

Each teacher in a school represents a similar family and sub-culture group at some point of change. He is operating in a regional and socio-economic society, of which the school is a unit. The teacher is a cultural mediator, who selects those values, patterns of behavior, and concepts of reality that have most meaning for him. He needs to be aware of his own values in order to appraise what he is transmitting to children.

What the child learns from the teacher depends on his cultural preparation to learn. The teaching in one classroom may be the same—with one teacher—but the learning will differ according to the individual children. They represent varied phases of culture change or reaction.

CONFLICTS IN ATTITUDES ABOUT ART. The place of the arts and artists in this process of culture change is somewhat elusive. Some anthropologists find that Americans tend to be unaware of the function of art in their society.[9,10] The artist has not been considered as having an important role. However, some families and some subcultural groups enjoy and cultivate the arts and teach their children to do so. Teachers find children with differing attitudes about art, depending upon their backgrounds.

Some people believe that our society places too much emphasis on practical education when there is serious need for studying the humanities, including art, as a means of improving the quality of living. Other people, fearing that our society may not survive in the competitive world, are fostering reaction, a "return to the three R's." These critics want to brush off as frills everything that is not reading, writing, and arithmetic. In a period of rapid change, such as we are now experiencing, the reactionary tendency becomes aggravated.

Fortunately there are many people, in and out of professional education, who can look critically at all phases of education in terms of man's whole economic, social, political, ethical, and aesthetic life. One of the great changes they consider is the increase of leisure time. Max Lerner points out that the earlier patrons of the great art forms found in Western culture came from the elite classes.[11] Perhaps the reason the arts have been slow in becoming central to American culture is that the culture core has not been in an elite or leisure-class society, but rather in the middle class. The core group has only recently become interested in the fine arts and is slowly becoming more aware of applied and industrial art.

In earlier days, the middle-class people worked long hours. People who work most of the time evaluate things according to their usefulness. Invention, as a force in culture change, is increasing the leisure of the large mass of people, who formerly had little free time. Because the people have more leisure and more money, they buy more things for pleasure and must, therefore, make many aesthetic judgments. As aesthetic value approaches the importance of useful value, the arts may be more closely integrated with American culture.

We respond to the cooking ware of primitive and ancient societies as works of art, but we seldom look at the useful products of our own society as art—yet they, too, often possess excellent design. The increase of leisure can mean the development of a new dimension to American life—the aesthetic response and the evaluation, by large segments of the society, of our culture.

CHILD-REARING PRACTICES AND ART EDUCATION

ENCULTURATION. Enculturation is the process by which children learn their culture. Much of this learning takes place before children come to school; it continues through much of their face-

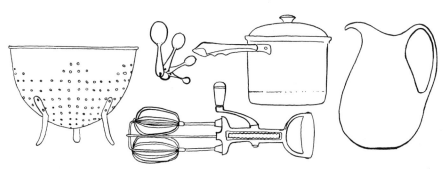

FIGURE 5-2. FAMILIAR ART FORMS

to-face group experience.[12] Enculturation, a major factor in personality development, contributes to the psychological environment in which children are learning habits and attitudes. Harsh and Schrickel[13] state: "The earlier view of personality as a kind of substance with inhering properties or traits is giving way to a dynamic conception wherein personality is viewed not as a thing . . . but as a complex of functions of interactive forces. . . ." *

The actions of parents and teachers encourage children to learn the habits of their subculture. Adults are often unaware of how apparently ordinary conversation implants basic values in the young. The following is a transcribed tape recording of a few minutes of conversation in a middle-class American family at dinner time. It will give you some idea of how values are taught over and over to children. The family includes father, mother, and three sons: Ronnie, four; Mark, three; and Jimmy, two.[14]

MOTHER: Ronnie, get your coat off and come get ready for supper.

RONNIE: No. (*no force—sounds more like an automatic acknowledgment.*)

MOTHER: Please? You take your coat off while you're watching the cartoon and then come get ready for supper.

JIMMIE: (*in high chair near mother in kitchen*): Ah-ya-ya-ya-ya-ya-ay- (*Pounds loudly on his plate.*)

MOTHER: Hey! Sh-h-h.

JIMMIE: Dadadadadadada.

MOTHER: No, you be quiet. We are going to get ready for supper now.

JIMMIE *continues pounding.*

MOTHER: No!

JIMMIE *pauses, then pounds more.*

MOTHER: Stop pounding *now!*

JIMMIE (*Pauses, then pounds some more*): Eat. Eat. (*Pounds.*)

MOTHER: Don't you do that any more. Come on.

JIMMIE *pounds intermittently.*

MOTHER: What do you want—milk?

JIMMIE: Mmmmyah—

---

* Charles M. Harsh and H. G. Schrickel, *Personality—Development and Assessment,* Second Edition. Copyright 1959 The Ronald Press Company.

MOTHER: No, you can't have it, Jimmie.
MARK: No.
MOTHER: No.
RONNIE: No.
MOTHER: Don't put your hands in your milk.
MARK: Why?
MOTHER (*loud, exasperated*): Oh, Jimmie! Now don't spill your milk in your plate like that. That's not *nice* to do that!
MARK: No.
RONNIE: No.
MOTHER: *Eat* your fish. You're supposed to *drink* your milk.

The values stressed in this short time are (1) being ready and punctual, (2) keeping clean and not making messes, and (3) being quiet. Over and over the mother stresses these points. The two older children help by repeating what she says. In further recordings it was found that the two younger children, Mark and Jimmie, resisted the mother much longer than did the older child. Jimmie would continue saying "No," but each time with less emphasis and finally after much encouragement would say "awright." The oldest child's experience with the family interaction was different from the experience of the two younger children—possibly because the mother's influence is stronger when she has one child than it is when her attention is divided among three children. The older child, before the others were born, missed this interaction with the larger group. Different regional, ethnic, religious, and social class groups will vary considerably, not only in values but in the way values are taught to children.

Differences in values influence children's behavior in art. From the information we have about Jimmie, Mark, and Ronnie, we can anticipate some problems they might have in art activities.

The first two values being taught—punctuality and cleanliness—if overstressed, might inhibit a child's work in finger paint, clay, papier mâché, or any material he might interpret as "messy." If he has to keep clean at all times and be on a strict time schedule, his freedom to explore and play with these media is likely to be curtailed. These three children, in an art activity, are likely to react to a teacher's suggestion quite differently. The two younger children may be much more self-directive and may need less encouragement to become motivated than would the older, more passive child.

Teachers motivate children by trying to get them interested and involved in reaching goals. Sometimes they encourage children to set their own goals. A child's motivated behavior is usually an interaction of his own needs and drives with his interpretation of the situation in which he finds himself. The teacher, by various methods, tries to arouse the child's curiosity, encourages him to try, and introduces things into the environment that may stimulate his interest. Sometimes threat of punishment is used to motivate the children to learn or perform. Whether the child is motivated or not depends on what the teacher does, how the child interprets it, and the way the child's past experience has prepared him for the situation. In the P-D process, the teacher's use of motivation takes place at Point II. He sets up the stimuli and contributes to the child's psychological environment. The way the child responds depends in part on his readiness, the values he has learned, the way he was taught them, and sometimes upon his place in the family.

When people are faced with value standards that are unfamiliar to them—when they are rewarded for a behavior in one situation and not in another, or conversely, punished for a behavior in one situation and not in another—because of differences in values among the persons in authority, they are experiencing *discontinuity*. For example, children who have always been rewarded for being obedient and doing just what they are told may have a difficult time in an art situation where they are asked to experiment with materials and are *not* told what to do. If they become anxious and afraid because they do not know what kind of performance will be rewarded, they may show the behavior of people under stress. They may (1) withdraw from the situation, (2) overcompensate by working extremely hard to achieve a "right" result, or (3) insist on doing something for which they know how they will be rewarded.[15]

Value differences in the subcultures of the home, the school, the church, and the peer group create the discontinuities children and adults experience. Part of our job as teachers is to help pupils to learn to deal with discontinuity, to learn that the rewards or

FIGURE 5–3.   CONFLICTS IN VALUE

punishments will not always be the same in every situation. Some adaptation is necessary in a large complex society, especially in a period of rapid culture change.

CHANGING AMERICAN CORE VALUES AND VALUES IN ART EDUCATION

Some of the anthropological studies described in Chapter 2 were made in times and places where the force of cultural maintenance was very strong. People knew their roles, and few deviated from them. Present-day Western culture is not so well-defined and is changing rapidly.

Studies of American core values are somewhat limited because the subject is so complex, but some of the values can be identified. [16,17,18,19,20] The core values that appear to be in conflict with goals in art education are organized in Figure 5–4. Three categories are shown to indicate differences in values that may be learned by any one child. The *traditional* values are those that have been handed down from generation to generation. The *emergent* values are those that appear to be developing in the process of culture change and the growth of "mass" society. The values in *art education* are those generally attributed to "artists." They do not represent the values of all art educators and teachers. The value conflicts described below do not occur in every child, but are, rather, tendencies toward conflict that can affect their learning in art.

VALUE CONFLICT I. COMMON MAN, GROUP MAN, AND INDIVIDUAL ARTISTIC MAN. In the development of the concepts of democracy, *equal* has often been interpreted to mean *average,* and the "common man" has been considered ideal. In an exploratory study of graduate students in education, Spindler has found a strong value placed on averageness as being descriptive of "the ideal American boy." The students put a major emphasis on sociability, well-roundedness, and ability to ". . . do many things quite well but . . . not [to be] an expert at anything in particular. . . ." This ideal boy is average in academic ability and in intellectual capacity. Furthermore, Spindler writes, "Individuality and creativity or even mere originality are not stressed in this concept of values. Introspective behavior is devaluated (even intellectuals are [suspected] by many). Deviancy, it seems, is to be tolerated only within the narrow limits of sociability. . . ." [21]

The ideal boy described by Spindler's students is not likely to exhibit the divergent behavior that is necessary for an artist. Other studies indicate that the artistic boy has personality problems, probably caused by the belief that the artist's role is a deviant one

	American Core Values		Ideal Values in
	Traditional	Emergent	Art Education
1.	common man	group common man	individual artistic man (divergent-creative)
2.	expediency and hard work	security	artistry and craftsmanship (quality before gain)
3.	reason as a basis for action	group planning before action	emotion combined with reason

FIGURE 5–4. SOURCES OF VALUE CONFLICT

in American society.[22,23] For this reason he has experienced a discontinuity throughout his school years, being rewarded by his teacher for artistic expression, but seeing no acceptable place in practical affairs for that expression. The teacher can help the artistic boy by pointing out the utilitarian values of art in society and at the same time encouraging him to depend on his own feelings for guidance, rather than on the pressure of conformity.

Artistic boys may be anxious because there is not a clearly defined adult role for their art interests, but artistic girls show fewer personality difficulties, probably because the roles of wife and mother do not exclude artistic production.

The traditional concept of the common man and the emerging concept of the group common man are strengthened in overcrowded schools. Lack of space and shortened class days often necessitate the neglect of individual expression. Opportunities for self-direction, so necessary in creative work, are not possible.

Along with his study of "the ideal American boy," Spindler has sampled (as a teaching device to help students become aware of their own and society's values) the attitudes of education students from 1952 through 1958. The report of his findings is used here for two purposes: (1) to point out a change in attitude toward the artist that may be taking place and (2) to illustrate ways in which innovation (in this case the entrance into the space age) and fear of catastrophe influence the values of a society.

The table shows, in categories, types of responses to open-ended questions. The questions covered a much larger range of attitudes, but only those most related to art are quoted here.

The investigator does not assume that this study is free from bias, because students may have discussed the test; nor is the sample necessarily representative of teachers-in-training throughout the country. But some interesting points can be raised. The pattern of change in the two questions is not the same except for a trend from a higher percentage of negative responses on both questions to a lower percentage with time. The attitudes about intellectuals are not as negative as those about artists. The negative attitude about artists does not shift consistently through time. Spindler feels that one of the most important implications of his

*TABLE OF CHANGING ATTITUDES**

Artists are——	1952	1953	1954	1955	1957	1958
Negative responses	46%	47%	22%	20%	35%	12%
Neutral responses	28%	25%	36%	20%	20%	25%
Positive responses	20%	25%	40%	45%	45%	60%

Negative answers were "bad, strange, weird, nuts, screwy," etc.
Neutral answers were "people, few, born," etc.
Positive answers were "creative, wonderful, exceptional, brilliant, geniuses," etc.

Intellectuals should——						
Negative responses	25%	15%	15%	16%	18%	4%
Neutral responses	29%	33%	38%	40%	47%	15%
Positive responses	35%	46%	40%	40%	25%	75%

Negative answers were "keep it under cover, get out of ivory tower," etc.
Neutral answers were "be more sociable, more human," etc.
Positive answers were "have their work be respected, thrive," etc.

Percentages do not always total 100, because not all students answered all questions.

* Unpublished material used by permission George D. Spindler.

study is that there is a small but consistent group of teachers in training or in advanced work who have negative attitudes about artists and intellectuals. These people will be helping to transmit their version of the culture to children. At times they may be in administrative positions and hinder the work of more creative teachers.

More encouraging is the indication that, at the level of attitude tapped in this kind of questionnaire, a larger percentage of students in 1958 were positive about their attitudes toward intellectuals and artists. Spindler comments, "The most important characterological implication is that these and other shifts in attitude may indicate a trend toward a more tolerant, relativistic attitude, that leaves room for deviant individuals and deviant behavior. In this new frame of reference everyone does not have to be average in order to be acceptable." [24]

The change in attitude may be the result of the entrance into the space age and the increased competitiveness among nations in exhibiting technological advances. In this changed environment, unprecedented situations are arising in science, economics, and international politics. Because new demands are made on people, creative problem-solving is necessary. Attention is being focused on the "uncommon man."

Contemporary man is continually questioning the values of his society. Children very often do not accept the values taught by the older generation. To meet the demands of the changing culture, children are having to choose among conflicting ideas presented to them—whether high achievement is more important than averageness, conformity than independence. The new values cannot be defined in a moral code of "right" or "wrong," but are rather a reflection of basic preferences.

VALUE CONFLICT II. EXPEDIENCY AND HARD WORK; SECURITY; AND ARTISTRY AND CRAFTSMANSHIP. The value on expediency has been growing since the beginning of the Industrial Revolution. The tendency has been to make more and more products in less and less time. Hard work, so necessary to the development of our country, has been measured in an accumulation of things. The two values, expediency and hard work, have led to the measurement of products by size and by quantity. The emergent value, security, probably has grown out of the knowledge that most people can survive economically without working hard, that they can in fact earn many conveniences and amusements on a moderate salary.

The products of the arts, on the other hand, are valued for their quality, a result of slow thoughtful work and the love of craftsmanship, as well as improvisation and invention. Time and speed have to be negated as an artist struggles to master his media and symbols to communicate his ideas. Industry can expedite technical problem-solving with computers, but no machine can help the artist to solve the problems of designing.

With the general value on expediency and hard work in our culture, many children are encouraged at home and in school to be punctual, to make their efforts pay off, to have something to show for their time. These children may have difficulty when asked to experiment without clear-cut goals. Primary children are often willing to enjoy the processes of art, but by fourth grade many of them are much more concerned about what they produce and how it will be evaluated. An interesting feature of the Alper study with finger paint (page 136) is that the middle-class children were more likely than were the lower-class children to want to take their work home.[25] The implication is that the middle-class parents, who most nearly typify the core culture, transmit to their children at an early age the value of showing accomplishments. There is some indication that lower-class parents are less concerned with their children's work in school.

One college instructor made an informal study of motivations of his students, roughly dividing them into two groups: those whose social group emphasized high achievement and those who had no such pressure. The former were less willing to explore; they wanted something to show for every minute of work they put in; and their fear of failure was strong. The second group explored more freely, but often had to be encouraged to complete their creative work.

In art education we are concerned not only with the product but with the kinds of experiences that will help children to develop creativity, confidence in their own ability, and a willingness to explore and invent. We want children to have free, less rigid experiences in art activities. To have a "freeing" experience in art, children must understand that it is all right to have less specific goals.

There comes a time when art in its more developed forms is also very hard intense work, requiring artistry and craftsmanship. Some people do not recognize that, while art must contain an element of play, it also requires skill, patience, and hard work. In their stereotypes of work and play these people cannot see two such "opposite" concepts involved in the same activity.

The artist can work hard, but he emphasizes the joy of working and the ultimate expression rather than expediency. He does not measure his output in units of product per unit of time. In art activities, the teacher can maintain the value of hard work and minimize the value of expediency by allowing flexible units of time.

VALUE CONFLICT III. REASON, GROUP PLANNING, AND EMOTION. Our heritage of democratic freedom has been based on the assumption that man is capable of reason, that logical thinking is the best way to solve our problems of life. During the pioneer days emotions had to be subjugated to the rational necessities of frontier living. Our society has come a long way in the use of reason in problem-solving, yet it has not become educated in the constructive use of emotion with reason. The arts, because they depend on kinesthesis and sensitivity, promote the integration of feeling with reason. Some pupils need help in overcoming conflicts about the expression of feeling. In our culture boys, especially, have been encouraged not to show emotion.

Art and Personality. A study was made on the personality structure of adolescent boys and girls by Louis Stewart at the Institute of Child Welfare at the University of California. While this study deals with adolescents, it has implications for elementary teachers because most early values are learned in the home and in the elementary schools.

ARTISTIC PERSONALITIES. Self-portraits of forty boys and forty girls of high school age were judged according to selected criteria in drawing, such as complexity, integration, naturalistic representation, symbolism, use of line vs. use of shading, aesthetic quality, technical skill, vividness of styles, vitality, etc. Three judges evaluated each picture on each variable.

Those portraits that showed the strongest "artistic ability" according to the criteria were given further analysis. Because these students had been the subjects of intensive study by the institute since they were in fifth grade, considerable information on their personality structures was available.

The experimenter found that the over-all pattern for boys in this group was "strongly suggestive of neurotic introversion, with symptoms of anxiety, low self-esteem, lack of social skills, and isolation from peers." For the girls the pattern suggested "creative and introversive tendencies, which, although accompanied by lack of interest in social contacts, are not related to anxiety, tension, or maladjustment." [26]

Stewart interprets the findings for boys as indications of cultural value conflicts. He stresses the deviation of the stereotyped idea of the artist from the average male in American society. Certainly the description of these boys is different from "the ideal American boy" reported the same year by Spindler.[27] Stewart feels that many artistic boys do not see a means of attaining adult male status and still continuing their artistic work. These boys may be experiencing "discontinuity" between their personal rewards from achievement in art and the lack of opportunity for reward from society. The full-time painter or sculptor is generally pictured as living in poverty. Master craftsmen, potters, weavers, rarely support themselves from their artistic work alone. The economic anxiety, Stewart feels, is closely related to the boys' adjustment problems.

Girls are not under the pressure to be "bread winners" in our society; success for women is not usually measured by the amount of money they can make, although goals for women are in a state of change and conflict. The young girl who is artistic may be in a better position than others. She has a goal acceptable for her sex and apparently not in much conflict with traditional sex role concepts.

The artistic girls in this sample showed few or no neurotic tendencies. Stewart also suggests that the introversive boys may have more adjustment problems than girls as the ". . . extroverted traits are so important in determining social acceptance and prestige" for boys at this period.[26]

The artistic boy is further separated from the mainstream of the culture in those communities where academic or practical studies are valued more highly than nonacademic or impractical studies. Art, however, is not far different in intent from English composition. Both subjects are symbolic, organized means of communicating. Letter symbols (organized through grammar) and pictorial symbols (organized through design) are both necessary even from the most practical viewpoint.

Some schools have emphasized group planning as a means of moving forward. Many improvements in business and industry are dependent on group, rather than individual, problem-solving. Some artists work very well as members of a team, but others can be far more creative alone. The artistic child may lose interest in art work if he is forced to subjugate his ideas to a larger plan.

The elementary school boy is not immediately confronted with attaining adult status and is not experiencing the pressures on adolescent boys to assume adult roles. If artistic children become more aware of the functions of the artist—the architect and industrial designer as well as the painter and sculptor—they may be prepared to go through the adolescent period with less conflict. If the trends noted by Spindler continue and a positive attitude toward artists becomes a part of the general value system in American society, the discontinuity will decrease for more people. Values change rather slowly, and sometimes they are held as ideals rather than as actualities. A person may approve of artists but hesitate to work actively in art. Also, changes in values may be noticeable in some segments of our society and not in others.

The three areas of conflict described are the most evident ones that teachers in art activities have to deal with in understanding children and in understanding the values that motivate the parents to instill certain ideas in their children. *One of the most difficult things a teacher has to learn is to recognize values in others, values that may be so different from his own that what he communicates is grossly misinterpreted.* The more a teacher knows about value differences within recognizable groups, the more easily he can learn to recognize how a child may be learning to respond. When the teacher is aware of cultural dynamics and of how values change, he will be better prepared to help children deal with the discontinuities of change in art activities.

IMPLICATIONS FOR PRACTICE

The immediate psychological environment plays an important part in the way children and adults are able to respond in art. In order to improve the environment, to encourage freer perceptual and creative activity, teachers should try to eliminate the threatening factors in the environment. While many artists can work under conditions of great threat, it may be that they are people with such strong drives to create that they overcome the fears. Freedom from fear increases most children's ability to respond to the environment.

OVERCOMING THREAT AND ANXIETY

Anxiety produced by continued failure can be overcome with the help of a patient teacher. Children who have failed in other areas may carry over their attitudes about themselves into the arts. *Often in art activities a child can get his first real success experience, if the teacher helps him to select a medium and process in which he is likely to succeed.* The teacher will need to help the child recognize that in some degree he has succeeded. Out of one success experience other successes can be built. If the teacher has over-all criteria of what constitutes success in art, many children will fail. But if the teacher can find a success each child has made in some phase of an art activity, the child can progress. Encouragement should be individualized; when pupils are regressing or are not continuing to develop, the causes should be investigated. Constructive criticism, in the upper grades particularly, is needed in keeping the child motivated to continue to develop his artistic potential. In a study of fifth grade children on the effect of praise or blame on "introverts" and "extroverts," it was found that praise, if continued, increased the output of introverts, and blame increased the output of extroverts. This study was made in academic subjects.[27] Since creativity in art is a more subjective, introversive activity, praise and constructive criticism may be the best method of teaching during art activities, but allowances for individual differences should be made.

Identifying possible threats to children requires vigilance on the part of the teacher. Many successful teachers keep a notebook handy all during the class day to record behaviors they might forget. A weekly review often identifies a pattern of behavior of some child that will give the teacher clues as to what may be frightening or inhibiting him. Art materials such as finger paint, torn paper, or clay may be threatening to some children who relate the material to past experience where they have been punished for getting "dirty," tearing books, or playing with mud. When a child is reticent about handling materials, a teacher can find a substitute so that the child can go on with his art expression in a medium he more readily accepts. Often after some success children can be led into expanding the range of materials with which they are happy to work. Sometimes the threat may simply be new things. Patient encouragement of the more rigid children to learn about, understand, and accept new things should help remove the threat. Occasionally a child who has had traumatic experiences that he cannot consciously remember may express fears the teacher is not prepared to deal with. In such cases the problem should be referred to the school psychologist.

The classroom environment is influenced by the teacher's attitudes. A teacher who accepts children for their individual worth, who has patience and understanding, will create a different psychological environment than will a teacher who finds it difficult to accept children, who has little understanding of them, and whose patience is easily taxed. The great rewards of teaching come from helping children develop their own potential. The teacher who has had success in doing this, who finds teaching personally rewarding, is likely to create a classroom environment which will be non-threatening to most children.

Enabling children to realize that they are accepted sometimes takes a great deal of time and effort. One teacher, particularly strong in teaching art, found it necessary to show Mexican-American children that she did accept them. Some of these children had learned that teachers did not always appreciate them, expected little of them, and liked them best when they were quiet.

This teacher worked with each child to help him find media and means of expression he particularly liked. She spoke Spanish some of the time in the classroom. Most of the children had been hesitant about using it at school, but eventually talked more freely in her classroom. Further, she showed examples of excellent Mexican fine arts and crafts to the whole class and in displays in the halls. All the children worked to records of Mexican folk music. Artistic expression and creativity flourished. A teacher who is genuinely interested in all the children in the class can help build a pleasant environment.

OVERCOMING DISCONTINUITY

The teacher is only one of many people who are teaching the child his cultural values. If parents stress conforming behavior, negate the value of activity in the arts, or come from a deviant subculture, real conflicts can be set up for the child. Parental indifference can also be a negative factor in the child's adjustment to school. The absence of reward may be as confusing to a child as punishment he does not understand. Part of the teacher's role is to help parents understand the values of the school.

We can gain some insight into the problem of discontinuity from anthropologists and social psychologists who are concerned with the problems of children who shift from one major culture to another. To a degree, a similar type of transition is faced by the child who experiences a discontinuity between his home variation of the subculture and the subculture represented by the school. DuBois suggests that the teacher should first help the child understand the differences in the rewards in the two groups, to encourage him to make an adjustment to more than one system of rewards and to understand himself in terms of the differences. This requires the teacher to be a "warm, supportive figure." [28] Hilda Taba, a specialist in intergroup education, has pointed out that not only the teacher but the class as a whole must understand differences in culture and support the individual child as he makes his adjustment. [29]

Art activities that are taught without relating them to the society and to possible adult roles may have little meaning for children. Art in all its myriad applications should be studied in the elementary school. Conflicts can be resolved by an understanding that art is work as well as play; that it is intellectual as well as emotional; that achievement in art is worth striving for.

A major objective in teaching children is to help them to appreciate and to make intelligent and aesthetic judgments about their surroundings. When children in the fourth and fifth grades are learning to see patterns in design relationships, rhythm, and balance, they can begin to see how they will use their understanding as adults. They can be introduced to a few functions of design in buildings, highway systems, airplanes, rockets, and interiors of homes. The roles of builder, engineer, industrial designer, and homemaker are seen in relation to art. Such learning not only gives children concepts of art as part of their lives but suggests adult vocations in the field of art.

SUMMARY

Threat and anxiety reduce the ability to respond to and organize visual information and to recall the details of objects seen previously.

Success experiences increase the ability to respond to and organize visual information. Failure experience tends to decrease this ability.

Continued success in general school experience helps children set more realistic goals for themselves and leads to further successes. Failure experience often leads children into setting unrealistic goals and into failing again.

Praise of more introversive pupils tends to increase their production; blame of more extroversive pupils tends to increase their production more than praise. Children are behaving more introversively in art, interpreting and expressing from the basis of their individual experience. Constructive criticism rather than blame is probably more effective in motivating children in their art activities.

Most cultures, at the present time, are in stages of considerable change due to innovation, cultural confluence, and catastrophe. These factors affect different parts of the culture in differing degrees. A given child represents his family, his subculture, and the core culture in some phase of the dynamics of culture change. These factors influence his attitudes toward art and his ability to perform in art tasks.

Art, not being central to American culture, introduces conflicts such as those between the common man and the individual, expediency and artistry, and reason and emotion.

Discontinuity can often be overcome when children are more sure of how they are going to be rewarded in each situation. Fear of failure and unrealistic goal-setting can be reduced by helping children succeed in some degree. Anxieties can be reduced when the threatening objects are identified and removed until the child is ready to accept them.

RELATED ACTIVITIES

Research materials and theory have meaning for us when we can relate them to our own experiences. Most of you have experienced anxiety in the classroom and, to some degree, value conflicts about art. It is hoped that the materials in this chapter have helped you to understand and perhaps resolve some of your own conflicts. To bring your new understandings into clearer focus, try some of these suggestions:

1. Write a short paper describing a discontinuity in reward that you have experienced. The conflict may be between home and school, between different classes, or between your peer group and your art class. Try to identify the differences in values in the two groups, the kinds of rewards given in terms of those values, and your own feelings during the experience.

2. Make a simple sampling of other students' attitudes toward art. Write a series of questions to ask each student and tabulate the answers. Cover such topics as these: art as an adult role; awareness of art forms used every day; what artists are like as people; what art is.

3. Observe children in an elementary school and watch their behavior in art activities, particularly when new materials are being introduced. Record the behavior as you see it. Compare your record with other students' records and discuss possible reasons for the children's actions and reasons for differences in the observations made. If possible, make a confidential case study of one of the children, using both your observation records and school records of the child's performance and background.

REFERENCES

1. Thelma Alper, Howard Blane, and Barbara Adams, "Reactions of Middle and Lower Class Children to Finger Paints as a Function of Class Differences in Child-Training Practice," *Journal of Abnormal and Social Psychology,* LI (1955), 439–448.

2. Hugh Kohn, "The Effect of Variations of Intensity of Experimentally Induced Stress Situation Upon Certain Aspects of Perception and Performance," *Journal of Genetic Psychology,* LXXXV (1954), 289–304.

3. Florence Goodenough, "The Intellectual Factor in Children's Drawings" (doctoral dissertation, Stanford University, 1924), pp. 21 ff.

4. Beatrice Lantz, *Easel Age Scale* (Los Angeles: California Test Bureau, 1955).

5. Pauline S. Sears, "Levels of Aspiration in Academically Successful and Unsuccessful Children," *Journal of Abnormal and Social Psychology,* XXXV (1940), 498–536.

6. Pauline S. Sears and Harry Levin, "Levels of Aspiration in Preschool Children," *Child Development,* XXVIII (1957), 317–326.

7. Leo Postman and Donald R. Brown, "The Perceptual Consequences of Success and Failure," *Journal of Abnormal and Social Psychology,* XLVII (1952), 217.

8. Ruth Benedict, "Continuities and Discontinuities in Cultural Conditioning," in *A Study of Interpersonal Relations,* ed. Patrick Mullahy (New York: Hermitage Press, Inc., 1959), pp. 297–308.

9. Clyde Kluckhohn, "Culture and Behavior," in *Handbook of Social Psychology,*

ed. Gardner Lindzey (Cambridge: Addison Wesley Publishing Company, 1954), II, 931–937.

10. Melville Herskovits, *Cultural Anthropology* (New York: Alfred A. Knopf, Inc., 1955), p. 264.

11. Max Lerner, *America as a Civilization* (New York: Simon and Schuster, 1957), p. 477.

12. Ralph Tyler, "The Individual in Modern Society," *The National Elementary Principal,* 1956–1957, p. 52.

13. Charles M. Harsh and H. G. Schrickel, *Personality—Development and Assessment,* 2nd ed. (New York: The Ronald Press Company, 1959), p. 375.

14. Malcolm McFee, unpublished ethnographic materials used with permission.

15. G. G. Thompson, "Multiple Responses to Frustration," in *Readings in Educational Psychology,* ed. Jerome M. Seidman (Boston: Houghton Mifflin Company, 1955), pp. 187–196.

16. Clyde and Florence Kluckhohn, "General Orientations and Class Patterns," in *Conflicts of Power in Modern Culture,* ed. Lyman Bryson (New York: Harper & Brothers, 1947), pp. 106–128.

17. W. Lloyd Warner and Paul S. Lunt, *The Social Life of a Modern Community,* Yankee City Series, Vol. I (New Haven: Yale University Press, 1941).

18. Margaret Mead, *And Keep Your Powder Dry* (New York: William Morrow and Co., 1942).

19. George D. Spindler, "Education in a Transforming American Culture," *Harvard Educational Review,* XXV (1955), 145–156.

20. Geoffrey Gorer, *The American People* (New York: W. W. Norton and Company, Inc., 1948), pp. 70–105.

21. George D. Spindler, unpublished materials used with permission.

22. Clyde and Florence Kluckhohn, "General Orientations and Class Patterns," in *Conflicts of Power in Modern Culture,* ed. Lyman Bryson (New York: Harper & Brothers, 1947), pp. 114–116.

23. Louis H. Stewart, "The Expression of Personality in Drawings and Paintings," *Genetic Psychology Monographs,* LI (1955), pp. 45–103.

24. George D. Spindler, unpublished materials used with permission.

25. Alper, Blane, and Adams, *op. cit.*

26. Stewart, *op. cit.,* p. 81–82. Reprinted by permission.

27. George G. Thompson and Clarence W. Hunnicutt, "The Effect of Praise or Blame on the Work Achievement of 'Introverts' and 'Extroverts,'" in *Educational Psychology,* ed. Arthur P. Coladarci (New York: The Dryden Press, 1955), pp. 422–431.

28. Cora DuBois, "Some Notions on Learning Intercultural Understanding," in *Education and Anthropology,* ed. George D. Spindler (Stanford: Stanford University Press, 1955), p. 101.

29. Hilda Taba. See *Education and Anthropology,* ed. George D. Spindler (Stanford: Stanford University Press, 1955).

6

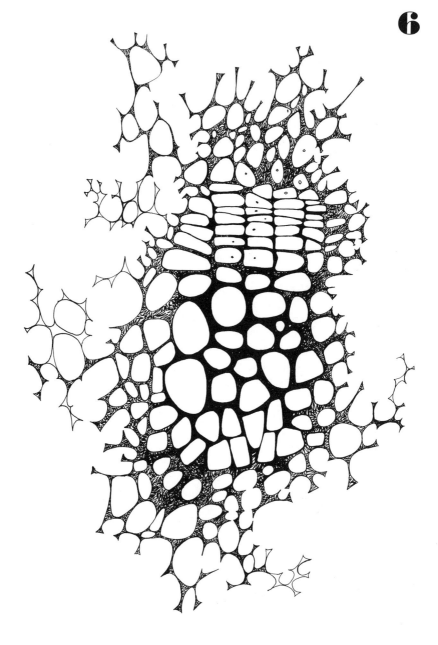

The Creative Process

What is "creativity?" What is a person doing when he is being "creative?" Philosophers have been asking these questions for centuries. Experimental psychologists are currently exploring creativity and giving us some information about man's capacity for achieving it.

One of the major objectives of art education is the development of the creative potential of children. To pursue this objective, art teachers need to gain much more understanding of the creative process. They need to try to discover what kinds of experiences encourage students to develop habits and attitudes that can lead to creative work. This chapter explores some of the current research in order to find directives for encouraging creativity in the elementary classroom.

DEFINITION. "Creativity," as used in this book, refers to people's behavior when they do such things as (1) invent a new pattern, form, or idea, (2) rearrange already established objects, patterns, or ideas, and (3) integrate a new or borrowed factor into an already established organization. A child is being creative when he delineates a different but recognizable symbol for an object, such as a variation on the symbol of the sun as in Figure 6–1. He is being creative when he takes another child's construction of building

FIGURE 6-1. VARIATIONS OF SUNS BY FIRST GRADE CHILDREN

blocks and rearranges them to represent something new. A group of children painting a mural may discover that an important idea has been left out. If they find a way to incorporate this idea into what they have already painted, they are solving their problem in a creative manner.

Some kind of creative activity is possible for almost everybody. J. W. Tilton, an educational psychologist, believes that most behavior is to some degree creative. He reasons that most situations people face are somewhat different from any they have faced before. They have to reorganize patterns or ideas, invent or borrow ideas, symbols, or objects to fill a void in a new situation.[1] For example, when two people are carrying on a conversation, each is creative as he tempers and adjusts what he is saying to the way he interprets the response of the other individual. He tries to find new words and new arrangements of words that will communicate his ideas more clearly. The creative child, in art, can likewise develop symbols to communicate his feelings and interpretations through his painting. The creative teacher changes and reorganizes ideas and symbols to meet the varied levels of understanding of the children in the class.

AREAS OF CONCERN. As art educators we are concerned with two major questions: (1) What generalizations derived from research on the creative process can we use in organizing art activities in the elementary schools? (2) What can we do to help develop the creative potential of more children?

"Creative potential" is a person's capacity for developing creative behavior. Environmental influences appear to inhibit the development of the traits of creativity. For this reason we cannot adequately evaluate an individual's creative ability until he has had optimum opportunity to use it. Our question then becomes, "What kinds of experiences and what kind of environment can we provide to give children more opportunities to develop their abilities in creative behavior?"

PERSONALITY TRAITS
RELATED TO CREATIVITY

Research into the nature of the creative process began with biographical and aesthetic studies of the lives of creative people. Studies have been based on artists' and scientists' own introspection into their creative activity. Only recently have controlled experiments in psychology tried to identify the kinds of behavior needed in different kinds of creative activities. A leader in this research has been the experimental psychologist, J. P. Guilford.

RELATION TO "PERCEPTION-DELINEATION." Creativity as viewed from the standpoint of the "perception-delineation" theory takes place at Point IV of the process. The three prior points, (I) *readiness* (all the factors of culture, personality, development), (II) *the psychological environment* (environmental influences on the child's behavior), (III) *information handling* (organizing detail), are all bases for creative behavior. At Point IV *the creative process* evolves from all the prior factors. The traits that appear to evoke creative behavior are (1) originality, (2) fluency, and (3) flexibility. Past experiences are drawn upon for explorations and inventions. Each of the points in the P-D theory functions in the development of the traits. We will deal with those traits that appear to be developed in elementary school children.

ORIGINALITY

Investigators have identified originality as a trait of creative people. They have found that the creative person in the sciences and the arts is able to see remote relationships, is willing and able to make "unusual or uncommon responses"[2] and to be novel and clever.[3]

ORIGINALITY IN CHILDREN. In children's drawings there are different levels of originality. A child's immature perceptual development may account for an unusual representation of an object. If a child has not yet become aware of size relationships, he may draw people and trees the same height. If he has not discovered how hands and arms are organized, he may draw a tadpole-like symbol for a person. The originality he expresses does not result from a purposeful disregard for realism, but rather from his symbolic representation of his level of perceptual development. This kind of originality is different from that used by the mature artist who, for another reason, paints people as large as trees or distorts anatomical structure.

Originality in children may be described as the ability to make *unusual responses,* to organize things in *uncommon* ways, and *to be novel* at their present level of over-all development. What might be called original in a child might not be original for an adult. What might be termed original within a given individual's experience might not be original for a larger group of people.

FLUENCY

The frequency with which ideas or symbols can be expressed in a given time is called fluency. If a child is fluent, he draws more symbols in an art period and thus has more opportunities to make novel responses. Fluency is a trait often found in creative people, but fluency without originality may not result in creative expression. A child who paints twelve uninventive scribbles is probably being less creative than a child who is inventing symbols and organizing them in one drawing.

Guilford identifies two kinds of fluency, *expressive* and *associational.* In speaking and writing, expressive fluency means speed in bringing forth words and combinations of words that express ideas. Associational fluency is the ease in building subtle relationships, one related concept on another.

In art, expressive fluency is probably evident when a child delineates symbols without any great effort. Associational fluency can be seen in drawings in which the symbols are carefully related to each other. Young children, who usually do not plan their drawings with care, but have this kind of fluency, may produce pictures that show refined relationships. Japanese children (whose paintings are shown in Plate III and in Figure 6–2) apparently have highly developed associational fluency. The children notice small details and integrate them skillfully in their art work, probably because they live in a culture where subtle relationships are stressed.

Verbal skills do not always adequately measure intelligence. A child may have a low score in the verbal part of an intelligence test, yet show high ability in the nonverbal part. The same child may not talk freely, yet he may be able to express ideas fluently with paint. Another child may have found his verbal expression quite adequate and may not feel a need for expressing his ideas in pictorial form.

FIGURE 6–2. BOYS IN SNOW (COLLECTION AL ZELVER.
SEE ALSO PLATE III)

Fluency in art may be determined partly by intelligence, and partly by culture, reward, and opportunity. In her analysis of artists and non-artists Eiduson found that the most important single difference between the two groups was that artists had early recognition of their artistic talents. This recognition led to ". . . many gratifying experiences and relationships . . . which tended to place a premium on artistic capabilities and helped crystallize these . . . activities in later vocational choice and performance." [4]

A CASE STUDY. Differences in fluency may be related in part to the kinds of experiences students have had. One student teacher experienced a great deal of difficulty with art activities. She appeared to be extremely slow in getting ideas with which to work, or in developing the ideas after she had them. She was above average in intelligence and could talk and write fluently. During a conference with her instructor she recalled an experience in junior high school, where the class had been required to draw pirate ships. The teacher, in front of the class, told the girl how poor her drawing was and tore it up. The student told her college instructor, vehemently, "I've hated art ever since!" After much assurance that she could overcome this feeling she was given encouragement to try again. She was given the choice of tools and materials easiest for her to use and the smallest successes were rewarded with more encouragement. Gradually she built up her fluency in art.

Several pupils in an elementary art class were very slow in working with torn paper, but had not been so with other media. Discussion revealed that they had been scrupulously trained not to tear books; tearing paper was like damaging a book, and might result in punishment. Here again we see the influence of past experience on fluency.

People differ considerably in their responses to frustration and failure, both contributing factors to low levels of fluency. If you lack ideas to work with, struggle fruitlessly to get them symbolized on paper, or experience difficulties in organizing your material visually, your trouble may be related to your past experiences. You may not have had opportunities to bring forth ideas in this manner, or you may have had a series of "failure" experiences in art. Because the process of communicating visually is so very complex, considerable patience with yourself and with your pupils is needed to develop visual communication skills. Continued opportunity for some degree of success, positive reward, and stimulating motivation are usually helpful in the development of fluency.

FLEXIBILITY

Flexibility, a trait often found in creative people, refers to a person's ease in changing his behavior, in meeting new situations, and in seeking new ways of solving problems.[5] *Degree of flexibility* means the level of ease with which a person responds to change. Where flexibility is weak we find *rigidity*. Rigidity describes behavior that is repetitious. The individual resists change in himself and in others. He stays within a narrow range of action, and resists moving into unfamiliar situations. *Flexibility-rigidity* describes a scale along which we measure behavior. Apparently some people are rigid in almost everything they do. Others are rigid in some situations and not in others, or flexible in most situations and rigid in a few.

To what degree these tendencies are inherited is not known. It is clear that they are affected by experience. Some of the experiences in academic training reinforce the trait of rigidity. If students are rewarded for conforming to the "right" as opposed to the "wrong" response, they will try to limit their behavior to what will get them good grades (being "right" on tests, using the "right" tool in the "right" way, saying the "correct" thing in class discussion).

If skills are taught in an authoritarian manner, the learner will probably be hampered in using them flexibly. If the skill is taught by the teacher as one of several "successful ways" people have found to use a tool or material, and if students are encouraged to explore other ways, more opportunity is given for flexibility to develop.

TYPES OF RIGIDITY. Rigidity can be seen in three types of behavior.[6] (1) *Slowness in reaction to familiar things.* Children who are hesitant in responding need plenty of time to formulate what they have to say, whether in words or in drawings.

(2) *Resistance to new or novel things.* This is related to "intolerance of ambiguity," an inability to respond to or accept that which is

not understood. A person might respond quickly to familiar things, but slowly to the unfamiliar. A child who has appeared to be quite flexible when using familiar art materials, may be quite rigid when working with unfamiliar tools and materials. A child might be very responsive verbally to familiar art forms, but be unable to verbalize about a new art form.

(3) *Difficulty in shifting from one type of motor-cognitive task to another.* A motor-cognitive task is one that requires the person to direct cognitively his motor skills—to use his body, his hands, his feet to achieve certain results. A highly skilled dancer has to use extreme concentration to make his body do just what he wants. A sculptor, working with a chisel, wants no interruption to interfere with cognitive control of his hands in his delicate operations. A child may have difficulty if he is taught one type of motor skill such as learning to write in neat rows, and then is asked to learn to control a large bristle brush. Somewhat different muscles and kinds of control are needed. If the teacher overstresses the value of orderliness in arithmetic papers, of staying in the right columns and keeping the borders clean, some children may find it very difficult to switch to the task of expressing an idea freely in art, when improvisation and exploration are goals.

We have referred to the Alper study on the effects of past experience (cleanliness training) on finger painting. To understand its implications for creativity we will review it in more detail.

CLEANLINESS TRAINING AND ART BEHAVIOR. In a study of nursery school children of different socio-economic backgrounds Alper compared finger-painting behavior to toilet training practice. As a group, the eighteen middle-class children had an average of 11.2 months longer toilet training than did the eighteen lower-class children. The middle-class standards of cleanliness were also much more exacting. Each child was asked individually to paint, and his behavior was reported by trained observers. Seventeen lower-class but only five middle-class children began to paint immediately. Seventeen lower-class and only eight middle-class children used both hands. Ten lower-class children and only one middle-class child used warm colors.

In another study with two similar groups, crayons were used instead of finger paints. The differences in response between the two groups were slight.[7]

Creative expression is limited if the child is working with a medium that is inhibiting to him. Prior training can influence a child's speed in responding, especially if the child perceives the new tools and materials in relation to past experiences in which he was punished. The teacher, however, cannot assume that all children follow the apparent cause-and-effect relationship indicated in the study. Some children may hesitate to finger-paint because it is a shift from their previous motor-cognitive tasks—they may not be accustomed to using their hands in this way.

Because there is such a wide range in speed of response, the teacher should allow plenty of time for some children to get involved in the activity. He might take intermediate steps to help the children to grow less rigid in responding. He should provide aprons to assure the children that they can keep their clothes clean. To provide adult authority for what he asks the children to do, he can demonstrate finger painting, using his whole hands and forearms. Sometimes he may need the parents' support for the activity.

Some parents do not see the educative values of finger painting, and some children have so great a fear of getting dirty that they refuse to touch the paints. In such cases it is unwise to force a child to become involved. The conflict arising in the differences in reward (parental approval or teacher approval) would be too great. One inventive teacher solved this problem by mixing bottles of liquid soap with food dyes while the children watched. Because soap was associated with cleanliness in the child's mind, it was not as threatening.

Flexibility is a necessary trait for a teacher, because the classroom is full of new situations. This is one reason why actual experiences with a variety of art materials are useful to the teacher-in-training. They give him opportunities to try new things, to explore and develop his potential for freer problem-solving.

To summarize, rigid behavior in art activities may be a response to (1) the medium or tool, as in finger painting, (2) the degree to which to task is unfamiliar and the ability to respond to novelty, (3) the nature of the shift required between tasks using different motor skills and cognitive controls, and (4) the child's ability to succeed within the time allowed him.

PAST EXPERIENCES

The experiences that an individual has had, his whole readiness for a perceptual task, come into play in the process of delineation. His past experiences are the basis from which he creates. Usually, a person who is highly talented in a creative activity such as sculpture or experimental physics draws from his wide experience, his fund of knowledge in his field, and his skills in seeing relationships between ideas, objects, and events. His traits of originality, fluency, and flexibility are often highly developed.

A wealth of background and the creative traits are necessary to the creative process. Why, then, do many children, without such a background, express so much fantasy and whimsy in their work? The answer may be that children have not learned the same organizing system as adults. They are more free to be inventive within the range of their experience than are many adults with much wider experience. But to encourage *continued* development of creativity, teachers need to provide children with varied and stimulating visual experiences.

PAST EXPERIENCE IN ART

Children's ability in art depends not only on their creative ability but also on their past experiences in art. Point IV of the P-D process represents the actual carrying out of an art expression. Creativity can be limited when a child has ideas to express but lacks a suitable means and medium to depict them. The child who is familiar with a wide range of materials, who has explored their possibilities for expression, has a better chance to bring his creative response into being. He is less likely to be discouraged by unfamiliar material.

In the primary grades the teacher selects materials that are easy to manipulate, materials that do not get in the way of expression. People of any age who are inhibited in their expression can find simple materials useful at first because some success is easier to achieve. Learning skills is not an end in itself. Skills are the *means* with which the expression is delineated.

During the intermediate years some children are ready to explore tools and media that require continued practice to develop the desired results. Perceptual and manipulative skills usually come with exploration and continued activity. Generally, skills in art, using a brush, drawing, modeling, can be improved during the elementary years by working toward expressive goals, trying to get the materials to do what the child wants them to do to reach those goals.

The teacher's role is to encourage children when their skills seem inadequate. Continued experience leads to greater skills and a broader repertoire of means of expression. When children have learned to use some tools easily, they can quickly learn to use other similar tools, particularly when the teacher encourages them to *see and feel* the relationship. If they have found several uses of the first tool and have been encouraged to be exploratory as well as confident with it, then learning to experiment with the new but similar tool will be easier.

Functional fixedness, being limited in the ways one can see to use materials, can limit the range of creative expression. This is why formal, authoritarian skill training in art in the elementary years is not wise. Neither is it wise to leave a child entirely to his own devices. By selecting challenging yet appropriate materials and by helping when necessary, the teacher can lead children into the development of skills that can serve rather than dictate their creative work.

DEVELOPING THE CREATIVE BASE. To increase the store of experience and information children have as a basis for creativity, teachers can help them develop more adequate means of getting information. To see the relationship between perceptual capabilities and creativity, let us review Point I of the P-D theory, readiness.

As we have learned, children differ in their habitual ways of orienting themselves to space and to their environment generally. Some depend largely on postural cues, others on the visual field. Many people can easily use both postural and visual cues. Because space-orientation is a learned behavior, it is reasonable to assume that those children who are able to use both kinds of cues are getting broader and more varied information about themselves and the environment in which they are moving.

We also learned that people tend to depend more on what they know than on what they see to get information from their environment. They make compromises between knowledge and visual information. The child who can use cognitive, visual, and tactile information has the better basis for being creative. He has more avenues for handling information.

The quality of creative behavior is developed by the range of experience and the imagination of the child. The teacher can enrich the experience of the child by giving him a stimulating environment in which to work. He can encourage both postural and visual responses. Children can study the environment as they already know it, and they can look for and analyze things they had not previously noticed. Such analysis should have meaning for the child and be within his range of acceptance, yet should also be exciting and interesting enough to challenge his curiosity. The classroom environment should be conducive to imaginative, inventive exploration.

Many children have the capacity for creative work but never get a chance to develop it because they have been inhibited in their attempts and have never experienced success. Many children can be creative if they are given enough time and encouragement. Others, who have developed fear of the ambiguous or the undefined, must be carefully prepared for new experiences so they can relate them to what they already know. Planning sequences will avoid abrupt shifts in the kinds of motor-cognitive activity necessary for success.

Creativity is more than mere personality projection; it requires invention, exploration, and some form of production. The creative potential is nurtured as these are experienced.

IMPLICATIONS FOR PRACTICE

Part of our obligation as teachers is to broaden the range of children's understanding, to help them see more relationships, to give them a wider base for creative thinking and action. At the same time our method of teaching should allow for the wide individual differences between children in responding to creative tasks, and it should encourage inventiveness in problem-solving, particularly in art. If children can learn that there are times when one does have to conform and other times when being somewhat different is also "right," they will learn to deal with both kinds of situations and not be limited to success in one or the other. The teacher should encourage and reward both types of behavior; he must make clear what he expects to be the outcome of his procedures, or the children may become confused.

A child who is learning to letter, to make legible and fairly neat papers, learns that he will be rewarded if he is meticulous about staying on the lines. Later in the day he may be given a large piece of paper and a big brush and encouraged to paint a picture of "what it feels like to be outside on a rainy day." In one instance he is expected to give a "right" rather than a "wrong" response; in the other he is to invent symbols of something that is very personal to him. The two tasks have different kinds of goals, requiring different conceptual and motor processes. If the child uses what he has learned in the first instance (to stay on the lines, to follow an outside criterion for what is "right"), he will be lost in the second instance without definite "orders" to guide him. If the differences in the activities are made clear to him, he has more chance of succeeding in both. But if the shift between tasks is made without this understanding, children may have failure experiences and learn to dislike some tasks because they do not understand the differences in reward. Because most classroom activity has been geared to learning specific skills, some pupils who have traits needed for artistic creativity are not rewarded and encouraged to develop them.

TWO TYPES OF THINKING PRODUCTION. Guilford has identified two basic patterns in the "thinking" process, which are related to the two examples (lettering and painting) discussed above. He identifies them as *convergent* and *divergent* [8] (see Figure 6–3). Much of the educational system is convergent, pulling ideas together. Too little opportunity is given for divergent thinking—expanding the ranges of relationships, improvising on a small factor, fantasy,

FIGURE 6–3. CONVERGENT AND DIVERGENT PRODUCTION

imagination, creation. Guilford identifies divergent production as related to creativity, in the arts particularly.[9] In complex problem-solving, both divergent and convergent thinking skills are needed. New concepts must be creatively imagined, but convergent thinking and production are needed to organize them so they can be understood by others.

Many people are capable of some artistic or scientific creativity, but, lacking opportunity for divergent activity, they have no way to develop their potential. For this reason, throughout this book we shall consider all prospective elementary teachers as potential artists and creative teachers, even though some may not have realized their potential.

Our objectives in developing creativity are (1) to give children wider ranges of experience and understanding, (2) to give them opportunities and rewards for developing flexibility, fluency, and originality, (3) to help them develop the communicative skills in art, which include (a) perceptual skills as a contribution to the creative base of the other skills, (b) eye-hand coordination as they are ready to develop it, and (c) familiarity with a wide range of tools and materials and opportunity to explore their possibilities.

SUMMARY

Creativity is the ability to invent new symbols and ideas, to improvise on established symbols, to rearrange established organizations into new organizations, and to integrate new or borrowed ideas into previously organized systems or situations. In the perception-delineation process, the creative act is at Point IV.

Personality traits that appear to be most related to creativity in the arts, as well as in the sciences, are originality, fluency, and flexibility. These are to a large degree learned behaviors, partially dependent upon the opportunity and motivation to develop them.

The factors that appear to hinder creativity are (1) rigidity in response to familiar material, to unfamiliar material, and to extreme shifts in motor-cognitive tasks; (2) too narrow a range of experiences and understandings; (3) limited development of information-handling skills; and (4) inadequate means of expression.

Much of the educative process is focused on convergent, rather than divergent, thinking and production. Children should be made aware of the differences in reward and motivation in the two types of behavior.

Teachers must allow for individual differences in the length of time needed to complete a creative act, in past experience with art media, and in the kinds of motivation that will have meaning for the children.

The creative base from which children work can be broadened by development of their information-handling abilities—learning to see both visually and cognitively, learning to use both visual and postural cues.

RELATED ACTIVITIES

Try some activities that will help you invent symbols or uses of materials. Start with a medium that you have enjoyed using. If you enjoy torn paper, concentrate on it for several days, seeing how many kinds of communicative symbols you can invent with torn paper. Explore the potential of paper as a medium; see how different weights and textures of paper respond to varied techniques. Use torn paper in different types of expression—for abstract design, to tell a story, as a teaching device for the elementary grade you hope to teach. After you have succeeded with a favorite medium, try some of each of these suggestions with a medium you have not enjoyed as much. If you are like the teacher-in-training who had to cover her eyes to endure immersing her hands in finger paint, you may look back on certain media with distaste. This girl enjoyed the paint when she was sure that it would wash off, that her clothes could be protected, and that the results could be exciting. It is important to be patient with yourself, to try to overcome what may seem disagreeable about the task, and to give yourself plenty of time to make adjustments to new tasks and situations.

REFERENCES

1. J. W. Tilton, *An Educational Psychology of Learning* (New York: The Macmillan Company, 1951), pp. 89–90.

2. J. P. Guilford, "Creative Abilities in the Arts," *Psychological Review,* LXIV (1957), 110–118.

3. J. E. Drevdahl, "Factors of Importance for Creativity," *Journal of Clinical Psychology,* XII (1956), 21–26.

4. Bernice T. Eiduson, "Artist and Nonartist: A Comparative Study," *Journal of Personality,* XXVI (1958), 22. Reprinted by permission.

5. Guilford, *loc. cit.,* and Drevdahl, *loc. cit.*

6. K. Warner Schaie, "A Test of Behavioral Rigidity," *Journal of Abnormal and Social Psychology,* LI (1955), 604–610.

7. Thelma Alper, Howard Blane, and Barbara Adams, "Reactions of Middle and Lower Class Children to Finger Paints as a Function of Class Differences in Child-Training Practice," *Journal of Abnormal and Social Psychology,* LI (1955), 439–448.

8. J. P. Guilford, "Traits of Creativity," in *Creativity and Its Cultivation,* ed. Harold H. Anderson (New York: Harper & Brothers, 1959), pp. 151 ff.

9. Guilford, *op. cit.,* pp. 142–161.

7

Theories of
Child Art

In this chapter we will review the ideas presented in Part One in terms of the perception-delineation theory, draw out useful generalizations with which to analyze existing theories of children's art behavior, and summarize the implications for practice.

PERCEPTION-DELINEATION

The theory of P-D has been presented as a framework to help us think about the complex process of a child's use of his past experience and his present interpretation of visual information in creating an art form. Art activities require the coordination of the child's intellect, emotions, and perceptual and motor skills. Many factors in his environment contribute to his readiness to use these traits. Learning in the classroom occurs to the degree that experiences are geared to the differences among children in each of the traits needed for art activities.

ART ABILITIES. The major art abilities are responding, expressing, designing, and creating. Perceptual skill is needed in order to be responsive to one's environment. The intellect is used for organizing and arranging to create a design. Emotion determines what is expressed, according to the artist's sensitive interpretation of life. Motor skills are necessary to create an art form that has quality and refinement.

All artists of note do not necessarily excel in ability to use all these traits. The training of some artists has so stressed the development of one of them, such as motor skill, that the others have been repressed to the point that a rich full art expression is never achieved. The problem for teachers is (1) to recognize how the environment influences abilities and (2) to help pupils develop abilities in their own patterns. The P-D process has been described to help you see the ranges of individual differences children may have, and some of the reasons why these differences exist. It is hoped that you can construct a curriculum in art that will help pupils develop their abilities more fully. The abilities needed for art activity are also necessary for most of mankind's attempts to understand his environment and to deal effectively with his fellow men.

Figure 7–2 is a reconstruction of Figure 3–1. In it are listed the variables that have been identified as influences upon children's behavior in art. We will discuss them briefly in review.

READINESS

Point I depicts the individual's over-all readiness to respond at a given time. It includes his present stage of physical and intellectual development and his perceptual development.

PHYSICAL AND INTELLECTUAL DEVELOPMENT. Height, weight, skeletal growth, muscle development, and intelligence do not

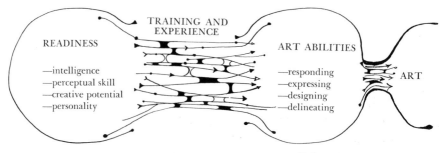

FIGURE 7–1. TRAINING AND EXPERIENCE

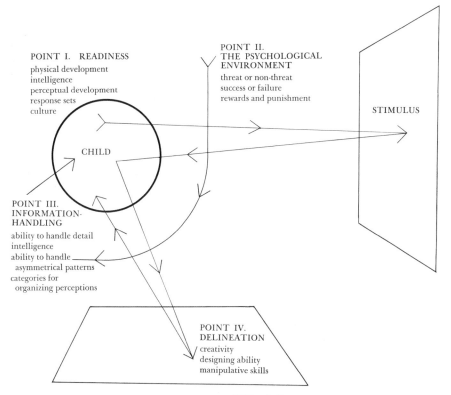

POINT I. READINESS

physical development
intelligence
perceptual development
response sets
culture

CHILD

POINT II.
THE PSYCHOLOGICAL
ENVIRONMENT

threat or non-threat
success or failure
rewards and punishment

STIMULUS

POINT III.
INFORMATION-
HANDLING

ability to handle detail
intelligence
ability to handle
  asymmetrical patterns
categories for
  organizing perceptions

POINT IV.
DELINEATION

creativity
designing ability
manipulative skills

FIGURE 7–2. PERCEPTION-DELINEATION THEORY

increase at the same rate within a given child. Wide ranges of growth patterns are found in children of the same age. We are not certain as yet how much physical structure affects art skill. Some evidence indicates that drawing ability depends more on how a child sees than on how well his hand muscles are developed. Age alone is an inadequate measure of stages of growth. Child growth is best thought of as organismic (each of the factors of growth at its present stage of development interacting with all the other factors of growth).

PERCEPTUAL DEVELOPMENT. Children grow in perceptual ability from seeing wholes to handling details, with wide differences at any age level. The ways in which children are taught to respond to their environment—learning about things cognitively or visually—determine in part their ability to handle visual details. The culture, which values certain things over others, directs perceptual training. Intelligence is related to information-handling; children with higher I.Q.'s tend to be able to handle more detail and more asymmetrical materials than are those with lower I.Q.'s.

RESPONSE SETS. Differences in personality, culture, and experience develop differences in the habitual ways in which people respond to their environment. These are called response sets. Rigidity is one personality trait that acts as a response set. Three types of behavior may appear as rigid behavior: (1) slowness in responding to the familiar; (2) slowness and little ability in responding to new things; and (3) difficulty in shifting from one motor-cognitive task to another.

The way people orient themselves to space is in large part learned, ranging from extreme dependence on visual cues to the resistance of visual cues and use of bodily feelings of uprightness. People who can freely use postural cues also can easily separate themselves and other objects from the surrounding field. They tend to resist authority figures in perceptual decisions. Young children are more visually dependent, becoming more posturally dependent as they grow older. The transition is parallel to the development of self-reliance as the child grows older.

CULTURAL TRAINING. The culture in which a child has spent his formative years and his own family variation of that culture influence strongly the kinds of things to which he will give attention. The attention-directing function of cultural attitudes, values, and beliefs encourages perceptual training in some areas and not in others. Sex roles or labor divisions often determine who shall have training as artists. Cultures vary in the amount of deviation that is allowed the individual.

THE PSYCHOLOGICAL ENVIRONMENT

How a child feels about his environment influences his perceptual ability and his work in art. The presence of a threat, whether defined or not, may cause anxiety that prevents satisfying work. Failure tends to inhibit children's ability to select and respond to visual experiences and to set realistic goals. Rewards and punishments are the means through which children learn what is a "right" way to behave. When there is discontinuity between values in different situations, children become unsure of how to behave.

INFORMATION-HANDLING

Ability to handle detail and asymmetrical patterns, along with general intelligence, helps children organize the visual information they receive. Perceptual training can develop the capacity to use detail. Learning categories for visual information, such as variations of color, enables children to handle more information. Much of the organizing activity goes on at a precognitive level.

DELINEATION

The creative process evolves from the preceding factors. A child's readiness for perceptual experiences is the basis for his delineation. Fluency, flexibility, originality, and past experience all contribute to creativity. A child's creative work is implemented by his ability to use the available materials. If he has had considerable experience and success with exploring a medium and knows several ways to use it, his creative expression is less likely to be inhibited. The child's wealth of background experience, from which he makes choices and devises new combinations, contributes to the quality of his work.

OTHER THEORIES OF CHILD ART

Current theories of child art found in practice today include (1) naïve realism, (2) intellectualist theory, (3) perceptual development, (4) the haptic and visual child, and (5) age-based concepts of developmental stages. We will discuss these theories and their implications for practice in terms of the P-D theory we have just reviewed, as supported by the research in Part One.

NAÏVE REALISM

This theory assumes that there is ". . . no difference between the physical object and its image perceived by the mind." [1] For

FIGURE 7-3. NAÏVE REALISM

example, it is assumed that a child looking at a car will have the same visual information to use in drawing the car that an adult who knows a great deal about industrial design or mechanics would have. According to this theory, the major differences between child art and adult art result from differences in motor control. It does not recognize that the individual is in part an information-handling machine and that prior learning, the culture, perceptual development, eye-hand coordination, and many of the factors of personality influence a child's readiness to respond to the visual stimulation of the objects in his environment. Furthermore, the theory does not consider the influence of fear and of past experiences on the child's art expression, nor does it recognize individual differences in ability to handle detail and asymmetrical design.

IMPLICATIONS FOR PRACTICE. Whenever children or adults are expected to draw in exactly the same way as soon as they learn the motor skills, the teacher is assuming the theory of *naïve realism*. One of the reasons many children learn to dislike art activity is that they have tried to draw the way the teacher has asked them, but they have not *seen* the object the way the teacher has seen it. This does not mean that we do not all see *somewhat* alike. Living in a similar culture we learn much the same visual symbols for things. Children can be taught to see objects with more careful observation, but the qualities they express about the object will be determined in part by their past experience and the way they are responding in the present situation. If children are being taught to draw in an academic way, with no allowances being made for individual differences, and with success and failure made evident by criticism or grading, their ability to observe will be inhibited. Children can be asked to expect individual differences, both in the kinds of assignments they will get from a teacher and in the results they will achieve.

Representational drawing is a form of visual communication. We have learned to see on a flat two-dimensional page symbols that mean three dimensions in both form and texture. Some non-literate peoples who are not used to getting information from photographs do not "see" what is communicated in pictures. They have not learned to "read" the flat symbolic pattern into their concepts of the three-dimensional world. Although most children can "read" pictures, they have not learned the details of the symbols enough to reproduce them, nor have they observed nature in enough detail to see where the symbols come from. Drawing, like speech or writing, is communication. It can be understood by many, yet it is unique to the individual. Among children, who have not yet learned much of our common visual language, great differences will be found. Forcing adult symbols on children inhibits creativity at their own level and leads to experiences of failure.

Naïve realism limits art activity to reproduction and does not include emotional and ideational expression, designing, improvisation, and invention. The theory does not consider the operation of culture in establishing goals for artistic activity. It assumes that the "realism" would be the same for all peoples. Studies by anthropologists show that the culture directs child growth in art by habitually using certain symbols to represent certain ideas.

INTELLECTUALIST THEORY

The intellectualist or "child draws what he knows" theory has been widely accepted. What a person knows about an object is his concept of it. One person's concept of an apple is made up of his impressions of taste, color, cost, observation of apple-growing, and all his other intellectual experience with apples. The concept does not necessarily include all the details that would be seen in

FIGURE 7–4. INTELLECTUALIST THEORY

a careful visual analysis of a present apple—subtle gradations in color and shade, small details of shape and texture.

In the intellectualist theory, the child's concept is considered to be the main factor in determining how he draws. In her original research, Florence Goodenough developed the "Draw a Man Test," which appears to measure intelligence by the amount of detail and correctness of relationships that a child is able to incorporate into a drawing.[2] The child with a more complete concept of "man" would draw more detail and would show a higher level of intellectual development than would a child whose concept of man contained less detail. This test has been the basis upon which much of the intellectualist theory has been built. Goodenough presents her study as an analysis of only *one* of the factors in the drawing of children; she recognizes that cultural factors are important, too.[3]

An important indication of the Goodenough study is that children's drawing is a form of communication and is more often related to their concept formation (what they know) about objects than it is to their visual analysis, thus supporting the statement, "the child draws what he knows and not what he sees." However, other research has shown that both processes, concept formation and visual analysis, are influenced by training and experience.

In terms of the research used in the perception-delineation theory of child art, what a child knows and his general intellectual capacities are important, but other factors—his cultural conditioning, success and failure experience, rigidity or flexibility, perceptual training, his orientation to space—are also in operation. Concept formation and visual analysis can be reciprocal. Knowing something about an object can improve the ability to observe its details. Careful observation will, in turn, increase knowledge about it.

PERCEPTUAL THEORY

Arnheim's theory is based in large part on research in Gestalt psychology.[4] The theory postulates that a *child draws what he sees—* that the perceiving process starts with undifferentiated wholes and proceeds towards more detail. To show that adults perceive generally in different ways from children, Arnheim describes drawings made by adults holding a pencil between the toes rather than the fingers. By asking adults to use untrained muscles he removed the variable of differences in motor coordination between adults and children.[5] The differences in amount of detail and kind of symbols used remained.

The study by French (p. 81) shows a *trend* from preference for more simple detail pictures toward more complex detail through the elementary grades. His study also shows greater ranges of individual differences in preferences for simple or complex pictures at each age level among children than among adults.[6]

The abilities to see detail and to handle asymmetrical material are related to intellectual ability, with wide individual differences at all ages. Culture is another variable. Arnheim recognizes

FIGURE 7–5. PERCEPTUAL THEORY

this and posits his theory that the child draws what he sees as only one of the important considerations in child development in art.[7]

HAPTIC AND VISUAL THEORY

Lowenfeld's theory of the haptic and visual tendencies of children, discussed in Chapter 3, is based on the assumption that space-orientation is a biogenic factor and not modified by experience. He describes the haptic child as one who is most dependent on his own feelings (emotional and bodily) in orienting himself to his world; the visual child depends more on his visual environment. More recent research by Witkin[8] and Linton[9] indicates that differences exist between children and adults in the ways they orient themselves to space. Younger children are more field dependent with wide differences at every age. Witkin reports that mother-dominance during growth, over-protection, restricted activity, and limitation of the child's curiosity by encouraging conformity, lead to dependence on the visual field rather than to independent use of bodily cues. Tendencies to orient oneself to space in one way or another are in large part learned.[10] Teachers can help children learn to use both types of cues in relating themselves to their world. Considerable care should be used in encouraging a very conforming child to develop kinesthetic responses to his environment. As he gains confidence in himself through such activities as rhythm and dance, and drawing what it feels like to run, to dance, or to march, he will increase the range of his responses.

DEVELOPMENTAL STAGES

Considerable effort has been made to identify children's developmental stages in art according to chronological age. This work started in Europe before 1900 when the child development studies began. These studies were often made by analyzing the drawings of one child or a group of children without knowing the conditions under which they were made or without having enough samples to make valid generalizations about all children. Some attempts were made to study children's drawings from different cultures. In the United States the work of Gesell and his associates, in their extensive studies of average child development, established norms for behavior.[11] The study at the Fels Institute by Sontag, Baker, and Nelson[12] and the work of Nancy Bayley in the Berkeley Growth studies[13] indicate that growth is more organismic than linear, and that at any given time all the variables of growth in a given child need to be considered.

The most widely used theory of developmental stages in art, that of Lowenfeld, was the first to make some allowances for individual differences that were not considered in the theory of naïve realism.[14] He has postulated the following developmental stages in art:

Scribbling, two to four years of age, when the child is marking with various kinds of strokes.

Pre-schematic, four to seven years, when the child is developing his scribbles into symbolic representation.

Schematic, seven to nine years, when the child has developed symbols he uses over and over again to mean certain things.

Dawning realism, nine to eleven years, when the symbols are becoming more "realistic."

Pseudo-realism, eleven to thirteen years, when the effort to achieve realism is accentuated.

The term "schema" is usually used to mean a flat drawing of a symbol that represents an object, and not a picture of the "real" thing as it exists in three dimensional space. Actually all drawing is schematic; no drawing ever achieves "realism" as the eye perceives it. In dealing with children's drawings, we more specifically could call them *flat* schema and *perspective* schema (in which the symbol represents space).

Another study of children's development in art was made at the Cleveland Museum. It is perhaps the most extensive research on child-art development to be carried on in many years, but it has not had wide publicity. This work, directed by Thomas Munro with Betty Lark-Horovitz and Edward Barnhart, was exploratory and not extensive enough to generalize for specific ages. But it does raise questions that challenge some of our theories.[15]

They studied dimensions of children's art more than symbolic development. A check list was developed from an analysis of the hundreds of children's drawings in the museum's files. The dimensions they found were (1) differences in *representation,* the use of color and clarity of outline; (2) *representational unity,* the relationship of all the ideas presented as in a scene; (3) *thematic unity,* the organization of line, shape, and color; (4) the quality of line used; and (5) the degree of completion of all the areas of the drawing. Further analysis was made of the use of flat schema or attempts at showing three dimensions, or a mixture of both.

The different age levels were studied, using the children from the museum's Saturday morning classes as subjects. Sample drawings from each child were collected. Specific motivating subjects were used, such as, "What you would like most to draw" and "Children playing out in the snow in a park." The drawings were then evaluated according to the check list.

The researchers say of their study that the differences found do not lend themselves to an easy analysis. Too many differences in children and kinds of art are possible. They found that the stages were not the same in each of the dimensions they studied. The ability to achieve thematic unity, that is, over-all design and decorative effect, increases to age eleven and then decreases so that fifteen-year-olds perform more like six-year-olds. In the study of the uses of schema there is a great deal of overlapping between ages and "levels of artistic expression." In Barnhart's part of the study 50 per cent of his sample, ranging in age from eight to twelve, were performing in the three stages he has identified— "Schematic, mixed schematic, and true to appearance." This suggests that the levels of development postulated by Lowenfeld's theory are too narrow in range and do not include all the dimensions of art behavior.

MENTAL AGE AND ART DEVELOPMENT. Mental age, which varies widely from chronological age, may be a better basis for identifying developmental stages in art. The tests of Goodenough[16] and the Easel Age Scale of Lantz[17] have related mental age to drawing ability. Neither, however, deals with creative ability nor the effect of the immediate psychological environment, although Goodenough does recognize cultural influence, as well as training and motivation. Children who are rewarded and have continued satisfaction in art activity will probably develop their potential more than children who have little satisfaction. But art products alone cannot be the sole measure of a child's potential. Some children whose products seem poor may do superior work when their environment improves.

Ability to see detail develops with age, with a trend from seeing an undifferentiated whole toward handling more detail. This trend is modified by intelligence; the more intelligent respond to more detail. Furthermore, culture operates as a strong director both in perceptual training and in rewarding artistic behavior. Perceptual training, the establishment of "sets" to see, rigidity-flexibility tendencies, habits of orientation to space, all contribute to a child's development in art. *Few of these things are directly related to a child's chronological age.* Culture also directs the kind of realism the child will attempt to attain, whether an effort is made to reproduce nature or to use the cultural symbols for things, such as those illustrated in Figure 4–6. The relationship between mental age and the amount of detail is not exclusive of other factors. For these reasons art products alone cannot be an accurate measure of a child's mental age.

When all factors are considered, only a very general concept of art growth as a series of developmental stages can be used. Probably children scribble before they invent symbols; the symbols become more definitive as they have more experiences; the symbols approach cultural "realism" when the motor, perceptual, and cognitive skills, as well as conditions in the environment, allow them to do so. The nature of the symbols the children invent is related to their total biopsychological-cultural experience.

The use of age as a criterion has been based on the assumption that biogenic growth patterns can be identified. Hallowell feels that we should abandon attempts to find relationships between art development and innate growth patterns, as the environment plays the major role in influencing the rate and direction of artistic development.[18] McCandles and Spiker posit that any attempt to find a relationship between changes in behavior (such as in art) and a child's age must also consider past learnings, physiological changes, shifts in the kinds of rewards society is giving him, and the child's changing status, which are only "incidentally related

to time since birth." [19] If an age-grading basis of modal development is necessary due to the age-grading system in schools, then
Figure 7–6 is perhaps a helpful, but necessarily general, attempt
to organize these variables on an age continuum.

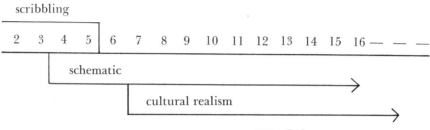

FIGURE 7–6. CHILD DEVELOPMENT IN ART

A schema or symbol is the major means of visual communication. The most exacting attempt to copy nature is still a two-
dimensional symbolic form for a three-dimensional object existing
in three-dimensional space. A drawing in mechanical perspective is
an attempt to show relationships between things as true to reality
as possible, but it only captures an instant of the experiences of an
actual perceiver looking with only one eye. Perception with two
eyes in a moving body gives one many views of a thing.

IMPLICATIONS FOR PRACTICE

Before a curriculum can be planned, before materials and
tools can be ordered, the nature of the class and the ranges of individual differences in readiness (Point I) should be considered. If
possible, the teacher should see anecdotal records, information
about family background, and intelligence test records. The
planning of the art activities is much easier if time is allowed for
teachers to observe the class they will have next year, and if records
are kept of each child's growth in such factors as ability to handle
detail, eye-hand coordination, and skill in using media.

The study of the Orotchen children and other cross-cultural
studies of children's art indicate that cultural values and cultural
training to see contribute to a child's readiness to see and draw.
Tasks and experiences that do not consider his readiness may result

in failure if the child has not been prepared for them. If children are going to go on a field trip to the beach or park, you may suggest that one way to record the experience is to paint it. Prepare them to see before they go. First consider their prior experiences with the things they are going to see. In an informal discussion, find out how much they already know. If your object is to develop awareness of small plant and animal life, bring into the classroom a few objects that they will see later in natural settings. Introduce both the visual and cognitive qualities of the things.

Point II of the P-D theory deals with the psychological environment the teacher helps to create. For most art activities encouragement, praise, and constructive criticism are effective. Be aware of possible discontinuity between what is done at home and at school.

At Point III of the P-D process pupils are handling the information they have received from their environment. They are doing this in terms of all their prior sets, their past experiences and motivation. You can help children learn about new things in their environment in terms of what they already know. Build one concept on another. For example, if children have already learned that forms change in size as they move farther away from them, then they can learn that color too changes as it moves farther away. The dimensions of their visual world can be broadened and made much more stimulating for creative expression.

Give children categories for organizing what they perceive. The categories of seeing, such as the descriptions of shapes (round,

FIGURE 7-7. PREPARATION, EXPLORATION, EXPRESSION

A. FIRST GRADE

B. THIRD GRADE

FIGURE 7–8. DRAWINGS OF TREES AFTER STUDYING BRANCHES

thin, long, narrow, bigger than, smaller than) and the way things change their shapes in space, give children more readiness to see and help them organize perceptions. Illustrate the categories with new as well as familiar things. This method helps to overcome the resistance that some children have to change and to novelty.

At Point IV of the P-D process the teacher becomes the catalyst for creative behavior. Up to this time, in understanding readiness, in creating a supportive psychological environment, and in helping children utilize and organize the stimulations they have been exposed to, the teacher has been preparing them for the creative act.

Past experience plays a large role at this stage. If children have had a great deal of opportunity for divergent, original activity, and have been successful in exploration of interesting materials, then the creative expression should come freely. If pupils have not had rewards for being original, take time to help them develop more confidence. In the primary grades most children have not yet been strongly trained in convergent behavior in school (finding the "right" answers, the correct way to do things), and may more readily become involved in creative art expression. But by fourth grade many of them are much more conscious of "correctness" or "incorrectness."

The selection of a variety of stimulating tools and materials is very important. The range of possible choices should not, however, be so great that children become confused or discouraged because there is too much to choose from. Constantly weigh the factors and choose the best way you can to enable the largest numbers of pupils to learn through art activity. Be flexible in planning because you will find wide individual differences in ability to organize detail and in motor and cognitive skills. Although a continuity must be developed within a given school, wide latitude should be expected in each class.

SUMMARY

The art abilities are responding, expressing, designing, and creating. Several theories attempt to explain the development of the abilities:

The perception-delineation theory is a framework in which the individual variables that affect art production are identified.

The theory of naïve realism assumes that children do not draw as well as adults only because they have not developed sufficient motor control.

The intellectualist theory (that a child draws what he knows) assumes that a child draws more detail as he learns more information.

The perceptual theory (that a child draws what he sees) assumes that a child draws more details as he grows older and sees more.

The haptic and visual theory divides children according to assumed biogenic tendencies in space-orientation.

Developmental stages are inadequate as bases for determining art behavior. Past experience, environment, and many other variables do not follow an age pattern.

REFERENCES

1. Rudolph Arnheim, *Art and Visual Perception* (Berkeley: University of California Press, 1954), p. 126. Reprinted by permission.

2. Florence Goodenough, "The Intellectual Factor in Children's Drawings," (Ph.D. dissertation, Stanford University, 1924).

3. *Ibid.*, ch. IV.

4. Arnheim, *op. cit.*

5. *Ibid.*, pp. 120–152.

6. John E. French, "Children's Preferences for Pictures of Varied Complexity of Pictorial Pattern," *Elementary School Journal*, LIII (1952), 94.

7. Arnheim, *op. cit.*, p. 127.

8. H. A. Witkin, H. B. Lewis, M. Hertzman, K. Machover, P. Bretnall Meissner, and S. Wapner, *Personality Through Perception: An Experimental and Clinical Study* (New York: Harper & Brothers, 1954), pp. 120–152.

9. Harriet B. Linton, "Dependence on External Influence: Correlates in Perception, Attitudes, and Judgment," *Journal of Abnormal and Social Psychology*, LI (1955), 502–507.

10. Herman A. Witkin, "Perception of the Upright," *Scientific American*, CC (1959), 54.

11. Arnold L. Gesell and Frances L. Ilg, *The Child from Five to Ten* (New York: Harper & Brothers, 1946).

12. Lester W. Sontag, Charles T. Baker, and Virginia L. Nelson, *Mental Growth and Personality Development: A Longitudinal Study,* Monograph for the Society for Research in Child Development, Inc., XXIII, Ser. 68, No. 2 (1958).

13. Nancy Bayley, "Individual Patterns of Development," *Child Development,* XXVII (1956), 45–74.

14. Viktor Lowenfeld, *Creative and Mental Growth,* 3rd ed. (New York: The Macmillan Company, 1957), ch. II.

15. Thomas Munro, Betty Lark-Horovitz, and Edward N. Barnhart, "Children's Art Abilities: Studies at the Cleveland Museum of Art," *Journal of Experimental Education,* XI (1942), 97–155.

16. Goodenough, *op. cit.*

17. Beatrice Lantz, *Easel Age Scale* (Los Angeles: California Test Bureau, 1955).

18. A. Irving Hallowell, *Culture and Experience* (Philadelphia: University of Pennsylvania Press, 1955).

19. Boyd R. McCandles and Charles Spiker, "Experimental Research in Child Psychology," *Child Development,* XXVII (1956), 77 ff.

PART TWO

THE ART CURRICULUM
IN THE
ELEMENTARY SCHOOL

In the first part of this book we studied the place of art in culture and the ways different cultures train children in art. We studied the ranges of individual differences related to art that are typical of the elementary classroom. Art activity, even in children, is a much more complex process than it appears to be; it involves the whole complex of values, attitudes, traits, abilities that the child has developed.

Part Two will help you to develop a curriculum in art and in the general classroom activity that is supported by art. We will discuss ways in which a teacher may allow for individual differences and still keep the activity meaningful for everyone. If you understand these differences, you will be better able to find adequate means for motivating many types of children into creative work and fuller appreciation of their art heritage. The information you have from Part One is your guide for solving classroom problems.

Each chapter approaches the subject differently. Chapter 8 analyzes ways of establishing objectives. Chapter 9 deals with the learning environment. Chapter 10 suggests a sequence of activities for the elementary school with a scope that allows for individual differences. Chapter 11 analyzes the design process as based on the psychology of perception. Chapter 12 describes classroom procedures for new teachers and reviews the basic elementary art media.

At the end of Chapter 12 is a suggested project that will give each teacher a working model and resource materials for teaching. All of Part Two should be covered to develop this last activity. The summary, Chapter 13, reviews the major generalizations from the foundations in Part One and their relation to practice as suggested in Part Two.

8

Establishing Objectives for Art Activities

In a democratic society the objectives of education theoretically evolve from the ideals and needs of the people. Ideals and needs vary from one community to another and change with time. School administrations and state and local governments often establish objectives in terms of their interpretations of the community's ideals and needs. Differences in interpretation, inadequate measurements, and changing values make the job of establishing objectives difficult in a complex society. School administrators, consultants, and teachers should have broad professional training to help them to evaluate community needs.

DIFFICULTIES IN ESTABLISHING OBJECTIVES

In some schools each teacher determines the objectives. An urban New England girl teaching in a rural Rocky Mountain community will probably interpret the needs of children differently from a girl who grew up in a rural community. If a school principal establishes the objectives, and if he does not understand the community, his objectives may be in strong conflict with those of the majority of parents. When some school boards establish objectives, only the values of the segments of the society they represent tend to be considered. Interpretation depends upon how well the interpreter understands the functions of the society and culture.

No measuring instruments are adequate in formulating a total picture of what our society is or should be. Public opinion polls and census statistics give some information on what people think and how they live. Books are written by thoughtful social scientists, as well as by "popular" journalists, purporting to describe the condition of our culture. All descriptions, whether based on statistics, samplings, or critical analyses, are subject to varying interpretations.

Those descriptions that are based on careful observation and analysis can be useful to a teacher who wants to understand the society; but it must be remembered that the picture is continually changing. What was a valid generalization five years ago may need to be discarded. Because of increased mobility, areas are losing their distinct characteristics. The structure of social classes is changing. Population grows at an increasing rate. Rural areas are no longer far removed from urban. The world shrinks constantly in terms of time and speed of travel. Isolation of groups becomes much reduced.

When cultures change as rapidly as ours, the identification of values to be maintained by the schools becomes more difficult. While a democratic nation has room in it for differing opinions on what the values are, a teacher must have some kinds of objectives in order to decide how and what to teach.

One function of education is to maintain the culture—its values, ideals, and patterns for living—through the training of succeeding generations. In art, this maintenance is difficult because the arts have not been generally recognized as central in our culture. We must set up objectives for art education in a society that surrounds itself with art forms, but that is generally unaware of the aesthetic qualities. We must work with many people who have negative feelings about artists and designers, so we cannot derive all our values about art education from the general public.

In teaching the values of art we have to make art meaningful to people of very different value systems.

Developments in educational research and philosophy do not keep up with the rapid changes in our culture. For this reason we must proceed as logically and intelligently as we can—using the best tools we have for evaluating the function of art experiences in the development of children.

SOURCES OF OBJECTIVES

One source of our objectives is our democratic society itself and the kind of citizenry needed to uphold it. To identify the objectives, we need to study our culture, our form of government, and the basic assumptions and ideals of our social organization. The second source is our own personal or subgroup philosophy. We have varying conceptions about the nature of man and the universe, what man's purpose should be, and how his potential should be developed. Our third source of objectives is our pupils, as we understand them from the viewpoints of professional education, psychology, sociology, and anthropology. This understanding will help us to allow for individual differences in the learning process. Our fourth source is the contribution of civilization's accumulated knowledge and expressions—the sciences, the arts, the humanities. In teaching art, our question is, "What can the rich heritage of the arts contribute to the training of children?"

OBJECTIVES FROM SOCIETY

Two reasons for the growing interest in art are the extension of leisure time and the increase in the number of people whose work does not give them a sense of personal reward because they do only a part of a job. One need of individuals in a mass society is to be able to find self-identification through meaningful independent work. To develop this capacity schools need to give pupils *opportunity to develop talent and skills in activities that contribute to their self-development.* The ability to organize and express ideas in art can give some people a strong sense of self-identification and achievement.

Leisure-time use of the arts is not limited to personal fulfillment. The improvement of homes and the appearance of communities depend on those residents who feel a personal responsibility and have time and skill to devote to the aesthetic quality of our cities and towns. There is also a need for an educated critical citizenry that insists that standards for city planning include the aesthetic as well as the utilitarian use of space. Poorly designed suburbs become drab slum areas very quickly. There is little opportunity for individuals to take pride in improvement of their homes if little or no possibility is left them to contribute their own aesthetic judgments.

Lewis Mumford has observed that our emphasis on increased physical power and the production of goods has taken our attention away from the art of living.[1] Some people appear to be more concerned with having and doing the "right" things than with being able to make independent judgments from a wide range of possible choices. We have well-designed products, but many are so standardized that only a very discriminating person will go off the beaten path to make independent selections.

WORK AND PLAY

Sayers and Madden have suggested that work may have the satisfying qualities of ". . . a deepening and broadening of purpose in . . . activity, . . . imagination and experimentation, . . . enjoyment of the activity from stage to stage, . . . 'pride of workmanship' [and] consequences . . . of deep and lasting significance."[2] In an age of automation millions must do work that has none of these qualities, work that has as its only purpose the earning of money to be spent. For this reason activity that is *not* a part of earning a living should have real purpose and meaning. We perhaps need to question the assumption that we should not work in our leisure time.

Art education can help to meet the needs of a mass society by developing the following attitudes in each pupil:

1. A capacity for aesthetic experience in work and play. Skills to express these experiences.
2. An appreciation of art as a way of life, permeating personal, community, and national planning.

3. A capacity for independent aesthetic judgment as a consumer and a producer, based on experimentation in design.

The following kinds of experiences will help children to reach these objectives:

1. Aesthetic judgment (how things appeal to us visually, their design qualities) should be part of the children's evaluation of most of the activities of the school. It can be used to assess displays in science and social studies. It can be part of the understanding of many of the things studied; the art forms of our own and other social institutions, the home, community, state, nation, and world. Design qualities can be found in the pattern and structure of forms of nature, in the relationship of numbers, and in music and poetry.

2. Opportunities to make choices, based on familiarity with design qualities (form, line, color, texture, balance, and rhythm) can begin at an intuitive level in the primary grades and at a more analytical level in the upper grades.

3. Individual communication through art should be a continuous part of the child's learning experience to equip him to make cultivated aesthetic judgments as a citizen. Art activity, producing and appreciating, then becomes part of the way of life. The stereotype of art as only "play" can be broken down.

CITIZENSHIP FOR DEMOCRACY

Democracy is an ideal that needs constant renewal and development—constant review by alert men and women. It requires citizens who have the capacity as well as the values necessary for democratic life. Seven major assumptions about the nature of man are intrinsic to the functioning of a democratic society.

1. Man has infinite value. The state serves the individual.
2. Man needs and has the capacity for freedom of choice.
3. He has equal rights with others to develop his own potential.
4. He has the capacity for self-government.
5. He has the capacity to work with others in "a teamwork of equals."
6. He is able to use reason.
7. He works for the future—towards his ideals.[3]

A man in perpetual possession of all these attributes is, of course, an ideal. The major function of state-supported educational institutions in a democracy is to develop man's potential toward this ideal.

The teacher has to make decisions about the kinds of experience he should give children to promote the ideals. There are few guide lines from research—either on the state of current values in American democracy or on the effective teaching of values to children. Decisions concerning citizenship training have to be based on logical analysis rather than research. Counts writes that "Democracy is more than institutions and ways of life. It is a great social faith . . ."⁴ Part of our obligation as teachers is not only to guide children into developing their capacities for self-evaluation, self-government, respect for others, and the rights of the individual, but to give them opportunities to see and experience democracy at work.

Values operate at ideal levels, as standards to work toward, and at actual levels, as practiced. For example, the ideal of equality of opportunity is held up as our standard, while in actual practice differences in geographic area, ethnic background, sex, and religion limit these opportunities for many people. We know that children work toward ideals only as they learn them from those adults with whom they identify. The kinds of values the teacher actually exhibits by what he does in the classroom have more effect than those he only talks about. Unless children are able to identify in some degree with the teacher's attitudes and values, they are not likely to learn much from him.

By studying the assumptions about the nature of man that underlie the ideals of democracy, we can form an idea about the characteristics of people that are needed in this society. This idea can suggest the kinds of experiences in art that, we hope, will lead to the cultivation of such characteristics in every citizen.

1. Supporting the assumption that man has infinite value, our objective is to give each child the opportunity to develop his unique potential through creative activity and opportunity for aesthetic experience.

2. As our society becomes more standardized, the areas for

freedom of choice become more limited. Our objective is to give children the opportunity for independent decision-making and action through art activity.

3. Children can have equal opportunities for developing their abilities because of the diversity of media and the flexibility of results possible in art activities.

4. By learning to evaluate their own work and the work of others, children can increase their capacity for self-government.

5. The art program can give children an opportunity to work together. The unique contribution of each child can be seen in group-planned and group-executed projects in art, in social studies, and in science.

6. The use of reason can be exercised along with expressive, intuitive activity. Self-criticism helps to unite the use of reason with the constructive use of emotion. One of our objectives is to help children become intellectually aware of what they are doing—to be able to evaluate their own work.

7. The processes of art necessitate the anticipation of new outcomes. This kind of behavior supports the democratic ideal of hope and work for the future.

ECONOMIC AND SCIENTIFIC NEEDS

Analyze the advertisements by employers in professional fields. The word *creativity* is used repeatedly in advertisements in such magazines as *Fortune* and *The Scientific American.* Industry needs people who have the capacity to reinterpret known relationships, to be inventive and willing to explore the unknown, and who are not satisfied with just one solution to a problem. Scientists and business people, as well as artists, need to be flexible, fluent, and original.

PHILOSOPHICAL SOURCES OF OBJECTIVES

To the degree that we share the values of democracy we share in part a philosophical basis for education. Our freedom of religion and philosophy allows teachers to have differences in their own basic assumptions and values. The teacher who is aware of his own philosophical values is able to relate them to the values of the society and to his obligations to this group.

The ideas one holds about the nature of man also relate to his ideas about beauty. Is the concept of beauty something that evolves through experience? Is it a universal "truth" that exists beyond man? Is it something man searches for but never finds in total? Is beauty in *things* or is it in the relationships and patterns expressed *through* things? Does everyone have the capacity to respond to beauty? Each of us should consider these questions to see how our ideas about teaching art relate to our basic assumptions.

These are broad philosophical questions. There is considerable disagreement among philosophers about their possible answers. But it is important for each of us, as teachers, to question and evaluate our assumptions.

OBJECTIVES DERIVED FROM THE NATURE OF THE PUPILS

The major need of the child in school is to learn many new concepts about the world he lives in and to find ways of organizing them so that he can respond intelligently to his environment. Art has at least four contributions to make:

1. It can help the child to develop visual sensitivity, to see more detail, to develop awareness of form and space, and to find more adequate ways of orienting himself to his environment. Art study can relate cognitive, visual, and tactile interpretations of things.

2. It gives the child a nonverbal means of organizing ideas, which supplements and reinforces his verbal learning. For children whose verbal ability has been inhibited, visual symbols can be a very important means of communication.

3. Art can give a child a direct means of constructive expression of emotion. Conflicts in values about art may have limited a child's opportunity to have aesthetic experiences, but this does not mean he has no need of them. Man needs the mirror of the arts, not only to raise his level of existence, but for his survival as a human being.[5] Art, like language and religion, is a cultivator of human experience, basic to development.

4. Because children differ in rates of growth, one of our objectives is to so construct the art program that every child can succeed at his own over-all level of readiness. We might call this our implementing objective—the objective that will help us to reach all our other objectives.

OBJECTIVES FROM THE FIELD OF ART

"Art comes from art," says Margaret Mead, "It doesn't just come welling up from the subconscious." [6] She is emphasizing that each artist uses his own creativity on the basis of prior invention in the arts. He inherits an art culture which conditions his taste.

Our ideas about art are influenced by the work of architects and industrial designers, like Mies Van Der Rohe, Walter Gropius, Henry Dreyfuss, Charles Eames. These people in turn have been influenced by such Cubist painters as Braque and Picasso.

"The Table" by Braque (Plate I) and the "Three Musicians" by Picasso (Plate IV) analyze the basic forms of the objects rather than just surface appearance. They are concerned with the structure and the patterns of relationships between structures. Cubism was an outgrowth of and reaction to Impressionism, which was an amplification of and reaction to prior art forms. Refrigerators, telephones, packages, gas stations, and hundreds of other products are in the direct line of art descent. Unaware of their pedigree, we look at them in terms of their usefulness and their fashion. Perhaps in the distant future a refrigerator will be in a museum as an art object of the middle twentieth century, and will be looked upon as we look at products of the Egyptian house.

"The Voyage" by Motherwell (Plate III) is an example of abstract expressionism in America. This kind of experimentation is still evolving in Western art. Its influence on product design is growing. Children who have learned to see relationships between experimentation in the fine arts and innovations in product design can evaluate and enjoy changes in all art forms. Many children are flexible. As they grow older they may become more set in their ideas.

If children can learn that art is a progressing, evolving thing and not a static "fine" art of some classic period—that it has been progressing and evolving through history—it will be more alive and real to them. Arithmetic is now being taught in terms of the patterns and relationships of numbers rather than by rote learning alone. This approach helps children learn to make many applications of arithmetic. Analysis of patterns and arrangements in art, and recognition of the many places similar relationships can be found, will help enrich children's responses to art far more than would memorizing names and dates of paintings and artists.

Another reason we have not used our art heritage more consciously is that our economy has been built on "conspicuous consumption." [7] To stimulate the need to buy, manufacturers each year introduce products "more lustrous and more dazzling" than the year before. [8]

How can awareness of the relationship of form and function affect the objectives of art teachers? Mainly, we are led to investigate art works, primitive and sophisticated, ancient and contemporary, not as single objects, but as parts of larger phenomena. This study can in itself be tremendously interesting. The arts, as they function in a society, can be made real to children by a study of American Indian groups and their costume design, pottery, basketry, housing, ritual, and religious service. On the basis of these concepts children can see the functions of art in contemporary culture. Their school, the library, the post office, their household tools can be seen as art forms of a kind.

Some of the values found in art that point up objectives for art education are these:

1. Art is a visual history of the development of cultures. *Objective:* The history of mankind can become more real to children through empathic learning of other periods and societies.

2. Art is the basis of much of our communication system. *Objective:* Children should become aware of visual forms as communication. They should learn to judge what to accept and what to reject, rather than to be passive receptors.

3. Art is a live reflector of our present culture. *Objective:* Children can see art as a growing, changing part of life through their own participation.

PLATE I

BRAQUE, Georges.
The Table. 1928.
Oil on canvas, 70¾″ x 28¾″.
Collection, The Museum of
  Modern Art, New York.
Acquired through the Lillie P.
  Bliss Bequest.

PLATE II

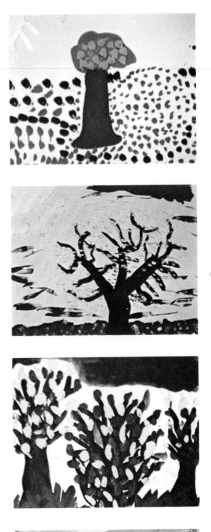

Spring Trees. Harriet, age 6.
Courtesy of Palo Alto Art Club.

Acacia Tree. Chris, age 8.
Courtesy of Palo Alto Art Club.

Trees. Jackie, age 9.
Courtesy of Palo Alto Art Club.

Spring. Susan, age 10.
Courtesy of Palo Alto Art Club.

PLATE III

Children Writing. Tokyo Schools.
Collection, Al Zelver.

MOTHERWELL, Robert.
The Voyage. 1949.
Oil and tempera on paper mounted on composition
   board, 48″ x 94″.
Collection, The Museum of Modern Art, New York.
Gift of Mrs. John D. Rockefeller, 3rd.

PLATE IV

PICASSO, Pablo.
Three Musicians. 1921 (summer).
Oil on canvas, 6'7" x 7'3¾".
Collection, The Museum of Modern Art, New York.
Mrs. Simon Guggenheim Fund.

4. Art is one of man's means for reflection of his personal and collective experience. *Objective:* Art activity helps a child objectify and organize his own feeling and interaction in living.

THE HISTORY OF ART EDUCATION IN THE UNITED STATES

Historically we have moved from the strict perspective drawing of Walter Smith to an almost laissez-faire situation of letting the children have complete freedom in expression today. Beginning in 1872, Smith directed the Massachusetts Normal Art School, which trained many of the teachers who established art activities in public schools in many parts of the United States.[9] At that time the idea of education for everyone was taking hold in the United States; drawing and crafts training were aimed at helping the children of working people learn practical skills. Drawing was not separated from actual design of objects. This relationship closely parallels art in many other cultures where the fine and applied arts are not separated.

The "art for art's sake" revolt of the nineteenth century was directed against poor manufacturing design. Its purpose was to separate art from manufacturing rather than to improve product design. When the fine arts as creative expression began to develop, they were set apart from the production of useful things. Industrial arts was established as a separate subject area in schools. Skills were emphasized but the aesthetic quality of design was neglected. Students copied their designs from other designs.

Other influences on art education came from the philosophies of William James and John Dewey in the early 1900's, and the resulting emphasis on child-centered education stressed freedom and opportunity for learning through experience. At the same time, the United States was exposed to the work of a European art revolt (Armory exhibit of 1913) against nineteenth-century realism, which had been the basis of art training. Cubism, expressionism, and surrealism supported educators who were encouraging emotional expression rather than literal portrayal. This movement furthered the separation of the fine and applied arts.

The Bauhaus school, transplanted to the United States from Germany just before World War II, has attempted to reconcile this separation. This school emphasized from the beginning the strong relationship between fine arts and product design. The Bauhaus training was visual and kinesthetic as well as productive. It made no separation between the materials traditionally used in the fine arts and in industry. Although the original Bauhaus is no longer in existence, teachers who have been trained in its philosophy are making a great contribution to art education in the United States, Canada, and Europe.

It is not clear how the attitude arose that art "appreciation" should be a study of something apart—a subject in which a student learned about art but did not use and become involved with it. The study of art for the sake of recognition or analysis rather than for use has contributed to the separation of the fine and applied arts.

Today, in shows of children's art work all these influences from the past can be found in the classrooms represented. Each teacher has been exposed to one or more of these trends in art education or to different stereotypes about art in our culture. Your awareness of cultural factors should help you to evaluate what you do with art in your classroom. Bringing art into daily living does not depreciate great art nor limit it as an expressive medium.

The general trend in elementary education today is to recognize individual differences in motivation and the kinds of tasks children are capable of, realizing that education has the function of helping children prepare themselves to contribute to and to live in a complex society.

SUMMARY

The objectives listed in this chapter are not absolute. They can become the means of stimulating your careful analysis of your own objectives in terms of a democratic society.

To preserve the individual's sense of worth and accomplishment in an age of automation we need citizens who have the capacity for finding and developing aesthetic experience in work and play. We need people who can make independent aesthetic judgments in the production and consumption of goods.

To further the democratic ideal we need individuals who respect their own worth and that of their fellows; who have the capacity to make free choices; who have equal opportunity for individual development, self-government, and the use of reason; who can work together as equals with others; and who plan for the future. In art activities, where a flexible program exists and individual differences are planned for, these qualities can be developed.

The arts can give children opportunities for exploratory inventive behavior that leads toward creativity, so necessary to our economic and social life.

As teachers we share the major objectives of democracy. Each of us has the obligation to clarify his own objectives in terms of the nature of our society.

The arts can help children develop their visual sensitivity, powers of observation, nonverbal means of organizing ideas and seeing relationships, and the constructive direction of emotional expression.

Experience in the arts can help children learn to understand other periods and other peoples through their art. By understanding their art heritage, children have a better basis for making judgments in art today.

The objectives in these areas are interdependent. As we work to help children become more creative, we can help their perceptual and organizing skills; as we help children become exploratory and inventive, we can help them maintain their independence.

As professional educators we need continually to utilize any research in sociology, social psychology, and anthropology that will help us in establishing and working toward our objectives.

REFERENCES

1. Lewis Mumford, *Technics and Civilization* (New York: Harcourt, Brace and Company, Inc., 1934), p. 5.
2. Ephraim Vern Sayers and Ward Madden, *Education and the Democratic Faith: An*

Introduction to the Philosophy of Education (New York: Appleton-Century-Crofts, Inc., 1959), pp. 211–212.

3. Ralph Gabriel, *The Course of American Democratic Thought* (New York: The Ronald Press Company, 1940).

4. George S. Counts, "The Core of the Democratic Tradition," in *Readings in the Social Aspects of Education,* ed. B. Othanel Smith, William O. Stanley, Kenneth D. Benne, and Archibald W. Anderson (Danville, Illinois: Interstate Printers and Publishers, Inc., 1951), p. 309.

5. E. Adamson Hoebel, *Man in the Primitive World* (New York: McGraw-Hill Book Company, Inc., 1949), p. 161. Reprinted by permission.

6. Margaret Mead in an address to the Pacific Arts Association, Asilomar, California, April, 1958.

7. Thorstein Veblen, *The Theory of the Leisure Class: An Economic Study of Institutions* (New York: The New American Library of World Literature, Inc., 1953).

8. Max Lerner, *America as a Civilization* (New York: Simon and Schuster, 1957), p. 868.

9. Frederick M. Logan, *Growth of Art in American Schools* (New York: Harper & Brothers, 1955), pp. 70–73.

Organizing the Learning Experience

Much of the success of the classroom teacher depends on how well the learning experience has been planned. The methods and practices presented here are suggestions to help you solve procedural problems in planning and in teaching the art curriculum. They are intended to help you work toward your objectives for the children more effectively; to help you plan for the group as a whole and for each child individually. To do this you must be aware of children's differences in ability and the implications these differences have for each stage of the educative process—determining children's readiness, creating a constructive psychological environment, introducing appropriate motivating experiences and materials, encouraging creative expression, and evaluating the results to help decide future tasks.

PLANNING FOR INDIVIDUAL DIFFERENCES

Some of the differences can be identified in school records. Intelligence tests measure a part of a child's potential.[1] If tests are given only on entrance to school and are not repeated at biennial intervals they cannot be assumed to be accurate. Environmental factors apparently can influence a child's test performance.[2] Anecdotal records of the child's performance in former classes will give you some ideas about how he has been responding. If possible, learn the attitudes of the teachers who made the anecdotal report.

Family background will give you clues to the kinds of visual experience and value training the children will have had. But, again, do not generalize too far. Social structure is changing so much that our assumptions about certain subgroups in our culture may no longer be valid. Also, detailed records for many children are not available. In many communities the turnover in pupil population is very great. Past experiences vary widely.

If art work is saved from one year to the next, you will want to know the conditions under which the work was done. Without this information the art work itself can mislead you about the child's ability. Stiff, stereotyped work done under the supervision of an uncreative teacher does not mean that the child cannot do different work in a different environment.

PERCEPTUAL READINESS

School records on intelligence tests will give an indication of the amount of detail the children can handle. In the primary grades you will use simpler visual stimulation than in the intermediate grades. If the class is above average in I.Q. range you can probably use more detail than if the class is in the lower range. But you will need to make allowances for the extremes in the class—those rarer children who see little detail but measure high on I.Q. tests or those low in I.Q. with ability to see a great deal of detail. The amount of previous visual training of the children will also vary. You can make a guess about where your pupils are in terms of perceptual development, but you must be *willing and ready* to change the visual motivation when necessary.

A third grade teacher creating a room environment for studying the art of American Indians could include simply designed objects with a few pieces of complex basketry or weaving. He could encourage the children to examine all the work for its craftsmanship and its ornamentation. If the class appeared to be uninterested in the fine, detailed objects, these would not need to be discussed until later. In the arrangement of bulletin boards and in the selection of movies or slides, the teacher could use materials to fit the range of the class, so that everyone would find something he is capable of responding to.

By working with the class in the discussion of bulletin board displays, you can discover which children find difficulty in responding to details. Undeveloped ability to handle the visual information may be the reason you get little response from some children. Try simple organization of the same display material. See if some of the children who were unresponsive before become more responsive now. Educators have long been concerned about the child whose vision is not adequate, but they have not been sufficiently concerned about the child whose physiological vision is adequate but who has difficulty organizing and using information.

An art consultant, familiar with the function of perceptual development, tried to help a fourth grade boy who was failing in arithmetic. The boy had been assigned a full page of multiplication problems, eight rows of six problems each. The art teacher covered every other row with tape to make four rows of three problems each. The boy did those problems successfully. Then the tapes were changed so that the other problems showed. Again the boy succeeded. The consultant's hunch was apparently right; there was so much visual information on the page that the boy was unable to separate out the parts and handle them one at a time.

ORIENTATION TO SPACE. One way to identify extremes in orientation to space is to set up two kinds of motivation and observe how children respond to them. Choose two stories somewhat similar in appeal and interest to most of the class. For the first story, divide the children into small groups, one for each part of the story. Ask them to pantomime the action as they listen to the story. If the story is an unfamiliar one, read it aloud to them at least once before they try to act it out. Watch to see which children are able to use their bodies freely in the action. These children have probably developed kinesthetic cues for relating themselves to their environment.

For the second story, ask the children to paint a picture telling what went on. See if the same children, who could use their bodies freely, also paint the second story as if they were personally involved in it, like the little boy who painted the storm in Figure 3–8. Observe the drawings of the children who were inhibited about pantomiming. If some of them are very literal, showing little action, little personal involvement, then you probably have identified very field-dependent children. Many of the children will probably be able to use both kinds of cues, and their familiarity in doing pantomime or enjoyment of reading will determine the ways they express their responses.

This is far from a controlled experiment, but it can serve as a basis for identifying extreme differences in space orientation. Because two different activities are compared, you have more information on the kinds of motivation that bring out certain kinds of responses in individual children. At the same time the children, by experiencing both kinds of stimulation, may have been motivated to expand the kinds of responses they can make.

After you have made some observations of the children's space orientation, use your knowledge to help the children to develop in whatever ways you can. The child who was too timid to take part in the pantomime may respond more easily with a hand puppet. He may be willing to make the puppet do things he would not do himself. The use of a puppet may help a child who has difficulty in using postural cues to get involved with story action. If he has made the puppet himself, he may feel more closely involved.

FLEXIBILITY-RIGIDITY. Children are not necessarily rigid or flexible in everything they do, nor are they rigid or flexible in the same things at all times. Record your observations of children's behavior carefully during the first few weeks to help you plan ahead. Record their speed of adjusting to new tasks. Specify areas where they resist new experiences. Watch how they work with art materials, especially in new tasks. For example, with a new class, set up your art table with assorted media such as finger paint, sponges, tempera, chalk, and pencils. Watch which children use the freer media (such as finger paint) and notice how long they take to get involved in it. See which children persist in using the cleaner crayons or pencils. Your record will give you some clues to which children need help in broadening their experience with materials. Later in the year, you can refer back to the record to find out which children need more encouragement to become more flexible, and you can see which teaching techniques bring the greatest response. You should always provide materials for (1) the general level at which most of the class can succeed and (2) the levels that include the abilities of extremes in the class.

ATTITUDES TOWARD ART

Children in the upper grades can be encouraged to think about and can respond to simple questionnaires about their attitudes. A general attitude questionnaire may include questions about art. Use simple questions:

1. Would you like to be an artist? _____
   Why? _____

2. Would your family like you to be an artist?_____

3. List some things artists do. _____

4. Check which kinds of people need to be artistic and tell *why* for those you select.

   Teachers _____   Mothers _____
   Policemen _____   Grocers _____
   Architects _____   Actors _____
   Men _____   Children _____

5. Underline the art activities you prefer—drawing, painting, wire sculpture, constructing with wood, printing, mosaics. Can you think of others?

This questionnaire will give you clues to how the child perceives himself in terms of art, and what attitudes he may have learned at home. Children may have acquired cultural stereotypes that separate art from everyday life. McDonald calls stereotypes "Concepts of people, places, or events, which have not been formed on the basis of adequate experience with events. . . . Stereotypes are developed because the individual does not think critically, does not observe, does not analyze." [3] A stereotype is a cognitive average of similar but different things, just as visual information is categorized by making perceptual averages. The less opportunity the individual has to observe and to think critically, the more likely his stereotypes are to remain unchanged. The teacher's role is to increase the range of children's understanding, observation, and evaluation, so that limited stereotypes are broadened into more useful concepts.

A child may have stereotypes of art and artists, or he may have had opportunities to develop less limited concepts of them through direct experience. If he has not known any artists, his concept of the artist is likely to be developed by the values he hears about at home. If parents and friends refer to artists in negative terms, the child's stereotype is likely to be negative. The high value this society places on conformity and being "ordinary" may lead many children to forming a stereotype of the artist as a deviant, although many kinds of people are artists. Working in art requires children to relate themselves to their concepts of artists and what artists do. Limited and negative stereotypes can be the source of considerable conflict in art activities.

CREATIVE ABILITY

Creative ability is a complex of traits that most people have in some degree. If we had adequate ways of measuring those traits in elementary grade children, we could compare their performance with that of successful creative people. Tests would not tell us about creative potential. They would give only an estimate of children's present development of those traits. Creativity tests are not yet available for use with this age group.

By observation the teacher can get some clues to a child's development of his creative potential. If the child invents variations on familiar symbols, if he relates and organizes several visual ideas, and if he paints or constructs novel things, he is showing *originality*. If ideas come quickly and easily he shows *fluency*. If he responds quickly to familiar motivation, accepts new motivation easily, and shifts motor-cognitive tasks readily, he shows *flexibility*.

If a child does not show these traits, he does not necessarily lack the potential for developing them. It is not possible at this time, by test or observation, to separate lack of potential and lack of opportunity to develop the potential. For this reason, teachers are encouraged to give every child as much reward for self-directed exploration as the classroom situation allows. Children who are reluctant to work independently can be given small tasks in which they can begin to succeed in being creative. Gradually as they gain confidence, their capacity for creative work can increase. Those children who have had their impulse to create stifled by extremely rigid home and classroom experiences may take courage if they realize that they will now be rewarded for creative expression. Occasionally some children will interpret such freedom to create as meaning freedom to do anything they want. Often by supplying challenging and interesting tasks, the teacher can guide them into constructive use of their motivation.

CLASSROOM LEARNING EXPERIENCE

Threats and anxieties, both real and imagined, can inhibit children's ability to respond visually and to organize and use the information they receive. Anxieties may be produced by the environment at school, or the child may bring them from home. A tense fearful child must be put at ease before he can perform up to his ability. Sometimes the teacher cannot eliminate all the threats in the classroom, but continued attempts should be made to make each child feel accepted by both the teacher and the class. Fear of failure, of getting dirty, of being "sissy," of discontinuity in reward, as well as other emotional disturbances from the child's own life can contribute to his anxiety in school.

THE PSYCHOLOGICAL ENVIRONMENT

To help overcome fear of failure the teacher can assure children that their art work is exploratory and they will have opportunities to try again if their first attempts do not bring what they want. Vigorous art activities need to be available for both boys and girls who may consider art "sissy." Conferences with parents and parent-teacher meetings should clarify the important art learnings for children. Such meetings will help decrease discontinuity between the home and school.

SOCIAL ISOLATES. To identify children who are rejected by the rest of the class sociometric techniques can be used. Adaptations of Moreno's sociogram technique can be related to art activities.[4] A question like, "Who would you like to have work on a mural with you?" may give insight into who the class thinks is "artistic." Another time, say, "We are going to visit a museum soon. Who would you like to sit with on the bus?" Several interesting questions might be answered in this investigation. Are those children most often chosen to help on murals the same as those chosen as partners for the bus trip? What is the difference in the clusterings of who chooses whom in the two patterns? What children are not chosen in either group? What pairs of children stick together? Who are the leaders in the class?

Not every isolate is necessarily in need of acceptance by the group. Occasionally very independent, self-contained children are content to work by themselves or with one or two others. Sometimes they are the most creative children. But others, needing acceptance in order to get enough confidence to achieve in school, should be given special help.

DEVELOPING THE CLASSROOM ENVIRONMENT. A teacher can use the following teaching technique in developing a better classroom environment for individual creative work. Early in the year, discuss individuality, the importance of each one as a unique, creative person. Stress the importance of *this* group as being different from any other class because they, as individuals, are different. Make a definite statement of your philosophy of art education, such as this:

"As artists we all have different things to say with our art, different feelings to express. All year we will have opportunities to say important things through art. Each of you can grow in art in somewhat different ways. And all of us can learn from each other."

By encouraging individuals, by helping them gain respect in the group, and by emphasizing the uniqueness of the group, the teacher can develop a dynamic class. In such a group extremely timid, anxious children can build stronger concepts of themselves. Overconfident, self-assured children can make more accurate evaluations of their own work.

Most children apparently are more comfortable with a consistent pattern of rewards and punishments. The teacher, as the authority figure, sets the pattern. If the pupils have some responsibility in setting up the system of behavior, they are able to follow it better than they can if the teacher makes all the decisions. The teacher and the class should discuss problems that interfere with learning and creative activity—such problems as the amount of noise that disrupts creativity, the ease of sharing tools and materials, the ways to improve the psychological environment so that everyone feels free to work.

OVERCOMING DISCONTINUITY. A major source of anxiety about art lies in the conflict in values between the children's home culture and what the classroom teacher is using as a standard. We found, in our analysis of American core values, areas of conflict and differences in the ways children are rewarded and punished.

To help overcome the stereotype about art as play, by those children who are motivated by the traditional cultural value of hard work, the work elements in art can be stressed. Their art activities should be a challenge—intellectually and creatively. They need to be made aware of the art professions, which require hard work. Intermediate grade children can begin to analyze the meanings of work and play in our society and the relative nature of the concepts. What is work for some is play for others. Do we work when we play? Do we play when we work? Is it all right to enjoy work? Such analysis will help children to overcome the stereotypes that work should not be enjoyed, and that anything one enjoys doing is of secondary value.

Children who want to rush through an activity because of the value on expediency need to be exposed to the value of the personal pleasure that can be derived from painstaking accomplishment. Field trips to superior craftsmen, movies such as those of Maria of San Ildefonso ("Pueblo Arts," University of Minnesota), who preserves the quality of Pueblo pottery, stories of Eskimo craftsmen ("Eskimo Arts and Crafts," Canadian National Film Board), whose lives depend on the quality of their crafts, show the importance of artistry and craftsmanship.

Whenever possible the teacher should help parents reduce

children's conflicts by helping them understand the school's objectives in art. Children can be encouraged to understand that rewards are not always the same in every kind of activity.

THE TEACHER AS A CATALYST. The teacher's enthusiasm and his breadth of understanding of art will enrich the psychological environment during art activities. If the teacher does not value art, he cannot expect to teach children to value it. The teacher who values art, and also understands the differences among children, can have a tremendous impact on the children's aesthetic awareness and creative development.

STIMULATING MOTIVATION

The crucial elements in education are curiosity, the desire to learn, and the ability to organize and express what has been learned. The curiosity of children is maintained in an environment that introduces new interests and new goals. Perceptual training enables children to see and deal with more things, giving them more sources of motivation. The way to provide these sources depends on (1) the interest level of most of the pupils and (2) the amount of visual detail they can handle.

BULLETIN BOARDS. A bulletin board can be made by the teacher before the children start to work, or it can be a goal for all to work toward. Pictures or objects or both can be displayed. Pictures that show relationships may be organized to present some particular aspect of art—the development of present art forms from earlier forms, or the use of photography in explaining a kind of work.

Figure 9–1 is a drawing of a bulletin board showing different crayon methods. With cement or wire, different kinds of tools can be fastened to a display board, and examples of the many uses and methods of application can be shown. The objective here is to stimulate flexible use of tools and materials.

INTERESTING OBJECTS. Another kind of motivation is to relate the task to a highly valued trait of the culture. One enterprising teacher of a third grade related work to aesthetic experience by bringing to class a box of what she described as "treasures" to help beautify the classroom environment. She brought a somewhat

FIGURE 9-1. TEACHING WITH A BULLETIN BOARD

rusty large-size juice can that became a container for brushes. Before being decorated, the can needed scouring with steel wool and cleanser and then careful enameling with metal paint. A highly oxidized copper bowl for flowers needed cleaning and polishing. Some art books needed covers to protect them for use in the class. A wooden bookrack needed repair and refinishing. Pupils who wanted to contribute to the visual quality of the room as part of their self-government organization volunteered to work with the treasures. When the projects were completed, the pupils discussed how it felt to work at making the room more pleasant for everyone. After this experience the children were encouraged to point up things that needed beautifying and, where feasible, encouraged to work on them singly or in groups.

Children's perceptual awareness can be broadened with equipment like colored spots, magnifying glasses, and shadow boxes to help them explore their visual world. The old fashioned focus card cut from cardboard with which an artist blocks out a surrounding area will help children concentrate visually on a specific area or thing. A light on a tripod or clip can be focused where it

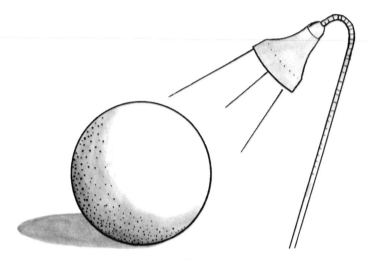

FIGURE 9–2. LEARNING TO SEE FORMS IN SPACE

is needed. Display boxes can be made of wood or cut from a heavy carton. The display box separates the object from the rest of the room and helps children observe more clearly, by separating the figure from the ground.

MURALS. The mural is effective in motivating children to use art as a learning device and a means of organizing and communicating ideas as a group.

A mural can be used during the introduction and culmination of a unit of work. A fourth grade class studying a major industry in their area made a mural showing the sources of raw materials, their preparation for market, the basic process of manufacture, their distribution, and their ultimate use. A large tackboard area was covered with butcher paper. The known objects and activities were painted in bright colors on separate paper, then pinned in sequence on the board. A list of topics to be studied was made as each area of the board was analyzed. Such preparation made a field trip to the factory more meaningful as the pupils' *readiness* to observe prepared them to look for and recognize processes. It also gave them an opportunity to invent visual symbols for describing the processes. All through the days of study children or groups of children contributed drawings and paintings of the parts of the mural. In order to do this they had to do research. As a topic was discussed the ideas of the children were organized. Finally, the important ideas were analyzed, a pleasing design was developed, and the parts of the mural were glued together.

This activity fulfilled the objective of using art as a means of communicating, reinforcing visual and verbal memory. It encouraged "teamwork of equals," the creation of unique symbols, the opportunity to learn to accept others' ideas, and also the interrelation of work and aesthetic experience.

Dramatic play is a technique teachers can use in helping children explore situations in social studies and human relations. It helps children to understand situations in which they are too young to participate. Dramatic play is an outgrowth of children's games: playing house, cowboys and Indians, cops and robbers. They are encouraged to act out and explore more complicated situations as a means of learning. Acting the lives of people in history and in other cultures makes them more meaningful. It helps children understand the roles of different people in their own culture as they try to act out those roles themselves. Some children who do not feel free to participate actively in the dramatic play can express their interpretation of the situation through art. The dramatic play enriches children's concepts of social situations. The added understanding can broaden the base of information to be used in art production.

FIGURE 9–3. WHICH IS EASIER TO SEE?

EXPRESSION

The expression of emotions through art gives a child an opportunity to externalize some of his reactions in the process of relating himself to his environment. Interpretation of his experience through art gives him opportunity to crystallize some of the nebulous reactions he cannot put into words. This kind of experience may lead to self-identification. The term "self-expression" seems a misnomer. It assumes a well-defined self that can be expressed, whereas the child is developing a concept of "self" as an interaction with his environment. Art expression is one means of expressing his sense of relation to other people and to things. He puts into form feelings about his changing experiences. The action of making a piece of art work contributes to the piecing together of his developing concept of self and his relations to others.

PROVIDING MOTIVATION FOR EXPRESSION. Teachers have too often assumed that children always have something they need to express. Many children have had to suppress their desire for expression at home, or they may lead such drab, uneventful lives that their capacity for expression has had little stimulation and exercise. When they do try to express feeling they use shallow sentimental symbols. These symbols have derived little meaning from the child's own direct experience. Art expression can be related more directly to the child's interaction with his world if he is given the opportunity and encouragement to develop his own symbols. But if most of his experience is vicarious, if he gets his concepts of the world mainly from adults' interpretations, his art is likely to be superficial. If he uses adults' stereotyped symbols, filling in outlines in coloring books, he may not have an incentive to look at the rich detail in nature.

In this age of television, push-button toys, and overcrowded classrooms, the teacher has particular responsibility to give children direct experience with living, growing, natural things, so that the capacity to see, feel, and respond will not be left undeveloped. Children can learn to deal with the actual visual impressions while they learn about the functions of things. If, in the elementary grades and high school, children are encouraged to see and respond through motivating art experiences, they will not grow up to be visual illiterates (unable to "read" the visual details in their environment). The ability to make aesthetic judgments and to be creative in the arts can be greatly increased if the child is aware of and can assimilate visual information from his environment. An important part of *teaching* art in the elementary school is providing the stimulation—the direct experience—that gives children subject matter for expression.

Creative expression can often be encouraged by an exciting experience. Stories about the culture of northwest coast Indians, locating them geographically and historically, can prepare children in the intermediate grades for understanding more about these people. A movie like "The Loon's Necklace" (from the Canadian National Film Board) has strong expressive quality. Experiences with such stories and movies can be used to provide motivation for making beautiful, expressive masks. In art period, the pupils can make masks that require skills appropriate to their grade level. Paper bag masks, papier-mâché masks over crushed paper, masks molded in clay or papier-mâché and cast in plaster can be used in a wide range of technical readiness.

After showing the film, have materials available for the basic structuring of the masks. If you wish, show the film more than once. For sustained motivation, tape-record the music and words from the film and play it while the children are working—or when they come back to work later to finish the masks. Music may cause them to be motivated more by the mood than by a desire to copy what they have seen.

One seventh grade class responded to the "The Loon's Necklace" by studying another Indian group. Masks appropriate to the Indians' ritual and belief were made; and then, after writing their own story and wearing their masks, the pupils acted in a school-made movie.

Art is more than expression. Designing, organizing, and arranging may develop intuitively in some children. These abilities are evident in the work of many small children. Figure 9–4A is an example of how a young child can design intuitively. This child, a six-year-old girl, is not organizing along a base line, as children who are learning to put symbols on a line often do. Her painting has pattern, perspective, order, and interesting breaking up of space. The child exhibits an intuitive sense of design; at this stage it would be pointless to teach her about design. This is an unusual drawing for a child of six. Many fifth and sixth grade children cannot do as well. Figure 9–4B is a drawing by an eight-year-old boy who has been able to organize a great deal of detail in a single picture. These paintings were made in a situation in which individual differences were recognized and strong encouragement to observe nature was used to motivate the children.

DESIGN. In the intermediate years many children express less intuitive design ability. The decline may be caused by their increased awareness of adult standards and of the stereotypes of popular culture on "realism" in art—calendar art, illustration, cartoon art. During these years opportunities to explore design and to see how relationships develop will increase children's sensitivity to design. In Chapter 11 we will discuss ways in which you can encourage exploration in design.

Perceptual skills increase as children develop awareness of the perceptual constancies and at the same time see how sizes, shapes, and colors vary depending on how far away and in what position they exist. When children are motivated to look for relationships

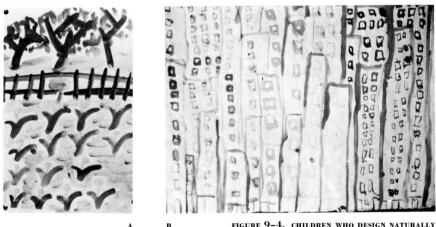

A   B   FIGURE 9–4. CHILDREN WHO DESIGN NATURALLY

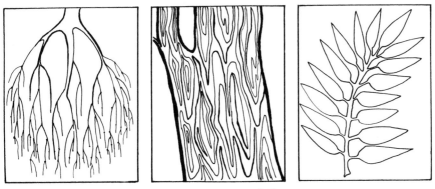

FIGURE 9–5. DESIGN IN ROOTS, BARK, AND TREES

and patterns, variations in form, line, color, and texture, their perceptual skills should develop.

SEPARATING FIGURE FROM GROUND. Many children have trouble separating figure from ground. Often they are dependent on the visual field and on authority figures, rather than on their feelings. To help these children learn to organize what they see, help them to look for pattern, the repetition and variations of similar things. If the class is analyzing the cycles of growth of trees, make a drawing of the tree without the leaves and with bared roots. Then place a transparent sheet over the drawing and on it draw the leaves and the earth. The pattern of the flowers and the bark can be shown in other drawings. Drawings made on clear film with plastic ink can be fitted into 2″ × 2″ slides, and details can more easily be pointed out.

To observe the actual plant, place it on a piece of solid color that contrasts to the color of the plant. Bright red of the same value and intensity as a green plant is not as good to show contrast as is a light yellow; red-green color-blind children will not see a difference. When the background is clearly different in color and value, plain instead of patterned, figure and ground can be separated more easily. The same techniques can be used in introducing a painting to the class. Help the children see the different parts, the patterns made by different forms, colors, and lines. On the blackboard, draw patterns of the different designs these forms make to help children identify them.

CHILDREN'S SKILLS

Motor skills can be developed as coordination and muscle development allow. A gross misuse of art is the attempt to use color books or mimeographed outlines. One consultant saw a first-grade child's art folder in which the classroom teacher had evaluated the child as poor in art and "messy" because he could not stay within the lines. The child, highly verbal, with evidence of slower physical development, was not ready to stay within the lines. Development of motor skills has a place eventually, but to evaluate a six-year-old child's total art ability on his coordination is not only unfair but also misinforming to the parent. The teacher's assumption, that coloring within outlines is a form of art, is a misconception. It has little to do with expression, communication, or design. This kind of erroneous evaluation leads to attitudes on the part of the parent and the teacher that may harmfully influence their behavior toward the child. The teacher who has assumed that the child is "messy" and not artistic will probably not expect him to succeed in other art activities. The mother who accepts the teacher's verdict may discourage his artistic attempts.

Skills in art are so varied, and so many techniques are available for children to use, that learning a specific manipulative skill (as is needed in playing a musical instrument) is usually not necessary. Skills that are more general in nature develop as children use tools and materials. The more they work with tools in a variety of ways, the more their manipulative skill develops. The more varied the activities, the more flexible the use of their hands becomes. Occasionally a teacher will see a child using a tool in a way that might be injurious to him. He should, of course, be told of the danger and helped to find a safer technique. When a child holds a tool like a crayon or brush so tightly that it cramps his work, the teacher can encourage, but not force, him to try other ways of using it.

In our study of the Orotchen and Zia Indian children, we found that perceptual training and motivation, rather than hand training, led to advanced drawing ability. Learning to be a sensitive, keen observer is probably the most important skill.

Dependence on postural or visual cues may influence the way children respond to tools. Some may be watching themselves using the tool; others are feeling their way with it. Since these dependencies are in large part learned, we can encourage children to learn to use both types of cues as they learn to manipulate tools. To lessen their dependence on *seeing* to control tools, children can do tasks like painting to music with their eyes shut. After they have become aware of the feeling cues that are available to them, they can learn to use these cues with their eyes open. Children who are more dependent on the "feel" of a tool can be encouraged to watch their brush as they use it. Both kinds of cues are needed in the development of sensitive control of tools and materials.

Whenever possible the choice of material should be left to the children because they differ in the ways they identify tools and materials. As a general rule, it is better to let a child work in a medium in which he has some confidence until he feels secure enough to try a new medium. *The particular medium is not as important as the symbols that are invented or the organization that is achieved.*

There has been a tendency to think that a new effect achieved with a new medium or combination of media is the major objective of art activities. While exploration of media must be encouraged, they are only the tools used to communicate—they are the vehicle, not the message. The art period should be flexible to allow a child enough time to complete an idea. Some art projects can be put away and worked on later. Others, particularly individually expressive drawings and paintings, may have to be finished in a single period, or the idea being expressed may not be recaptured.

TRAINING IN ART

When art is thought of primarily as a means of "self-expression," it is not being used fully. When art is thought of as a means of relating to the world, it becomes a broad subject with infinite possibilities for learning. Children can be encouraged to look outside themselves, as well as inside, for ideas. They can learn to see the aesthetic qualities of the physical world. They can learn to find satisfaction in improvement of their skills.

ART FOR PRESCHOOL CHILDREN. Successful early training has been shown by Dubin at the University of Chicago.[5] Children aged two to four were divided into two groups, control and experimental, paired by age, sex, and interest in art (to the extent possible). In the fall the children drew and painted as they wished in a normal nursery school situation. The drawings were then classified by Marian Monroe's categories of child development, and each category was numbered: *scribble unnamed* (one point); *scribble named* (two points); *diagram*—lines, masses, colors with a sense of relationship between (three points); *design*—an obvious rhythmic pattern (four points); representation of a recognizable object (five points). The average score for each child was recorded.[6]

During the winter the control group received no training, but the experimental group was given individual training. Scribblers unnamed were encouraged to verbalize about their drawings; scribblers named were encouraged to deal with the wholes and relations of parts in their drawings. The experimenter would say, "If you look carefully you can see that there are lots of parts to your picture and they make something nice all together."[7] Children who drew diagrams were encouraged to describe the parts. Designers were encouraged to achieve more recognizable forms. Children who did representational work were encouraged to be aware of the aesthetic qualities, such as color and composition. The experimenter did not attempt to direct the nature of representation but allowed the child to represent as he wished. [It must be added here that representation should not be the only goal, that designing ability should also be encouraged.]

In the spring the two groups worked again under equal conditions in a nursery school. The drawings of both groups were then evaluated by the original criteria, and compared with the averages recorded in the fall session. Both groups showed improvement. The control group shifted from a mean score of 1.52 to a mean of 1.75. The experimental group shifted from a mean score of 1.70 to a mean of 2.48. In total the trained children *gained* almost three and one-half times as many score points as the untrained children. Even though a slight difference in groups existed at first, the rate of gain was much greater in the experimental group.

Thinking of art as merely "play" is missing an opportunity for creative teaching. Try such encouragement as, "What a rhythmic design you have made—the rhythm is like singing—

could you make another painting with a different kind of rhythm or pattern?" In this way the exact nature of the task is not determined, but the child's use of his problem-solving and creative ability is encouraged. You are working here at Point III of the P-D process—helping the child to integrate new concepts into what he has already done, and then to do something with the new organization. In the language of Gestalt psychology you are helping the child integrate a new vector into his field of operation. This gives him a basis for new behavior, which, if used in a drawing or painting, we call creative expression.

The uses of art in other learning activities can be evaluated according to the kinds of experiences the children have. If they are learning that art is related to many phases of their experience, if they are relating, organizing, and expressing ideas creatively in visual forms, then the activity can be called an integrated art activity. However, if the teacher uses map-making, charts, graphs, that allow little creativity and reorganization, as the only kind of art activity, then the art program is being misused.

Much of the learning in elementary school consists of concept formation—learning meanings of words, facts about countries, the mechanics of arithmetic, the uses of science. Reading is a cognitive organization of words. Looking (at the physical world, at pictures, at nonverbal symbols) requires visual organization. Verbal and nonverbal organizations, although not separate functions, are somewhat different. *Concepts are evolved from experience, but if the experience is limited by lack of visual awareness, the quality of the concept will be poor.* If a child is learning about the transportation of goods by boat, the words and their verbal meanings alone will not mean much to him if he has never seen a boat. Pictures, movies, and field trips to harbors will help, but only if he can organize what he has seen. He can do this by looking at related details in what he actually sees and what he reads, listens to, and thinks about. In this way his concepts will be more complete. They will have more meaning because of his own experience.

A Classroom Study. The paintings of trees (see Plate II) were made by primary grade children in a Saturday morning enrichment class. The teacher took the children on a "looking expedition," leaving their paints behind. She called particular attention to the acacia trees, encouraging the children to look as hard as they could, to touch the bark and the fallen petals, to smell the air, so that when they came back they could paint a picture of what it is like to see an acacia tree on a spring day.

When they returned to the classroom, the paints were all ready—with a variety of brushes and colors to choose from. Each child created different symbols of trees, of the feeling of spring air. They were particularly expressive of the *essence of spring,* of the tree's "being," not just static pictures of trees.

The teacher of this class was particularly gifted in getting children to become involved with the interesting minutiae of detail all around them. Because she was herself aware, she was able to inspire children.

This class represented a fairly wide cross section of society. Many of the parents wanted their children to learn to draw, and this teacher was to help both parents and children set more creative goals for the class's work. She had them for only one hour a week, but her understanding and training in individual differences among children in art, and her skills in motivation enabled her to help the children make important gains in creative invention and expression.

In terms of the P-D theory this teacher (1) helped develop the children's readiness by arousing their curiosity about an expedition and preparing them to look for certain things, (2) created a psychological environment of play and delight, (3) helped them individually to understand the new stimulation by feeling, seeing, and smelling—giving them several ways to get information to stimulate their creativity, and (4) having appropriate means ready for their creative expression.

EVALUATION

Evaluation of art products and experience in terms of letter grades is difficult, and does not tell the next teacher or the parent much about the child. Teachers may give a high grade for various reasons—"talent," neatness, or good behavior. Still others may be concerned with drawing ability alone as a function of art. Some children excel in copying nature, others in designing and organizing, others in inventiveness. The trend away from letter grades for primary children is encouraging.

"Talent" in art has never been clearly defined. The traditional concept that one is born with talent is too simple to explain the complexity of a child's development in art. Mendelowitz considers talent mainly a matter of opportunity and reward.[8] These are certainly important factors, but there seem to be inherent traits that "talent" also comprises—intelligence, eye-hand coordination, and intensity of drives.

Evaluation can be used educationally as (1) a tool for teachers in recording individual differences to help plan for the continuing art program and (2) a means of helping parents understand the teacher's evaluation of the child's development. The following questions are suggested as criteria for the teacher to use several times during the year, for curriculum planning and parent-teacher conferences.

A. *Evaluation of art products.* Does this child:
   1. Show increased awareness of his environment?
   2. Use more than one type of subject matter?
   3. Change and develop his symbols?
   4. Show signs of increased ability to organize symbols?
   5. Like to work with a variety of media?
   6. Express feelings as well as ideas?

B. *Analysis of behavior during art.* Does this child:
   1. Move easily from one task to another?
   2. Have an interest span long enough to carry out his ideas?
   3. Have adequate motor skills to facilitate his expression?
   4. Respond readily to most kinds of motivation?
   5. Appear to be enjoying himself in art activities?
   6. Seem to feel at ease, that is, not show conflict?

C. *List of media used.*

Your answers will suggest changes in motivation and kinds of tasks for the class and for individuals who need special encouragement. This is not a basis for a letter grade in art, but it will help you in parent-teacher conferences. It is also a means of keeping records for the next teacher. When an entire school uses specific criteria in recording art progress, each teacher has a better understanding of the experience of the class and a basis for planning ahead.

It is useful to save a typical art product of each child every week or so. Every few weeks the collection can be analyzed for changes. Samples of a child's work at conference time, with a description of change, may be more meaningful to parents than sending home a picture every day. Some children are so pressured to show what they have done in art that they insist on taking things home regularly. If this need is strong, it is usually best to comply and discuss reasons with the parents. Usually enough things can be saved to help you keep adequate records.

SELECTING WORK FOR DISPLAY. When a teacher is selecting children's work to display in the room and in the hallways of the school, he should decide whether he is displaying the work for the *children,* to help them see their own work in relation to that of others, or whether he is using the display to show the administration and visitors the high quality of work in his class. Actually both demands can be met. The children and the teacher can organize an interesting display of their work. It is a design problem in itself. If all the children's work cannot be shown at once, they should understand that each will have his turn. Displaying work should not be a form of reward or punishment; if some of the children in the class are experiencing failure because their work is never selected, display is being misused.

Evaluation of Personality. Interpretation of children's personality traits through drawings is much too uncertain a field for the amateur. Even for the highly skilled psychological clinician the use of art products alone is insufficient for diagnosis. Many factors are in operation in the P-D process when a child draws or paints: experience and training, threats and anxieties, motivations and rewards, individual patterns of development, past successes and failures, rigidity-flexibility patterns, habits of relating to the environment, cultural direction. Anecdotal records, as well as drawings, may be useful to a psychologist in understanding a child's problems.

The classroom teacher's observation of a child's work is based on his own "sets," but because the teacher may know more about the child than anyone except the parents, his observations should be considered a significant part of the total evaluation.

SUMMARY

Children's individual differences can be understood in part from school records, but adequate tests of artistic ability are not available. Observation of behavior during art tasks will help.

Continued evaluation of the classroom environment is conducive to creative aesthetic activity.

Motivation towards specific objectives should be geared to both the general level of the class and the ranges of slower- and faster-learning children.

Art includes both expression of emotions and organization of visual knowledge. The child's expression is more important than the medium used.

Training in art includes helping children develop readiness and interest in a task, creating a psychological environment conducive to creativity, helping them incorporate new things into what they already know, and then providing the tools and materials with which they can express their ideas.

Evaluation is needed to help the teacher develop the program, to work with parents, and to give the next teacher a useful record. Letter grades have little value in art.

Analysis of personality as evidenced in art works should be made only by a highly trained clinician.

REFERENCES

1. J. P. Guilford, "Creativity," in *Readings in Educational Psychology,* ed. Jerome M. Seidman (Boston: Houghton Mifflin Company, 1955), pp. 224–225.

2. Lester W. Sontag, Charles T. Baker, and Virginia L. Nelson, *Mental Growth and Personality Development: A Longitudinal Study,* Monograph for the Society for Research in Child Development, Inc., XXIII, Ser. 68, No. 2 (1958).

3. Frederick J. McDonald, *Educational Psychology* (San Francisco: Wadsworth Publishing Company, Inc., 1959), p. 157. Reprinted by permission.

4. J. L. Moreno, *Who Shall Survive?* (Washington: Nervous and Mental Diseases Publishing Company, 1934).

5. Elisabeth Ruch Dubin, "The Effect of Training on the Tempo of Development of Graphic Representation in Preschool Children," *Journal of Experimental Education,* XV (1946), 166–173.

6. *Ibid.,* p. 168.

7. *Ibid.,* p. 169.

8. Daniel M. Mendelowitz, *Children Are Artists: An Introduction to Children's Art for Teachers and Parents* (Stanford: Stanford University Press, 1953), pp. 3–15.

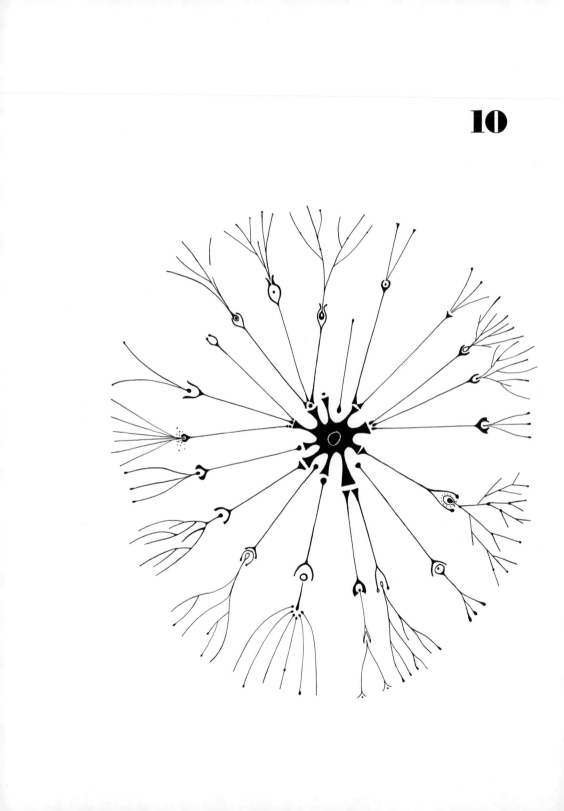

10

Scope and Sequence of an Art Program

After developing our objectives for art activities and our understanding of children's individual differences and their implications for teaching, we are ready to plan a long range curriculum. Sequential planning within a school or a district is desirable to avoid both repetition and large gaps in the sequence of learning. If the same media or tasks are used in the same ways year after year the children may find art activity tedious and uninspiring. But the suggested grade level sequences in a school's plan should be used flexibly, as a rigid child of ten may be helped by the methods used with a six-year-old.

Three kinds of art activities are effective in the classroom: (1) art learning activities, (2) self-directed art activities, and (3) integrated art activities. *Art learning activities* should be given regular, but flexible, amounts of time in the total curriculum. Specific learning in art is the nucleus from which art spreads to the rest of the program. *The self-directed activity* takes place when children voluntarily go to the art corner and select a medium to work with as they wish. *Integrated activities* take place in relation to other areas, such as social studies, music, science. Pupils make murals, puppets, posters, bulletin boards, science displays and illustrations.

THE PRIMARY YEARS: ART LEARNING ACTIVITIES

In the primary years art learning experiences are used to increase the numbers of things children will respond to, to increase their ability to relate and compare things, and to enlarge the means they have for expressing their responses in art forms.

1. They can have experiences that increase their visual awareness. They can be motivated to *observe*, to *watch for relationships*, and to *look for more detail*.

2. They can be encouraged to maintain and develop their *curiosity* and *creativeness* by being given many opportunities and rewards for inquisitiveness, flexibility, and originality.

3. They can begin to learn that there are different ways of working in different situations. They can be helped to overcome stereotyped ideas about work and play.

4. Their means of creative expression can be increased by exploring media.

5. Visual language can parallel verbal language in the learning of similarities and differences.

6. They can relate their own work to the art in their environment and in other cultures and periods. They can begin to make aesthetic judgments.

ABILITIES DEVELOPED DURING LEARNING PERIODS

PERCEPTUAL SENSITIVITY. In the primary grades seeing likenesses and differences, bigness and littleness, roundness and sharpness of things is very important. The teacher, aware of the effects of perceptual constancies, can encourage children to observe. Some observation can be done of objects they like to draw and paint. This is not teaching drawing; it is teaching *looking,* and the drawing will follow as the child develops the motor skills. The emphasis on looking leaves him freer to develop his own symbols for what he sees.

A child, when dealing with visual complexity, has to abstract from this visual information those things he needs to know in order to respond. The amount of detail he will use depends in part on his past experience, his visual learning, and his intellectual ability to handle and sort information. If you can show him how to look for details and their relationships to one another, you can help him handle more visual information. Besides the word categories that indicate size and shape (big, little, small, tiny, round, sharp, square, narrow, and wide) children can learn to see patterns in color, line, light, and shadow. They will be better able to handle more complex information if they have skills for organizing it.

Belief in the theory of "naïve realism" has led to the assumption that all a child needs to do to respond to the complex visual information in a painting is to look at it. Learning to see and respond to complex forms of art, whether a mural, a stained glass window, sculpture, or architecture, requires learning rather than casual observation. We start with simple patterns and qualities of line and color to begin training children in this direction.

An excellent book for the classroom is Helen Borten's *Do You See What I See?* [1] Since it is a picture reading book, children who are having difficulties in art may learn by reading about the visual elements of art (form, line, and color). Using this book to motivate children to look at form and beauty in nature and art, the teacher can lead them into making further responses—relating feelings to perceptions. "Where do we see jagged angular lines?" "How do they make us feel?" "What kind of lines do soft rolling hills make?" "What do circles do that squares do not?" "What colors make us feel quiet and sleepy?" "What colors wake us up?" "What shapes are like our white rat?" "Is he like a pear, a cucumber, or a football?"

Compare, relate, organize—in this way you can teach children to see richly and aesthetically. When they look at a new painting, help them see the patterns made by colors and lines. Ask them to show where the lines go and how lines hold the picture together. Compare the ways different artists use color to make lines. Help them see functions of lines in their own art work. Help them see how lines, forms, and colors make objects, as well as paintings, beautiful. Include touching and feeling as other ways to become familiar with the quality of things, particularly when "looking" at textures. Touching things will encourage the exploration of tools with which to make texture effects. A choice of media is important so that the flow of ideas and the creation of symbols are not stopped by unfamiliar or disliked tools and materials.

CREATIVITY. Fluency, flexibility, and originality are traits of creative people. Although further research is needed on the kinds of psychological environments that enable different personality types to be more creative, we can get some help in curriculum planning by having the development of these traits as objectives. We want to help each child express ideas freely. Even though a child may have a potential for fluency, fear of making a wrong response, or continued punishment for talking too much, may prevent the realization of this potential.

Self-directed art is not enough. Some children will not communicate ideas and feelings fluently. During art learning experiences the teacher needs to encourage communication specifically. Many different kinds of motivation can help children to get started. Cognitive, audio, visual, and tactile stimulation can come from listening to stories, poetry, music, and taped recordings of interesting sounds; from touching shapes and textures; from studying objects in strong light, clearly separated from any confusing background.

Encourage primary children to explore, particularly with the symbols they use, to find ways to change and improvise on known symbols. Encourage children to accept multiple solutions to art problems. Discuss with them the many ways their art work is unique in organization and design. You may find conforming children who need strong motivation to lead them toward more flexibility. For example, find a small object that will interest the children. It might be a mechanical toy that dances to a music box. Instead of just winding it up and letting it play, set the stage. Ask some of the children to come up for a game. Ask them one by one to feel the object with their eyes shut. Then have them turn their backs and listen to the object. Finally, show them the object itself. They will be better prepared to see after using their senses of touch and hearing. Display the object against a plain background so that its visual qualities can be clearly separated from those of the rest of the room.

Immediately after this sensory experience ask the children to select from the art materials which you have ready for them. Encourage them to make a picture of what they experienced, heard, or saw. Children whose pictures show little originality may be rigid as a result of anxiety, failure, or limited experience. Try to reduce their anxiety by accepting and encouraging their work. Be sure that they realize that your objectives include *individuality of expression*. Gradually lead them from one success to another. Careful planning of motivation and materials will help these children to respond and to succeed to some degree.

Since rigidity is usually learned, young children may not have had many experiences to make them rigid. By encouraging and maintaining their flexibility at this level, their creativity will have more chance to develop.

It is most important that the child's efforts be accepted; that success be found in what he does. Freedom from fear of failure comes after one has learned that success is possible, after self-confidence is established.

The following case study by an art consultant trained by Schaefer-Simmern shows how symbolic fluency can be developed even in a child who is considered mentally retarded.[2]

A Case Study. An art consultant was asked to work with a fourth grade class of mentally retarded children. The case of Sara, age nine, will show the ways in which an inhibited child can be led into stronger communication with others through skillful teaching in art. This case is described here because the techniques used are appropriate for primary children.

The consultant found that her best technique for working with children was to encourage each child individually. In this case the children were asked to draw variations of their initial drawings, until they reached a plateau and no new inventions for communicating visual ideas came forth. Then new stimulation was needed.

Sara was not reading, could not do simple arithmetic, was not interested in school, was a social isolate, would not talk to either the teacher or to other children, who, in turn, avoided her. The consultant asked the class to draw trees. Sara responded by drawing a simple figure of a tree. The consultant reports:

> When I asked Sara how she liked her first drawing she didn't look at me or even answer me. I then asked her if she would like to make another picture of a tree. Without answering, she started to draw. This time she added small branches to her larger ones. When I asked if she would like to make a larger drawing of her tree, she beamed and started immediately. This time she added still more smaller branches to the larger ones. It was a very beautiful drawing and highly organized. When I thanked her for her picture she asked me if she could have another piece of paper.
>
> The classroom teacher was surprised at this for it was the first time she had seen Sara draw a picture or talk freely with a stranger.[3]

An early drawing, Figure 10–1, shows considerably more detail than her first drawing. The next week when the consultant returned she found the child beginning to read. By the end of ten weeks Sara had made many strides. She had gained status in the class by excelling in her art. Her concept of herself appeared to change as she became part of the class and sometimes a leader. She participated in games during recess and other children wanted to sit by her in class. Figures 10–2 and 10–3 show her drawing at the end of ten weeks.

The consultant worked closely with this child, beginning at the level where she was and continually encouraging her to produce, accepting what she did, and leading out from one success to another. Through this process the child was given four important things: (1) a means of communication and expression, (2) a means to succeed, (3) the acceptance and encouragement of an adult, and (4) acceptance from her peers.

Although we do not know what factors may have inhibited Sara, the progress she made indicates that her mental retardation may have resulted from continued failure or from anxiety and threat.

The relationship between her learning to symbolize visual details and her beginning reading may have been coincidental. But

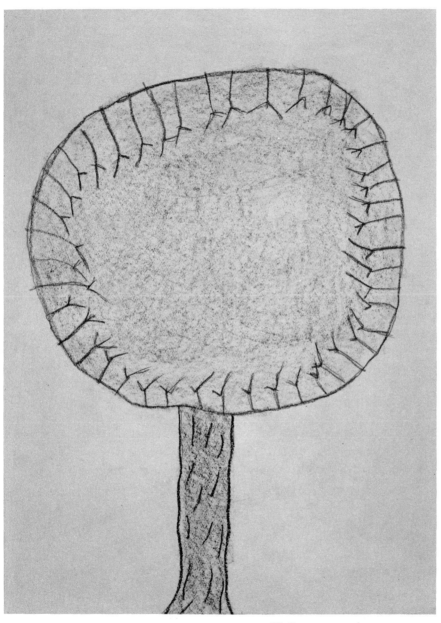

FIGURE 10-1. ONE OF SARA'S FIRST DRAWINGS

FIGURE 10–2. A LATER DRAWING

FIGURE 10-3. A LATER DRAWING

confidence, ability to use more detail, and having an avenue for communication in art would probably contribute to a better psychological environment for learning to read.

The attitude of the consultant is a very important variable in the success or failure of such a teaching method. This particular person has a basic acceptance of all children and believes that all have potential abilities that can be developed.

Individual Expression. We often assume that all children have some strong feelings they want to express. Children may lead uneventful lives with little to motivate expression. Other children may have such feelings of anxiety or hostility that it would be unwise to encourage them to unleash their feelings too fully in the classroom. But both types of children can sometimes learn to express emotion constructively in art if the ideas they are expressing are *somewhat separated from their own experience.* This separation enables them to be more objective, particularly when their emotions are related to inhibition or fear. For example, speech therapists use puppets in working with children who stutter. The child, talking for the puppet, often stutters less than when he is talking for himself. Gradually through such therapy the child is enabled to improve his "own" speech.

In art activities, motivation that is somewhat removed from personal experience may give some children more opportunity for expression. Almost all children respond to music. With a whole class participating they can respond to rhythm in music and art in several ways. The rhythm, mood, and pattern of the music gives them an "outside" structure through which to express their feelings. A variety of musical forms should be used, so the children can see that their individual responses differ from one piece to another. Three excellent compositions that encourage different kinds of responses are Aaron Copland's "Red Pony Suite," Virgil Thomson's "Acadian Suite," and Offenbach's "Gaieté Parisienne." Responses can be made by dancing and by drawing with easy, flowing materials such as paints and inks.

Children can learn that rhythm and repetition take place in music and in art and are means for expressing different kinds of feeling. Gluck's "Dance of the Happy Spirits" has a lilting dance-like quality. Tchaikovsky's "Sleeping Beauty Waltz" may be familiar and easier for them to respond to. When they have developed skills in this kind of interpretation, play Bartók's "Suite for Children." This music, a group of Hungarian folk song arrangements, has quick changes of mood. Eric Coates' "Knightsbridge March" has a brilliant marching rhythm in contrast to the dancing rhythms of the other compositions.

In responding to strongly rhythmic music, pupils can use instruments they have made, jingle clogs, tambourines, maracas, and drums. Several members of the class can play the instruments, while others work with art media. Opportunity to play the instruments may help some children get the "feel" of the rhythm more clearly. They can compare ways different kinds of music and sounds influence their art work. Interpretation of music leads children to increase their range of expression. It lays a foundation for understanding design (rhythm, pattern, repetition, variation) in

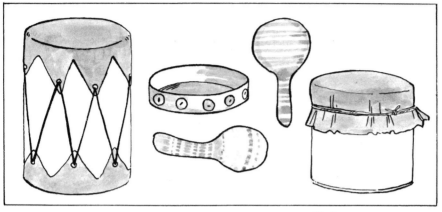

FIGURE 10–4. MUSICAL INSTRUMENTS

other media of expression. It does not take the place of self-directed art activity, where the child works by himself when he is ready, but it should increase the variety of ideas he can express in his self-directed work through the use of postural, kinesthetic, and auditory cues.

DEVELOPING SKILLS. The child can develop pride in craftsmanship by working with a tool until it behaves as he wishes it. At this level the standards for such skill should be established by the child more than by the teacher. Some children will depend on the feel of a tool, others on its appearance, to guide their experimentation. Encourage them to use both types of cues. Allow for differences in eye-hand coordination. This kind of teaching of skill does not produce the failure experiences frequently observed where specific techniques are assumed to be right and children made to try them regardless of their readiness. When a child wants to learn a specific skill the teacher should help him or ask someone to help, such as the art consultant.

To help pupils learn how to handle tempera, you might proceed as follows. The children have been on a field trip to the city and have ridden on the subway—many for the first time. Before going, you had told them about the subway, how it speeds along in the dark and then suddenly comes to a brightly lighted station. You had asked them to look for all the patterns of light and colors they would see as they got out in the station. Back in the classroom some of the children want to make a picture of what they experienced. Some choose paint and brush to do this. Encourage the children to see how many kinds of textures paint can have—how they can spread it, smoothly or roughly, how many kinds of brush strokes they can make. Ask them to try the colors on white, black, and colored paper. Give many suggestions for them to try, and encourage them to judge whether they got what they wanted; if they did not, ask them to try the paint in another way, such as with sponges. This kind of experience leads to versatility as well as to practice in using the skill. You are combatting "functional fixedness," the tendency to use a tool in the first technique learned. When a child finds one way that is successful and stays with it too long, give him new experiences that lead to the necessity of trying new ways of using the medium.

EVALUATING AND INTRODUCING A MEDIUM

When you select a medium to introduce you are making an educational decision. Your knowledge of the foundations of art education helps you to understand the nature of the process and the kinds of individual differences you must allow for. Children vary in (1) their tolerance for new and unusual tasks, (2) the time it takes them to shift to using new tools and materials, and (3) their attitudes developed from related past experiences.

In introducing anything new, relate it to similar things they have already used—watching for possible reactions of nonacceptance. Overcome resistance to it by your own enthusiasm and interest, and by encouraging rather than insisting that pupils use it. Even in art learning experience, every child should not always be required to use the material presented. After success with a medium that is acceptable to him, the child can be encouraged to try others. Most of the class will usually accept a new material, but any one child may be slow with any one medium. On rare occasions a child will be so inhibited by past training, such as fear of getting dirty, that you may have no success in getting him to try a certain material. This does not mean that he must fail in art. Your objectives are not limited to uses of certain materials; there are many ways for a child to experience success in art.

To allow for children who are slow to accept new things, your presentation of a new material can include a reanalysis of the past one. A child who may not begin to work in a medium the first time it is presented may be ready the second or third time.

It is not possible to know all about a child's past art experiences, but within a school district you can learn what has been done in prior grades and kindergarten. If possible, find out what *ways* the materials were used, as attitudes develop from actions as well as from things. For example, if a child has used crayons for learning color names and for filling in so many red apples or yellow bananas in an arithmetic lesson, his attitudes toward crayons may correspond with his attitudes toward arithmetic and how well he could stay within the lines. If, on the other hand, he used crayons in exploratory ways, discovering many ways to use them for expressive effects, he will have less rigid attitudes towards the medium.

When a new pupil arrives, part of his introduction to the classroom should be a tour of the art area. Ask him which materials he has used, which he liked best, and which he liked least. This discussion will introduce him to the art materials available to him and will help you to assess his readiness.

Decisions about when to use a new medium should be considered in terms of the whole class, as well as of individuals. Ask yourself the following kinds of questions in order to make a decision.

1. If I introduce a new medium now, will those members of the class who are motivated by the values of expediency and getting things done as quickly as possible neglect their further exploration of familiar materials?

2. If I do not introduce a new medium soon, will those children whose attention span is short, or who are unable to work in much detail, lose interest?

3. How can I encourage further work in the media we are now using, adding new dimensions to keep both groups' attention?

At the same time that you increase the number of materials the children can work with, you should encourage them to experiment with familiar materials. A superficial use of many materials will not contribute much to growth in creativity and expression. Too limited a range of materials can inhibit the growth and success of those pupils who have not yet found enjoyable avenues of expression. *The most important thing is what a child says with his art; the medium he uses to say it is of lesser importance.*

When all these factors are considered, you may decide to introduce the new medium, but you need not insist that everyone try it during the art learning experience. It can be available for self-directed art activities and it can be brought up in art learning periods several times—encouraging creative use of the medium each time.

Part of the decision depends on the nature of the medium. For example, gold and silver foil papers have so much glitter in themselves that the child may feel satisfied without having to invent much. Crayon etching (scratching through black ink or crayon to colored underlays) gives exciting color experience. Often children enjoy the entertainment without making attempts at symbolic creation. Both of these media can be used most creatively, but the teacher's question is, "Are these children ready to be inventive with this medium, or will they stop with just the exciting initial effect?"

THE PRIMARY YEARS: SELF-DIRECTED ART

So much of a child's activity is teacher-directed that he needs some opportunity for constructive self-directed activity. In art, he can have such activity while the teacher works with small groups in other subjects. The child may work on an individual or group project. In the art corner he can find many materials.

New media, after being introduced in the art period, should be available for free time use. Less frequently used art and craft materials can be rotated as the need arises. As a general rule, *too many choices confuse children; too few choices are frustrating.* Be sure to save some new things for later in the year and later in their schooling. Often the selection of a new medium will coincide with its use in integrative art activity, such as a mural for social studies.

Watch children's activities during the free choice periods. What they produce will be clues to their interests. These interests motivate them in other areas and other art activities. A child who draws trains may enjoy reading books about trains. A child who reads about trains can learn to see and organize visual stimuli of trains by drawing them. If a child persists too long in drawing the same thing, encourage him to read more about it; then try to expand his reading to related objects and encourage drawing of these objects.

Recognition of Self-directed Art. Free choice activity should be given some recognition. A child feels rewarded when the teacher asks to save one of his drawings. Displays can be made of free choice art activity. The child can keep a folder of things to take home. Art work that is preserved for anecdotal records should be marked, "self-directed," "art learning" or "integrated art activity" to tell you and the next teacher the most about the conditions under which the work was done. Comparisons of self-directed work with art in the other areas will give clues to the child's independence and self-motivation.

THE PRIMARY YEARS:
INTEGRATED ART

Art underlies most of the other learnings of the elementary years. It functions wherever symbols or objects are organized as part of the classroom design. As language, art helps children to organize their learnings and to reinforce their verbal concepts. The symbolization in graphs, charts, and models necessary in all levels of scientific study demonstrates that words alone are inadequate to structure the patterning of relationships. Learning to see aesthetically, as well as visually and cognitively, helps to make elementary science more meaningful.

ART IN ELEMENTARY SCIENCE

Major objectives of the science program are to develop children's curiosity, to encourage them to see relationships and differences in the interaction and growth of plants and animals. The design of a snail's path across the sand, the structure of the shell that protects an animal, the pattern of the roots of a plant reaching for food and water are sources of aesthetic appreciation. Learning to see structural beauty can help children remember visual detail. Also they can enrich their potential for creativity in art through the source material in science. The research that shows that people trained in the visual arts see more detail leads us to feel that using art with science can strengthen children's perceptual training and visual space manipulation (being able to think of things in three dimensions).[4]

Transfer of training from one field to another does not take place automatically; but the use of principles, concepts, skills, and attitudes learned in one situation can be applied to other situations.[5] To reinforce children's transfer of learning between art and other subjects, direct references should be made, showing them how the same ability or organizational pattern operates in both situations. For example, children may have learned to look for design in art and outdoors, but may not see it when they look at things under a microscope. Show them that similar kinds of patterning are present. Help them look for the particular form of order and variation when they look at nature in finer detail. Children may be able to see design in abstract forms, but when they look at pictures of real things they are so concerned with the *things* that they fail to see the organization. Encourage them to look at the basic forms, lines, and colors. Sometimes looking at a picture upside down helps this transfer of training to take place—the things have to be set in an unreal position for the child to see the pattern.

ART IN SOCIAL STUDIES

The social studies program is often organized with a change of focus each year, expanding from the home as a social institution to the neighborhood. In the first grade a model house may be made. The children furnish the house by sewing curtains, molding *papier-mâché* plates and clay bowls, making small rugs with a loom, and making or choosing pictures for the walls. The wall dividers can be painted or covered with pupil-designed wallpaper. If choices are made for reasons of function and beauty, the children are learning to be discriminating.

In second grade the focus shifts to the neighborhood, the

people who work and live in it, the distribution of foods and supplies, the sources of raw materials and the ways we use them. The influence of art can be found everywhere. Awareness that art is involved in so much of life precedes any aesthetic judgment about the quality of the art.

Third grade deals with the people in the community, their functions, their interdependence, and their relation to other communities. Dependence on the artist and designer can be stressed. Awareness of the functions of art in the community can be further developed.

In the primary years children are often taught the roles of the people who serve their community, the policeman, fireman, grocer, lawyer, doctor. They should also be aware of the building and landscape architects and the industrial designer. The architect who designed the school should be well-known to the children who use his building. Field trips in the social studies can be reinforced by aesthetic observations.

In simple ways, through pictures, bulletin boards, slides, field trips ask children to identify where an artist or architect has been at work. Give them clear workable definitions of architects and artists.

Architect means *chief worker,* the one who designs how buildings are to be built.

Artists make pictures instead of stories to tell us things. Artists also design and create things we use.

BEGINNING CONSUMER EDUCATION. Opportunities to make choices and to question one's choices can begin early. To develop independence in aesthetic judgment, early training in making choices and thinking about reasons for choices are important. Children need two things to help them develop independence—(1) freedom to choose and (2) continued experience and learning to develop a capacity to choose. An art file containing prints of paintings and photographs of well-designed objects should be available. From it the children can select material for their bulletin board. Choice-making can be made the subject of class discussion. Short paragraphs explaining why the pictures were chosen can be displayed with the pictures. Primary children can discuss what they have done, while the teacher writes their conclusions. Some children in second and third grade can make simple statements of what they think about the pictures. These paragraphs, in the children's own words, can be made into reading charts. Continued evaluation helps primary children grow up in an environment in which the art around them is recognized as part of life—advertising, architecture, product designs, and painting.

THE INTERMEDIATE YEARS: ART LEARNING ACTIVITIES

The intermediate years of the elementary school, grades four through six, are particularly crucial in children's development in art. Generally speaking, less time is given to art. At the same time, individual differences become more pronounced. The range in abilities is wider, and experiences are more varied. More cultural values have been learned, so differences between children from different subcultures may widen the gaps between groups.

The purpose of this chapter is to show sequence in art training, but some of the suggestions for the primary grades are appropriate in later situations. Some of the children may have had very little art experience prior to the time they enter your class. In this case you need to begin where they are. The suggestions for the intermediate years are planned to be built on experiences of the primary grades. If you plan to teach in the intermediate grades, you will need to understand what has gone on before.

DEVELOPING TASTE

Children's levels of aesthetic taste can be raised by exposure to, and training in, the fine arts and superior product design and advertising. Understanding will come as the relationships are seen between pupils' symbolic inventions and those of the professional artist.

A ten-year-old's painting of patterns of city streets may be compared with a print of Mondrian's "Broadway Boogie Woogie." When the child sees the likenesses and differences between the two, he may respond in a number of ways. He may find his own interpretation more acceptable, or he may become more receptive to abstract painting. If he shows interest he may be told about the Museum of Modern Art, which owns the Mondrian painting; he may look through the museum's publications to understand its social function, its encouragement of good design in industry as well as in the fine arts.

LEARNING THE ARTIST'S ROLE IN SOCIETY

The role of the designer can be explored in visits to the studios of architects and city planners. The art director of a store can show children the implementing of an idea for a window display or an advertisement. A visit to a creative painter or sculptor may help break down stereotyped attitudes about artists. Children may be allowed to see paintings in various stages of development and to watch as the artist works. Discussion should be directed away from the building of new stereotypes.

In selecting an artist or craftsman, be sure that he is willing to accept children, and that his work is truly creative. When children are exposed to unimaginative work such as extremely representational painting, they may feel that their more childlike interpretations are "wrong." Many traditional painters, however, are very expressive and inventive in their interpretation of nature. At this age children can begin to learn that artists have different purposes in what they do. Some interpret nature graphically; others express their feelings about things; still others analyze the structure and form of nature, disregarding its surface appearance. Today there is considerable emphasis on expressing the essence of experience rather than interpreting the nature of things. If children are exposed to many kinds of art, it is not always necessary that they know the differences between expressionism, cubism, and abstraction.

PERCEPTUAL TRAINING

During these years children are learning many new concepts and the complex relationships between them. Their perceptual training can parallel their cognitive training. Through the elementary school, children have opportunities to develop verbal skills and means of communication through language. Because of the assumption of "naïve realism," that skills in perception are not needed, children may grow up with little help in perceptual learning and communication through pictorial symbols. If your intermediate grade children have had simple training in perception in primary years, continue to increase their ability to assimilate, organize, and communicate through art.

HANDLING COMPLEXITY. Increase the number and kinds of systems the children can use for organizing complex visual experiences. In a painting, they can look for the obvious pattern of line and then for the more subtle patterns. This can be done by separating lines of different colors, different kinds of lines—sharp, smooth, curved, angular. Look at Picasso's painting in Plate IV; here are patterns of straight lines, of rounded lines, of subtly moving lines. The pattern of values can be studied, the very light areas, the very dark areas and the intermediate steps in between. There is a pattern of shapes, in this case mainly rectangular. Help the children see very small rectangles and very large ones and the more subtle differences between big and small, near and far. Let them look for the patterns of colors, how they are repeated in different values of the same color.

To help them conceptualize what they are learning to see in space, use a colored slide of nature in which great distance is shown, with objects in the foreground to make comparisons. Encourage them to translate what they see in visual space into written descriptions. Give them more categories for describing space, such as close, distant, in front, behind, above, below, near, and far. Help them make comparisons in terms of relative position in space, such as "the train close by is as big as the mountains far away."

Instead of imposing a traditional color system on these children encourage them to describe all the differences they can see. Using tempera or water color, encourage pupils to mix as many kinds of blues, greens, reds, yellows as they can. Mix color with black and white to see differences in values.

COGNITIVE AND VISUAL LEARNING. Explore with children the way forms, colors, and shapes change as they move in space and light. Most of the pupils will not have learned this in the primary grades. Those who have begun to learn to discriminate can increase their ability. They can be more analytical of these changes and can see in more detail. Strong spotlights help separate objects from the background so that children can more clearly observe how the forms change as they move in space. The light makes strong lights and shadows, making edges clear cut and easy to see. Explore each of the constancies, shape, form, color, and size.

This practice develops the capacity to see *visually* as well as cognitively. For example, your pupils know their school building very well, but *how* do they know it? What kind of cognitive concepts do they have about it? Probably they know the pattern of the halls and where their classroom is, the lunchroom and principal's rooms, the way to the playground. But probably only a few have paid attention to the different colors used, the architectural form of the building. Few have learned to look for the aesthetic values in the building, the design and light patterns made by the planes and lines. Figure 10–5 shows two drawings of a school building, one showing mainly patterns of dark and light and the other the patterns of line.

Black and white slides and photographs taken in bright sunlight of any school building can be useful in teaching children to

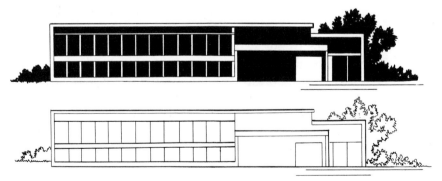

FIGURE 10–5. PATTERNS OF LIGHT AND DARK AND PATTERNS OF LINE

look aesthetically as well as cognitively. In a semidark room show the slide, using a large sheet of newsprint for the screen. With colored chalk the teacher or one of the pupils can draw the pattern of lines the photograph makes. Another drawing can be made using black and white chalk on gray paper to show the patterns of dark and light. This is abstracting, taking from the complete photograph certain elements to analyze for their aesthetic quality. It is also perceptual training, helping children learn how much goes on in perceptual organization, how much there is to "see" if one takes the time to look.

Similar kinds of abstracting can be made by analyzing the patterns of colors in a landscape. The patterns of varieties of shapes, the subtle differences in size and shape, can be made without too much emphasis on what the "thing" is.

DEVELOPING CREATIVITY

During the intermediate years creative ability appears to decrease for many children. Since decrease is not found in all cultures, we can assume that many of the reasons for its occurrence are cultural, differences in the way the children are rewarded. In American culture the pressure to conform to the peer group is beginning to be felt by fourth grade. Children seem to have less motivation for independent expression. To counteract this trend, the teacher can encourage and reward independence, can make clear to the children the rewards they will get for originality. The need for creative behavior can be made apparent in a study of the lives of many of the great men and women, now and in the past, whose contributions to our way of life have been an outgrowth of their independent creative thinking and action.

Make clear to the children that they need not fear failure in something they try. Exploration and attempts at invention are valuable in themselves. Show them that many of the problems they will have to solve in art and in life do not have clearly defined right and wrong answers. Show them that there are many possible good solutions to design problems. In discussing the results of their own work, show them how many different ways they have expressed and organized ideas so that they communicate clearly.

Materials that are easily manipulated help children explore

differences in the ways they organize things. Mosaics, cut paper, and torn paper make rearranging and shifting form, lines, and colors easy. Many children need encouragement in becoming more flexible by shifting their original idea, improvising on it, and changing it. Exploration with a medium, seeing how many ways can be invented to use it, helps keep children from becoming rigid about the uses of tools and materials.

Some technique should be used to sustain interest in a task that takes considerable work before a satisfying art product is made. One teacher used the technique of suspense. During an art learning period she introduced the children to crayon etching, but she only went as far as showing them how they could get the thick crayon on the paper, dust it with chalk dust, and then cover it all over with black ink. With considerable enthusiasm she encouraged them to get their sheets ready for a surprise they were going to have the next day. She stimulated their interest by having them guess what they might do—but did not tell them. On the following day she asked each child to take out his black drawing; then she began to describe the wonderful pictures that were hidden under the ink. Each picture in the room was different, because each child would use his own imagination to find it. Demonstrating with different points, a dry pen point, a nail, the prongs of a fork, the teacher showed how scratching through the ink revealed colored lines underneath. Then when each child had his tools ready she introduced another incentive. She played a taped recording she had made at a county fair. Most of the children responded easily and delightedly to the music of the carousel and the Ferris wheel, and the cries of the barkers. Some children needed further attention and encouragement. Moving around the room, helping individuals while watching the whole class, the teacher soon had everyone working.

A discussion followed of how sounds communicate ideas to us, and how out of our experience and memory we imagine pictures. The variety in the paintings was pointed out. Each child remembered somewhat different things. County fairs from many parts of the country were recalled. Something of value was found in each drawing. The children who had never seen a county fair had been to an amusement park, but one child had had no experience with either. The teacher pointed out how wonderfully inventive this child was to imagine things he had never seen.

The discussion went on to an evaluation of future uses for the new skill. Some children were eager to try again during their self-directed activity. Others wanted to learn more by continuing it in the next art learning period. A few pupils had suggestions for its use in other class work.

CREATIVE PROBLEM-SOLVING IN DESIGN. As children become more critical of their work they can become conscious of what they are doing in design. Some of the principles of design such as balance of unequal things and the influence of every part in a design on every other part, can be adapted to the child's level of understanding. Informal discussion of the principles is appropriate and leads to discoveries of how nature designs, with infinite variety yet with patterns of similarity and unity. Children can analyze each of the properties of design—form, line, color, and texture—and see how they interact upon each other. They can experiment with them so that their designs are interesting and easy to see. They can think about the design qualities and use them as a basis for evaluating their own work and making aesthetic judgments, particularly in the intermediate grades when their more natural child-like designing ability seems to decrease.

Children vary considerably in their ability to handle complex visual details. If designing is an unfamiliar task, some children will need particular encouragement. The subject may be too abstract for them to deal with, but many can profit from the experience. The practice of leaving the study of design to the high school was a reaction against the more academic study—practicing set "principles"—which has not been considered effective in the elementary grades. Creative problem-solving in design can be adapted to the most simple processes. In Chapter 11 we will study the nature of the designing process so that you can help pupils work at their own level.

SKILLS

During art learning experiences children can increase their skills with familiar materials and can learn to use many new materials. More complex printing methods, paper sculpture, weaving, pottery, mosaics, and a variety of paints and brushes can be introduced. The number and the sequence depend on the readiness of the class. As children's perceptual and creative skills develop, the means for developing broader ways of expression need to be provided.

THE INTERMEDIATE YEARS: SELF-DIRECTED ART

If the art learning experience has been rich and has dealt with individual differences, the self-directed art activities will go on freely. If pupils know where to find and how to return materials, then more things can be available at any one time. Because most classrooms have limited storage space, some rotation of the art materials available for self-directed art is usually necessary. Several selections should always be available, particularly as new media are introduced during art learning experiences.

Children differ in the amount of self-discipline they have learned. If their previous teachers have dictated every step, little self-discipline will have developed. Also, rejected children who are getting attention through aggression may find self-direction difficult unless the teacher gives them duties or finds some other way to make them feel accepted and wanted.

Discipline problems often show up during free choice periods. The sources of these problems can usually be found in (1) rejection at home, (2) discontinuity about rewards, (3) continued failure experiences, and (4) boredom with a repetitious or too difficult task. If the child understands that he is accepted, he loses one reason for being rebellious. If he knows the reward and punishment system, the limits of acceptable behavior, and if he can find an activity that is challenging but not beyond his ability, he should be able to work without bothering other children.

The apparent decrease in creativity beginning in the fourth grade may limit children's ability to be self-directive during those periods when they are free to choose their activity. One reason may be that the goals in subject matter are more specifically established in the intermediate grades. It could be that there is too much discontinuity in reward between their academic learning and art. There may be differences in the attitudes of teachers who choose to teach in the primary grades and those who choose the intermediate grades. The latter may have more interest in cognitive learning and may neglect visual and aesthetic learning. This attitude may never be recognized by the teachers themselves.

To continue the development of creative ability every child should have time for his own exploration in art activities, in creative writing, and in solving problems in science. Learning to solve a problem flexibly, to deal with ambiguity, to reinterpret, and to accept change are necessary skills for living in a dynamic society. Margaret Mead has pointed out that we have to train children in problem-solving for problems we cannot now imagine.[6]

The contribution of the self-directed art program is to give each child an opportunity (1) to direct his own exploration in art, (2) to let him use what he has learned in his own way, (3) to give him time to work at his own rate, and (4) to give him freer choice among media.

THE INTERMEDIATE YEARS: INTEGRATED ART

Curriculum patterns vary throughout the country. The sequence suggested here is only one pattern. Teachers should explore possibilities for using art in the curriculum established in their own schools. These suggestions are given to help you find *ways* in other systems.

FOURTH GRADE. Fourth grade children are becoming acquainted with larger areas, learning the geography and history of their state. History can be made to seem real by trying some of the processes of production used in earlier periods. For example, let children work with native clays, locating and preparing them. Let them try making tinware, hammered copper, and weaving. The different cultures that have entered the area can be studied through the things settlers made to enhance their way of life. California children can study Mexican, Indian, and Spanish art, all strong influences on the early settlers. State history and related cultures are very different in New York, Wisconsin, Louisiana, and Montana.

But forms of art can be found in the history of all regions and in the related cultures.

FIFTH GRADE. In the fifth grade the development of the larger society—the nation—is stressed. Art forms of all the ethnic groups can be studied, even though the actual production of all the things is not necessary. The growth of social institutions can be explored. Include those that support the arts—libraries, art galleries, symphony orchestras, theaters. Most art galleries and museums have educational directors who want children to learn not only what is in their galleries but what the function of the gallery is in the community. Many have slides, paintings, and books for rental to schools. They have trained lecturers, who can guide children in the galleries. State boards of education, colleges, and universities have film rental services.

Social studies curricula often neglect to include the institutions devoted to the aesthetic growth of the community. Through your training in art education you can enrich the social studies program. The pupils can write to local and national galleries and orchestras for pamphlets, program advertisements, and catalogues for information and display. Some galleries have instructional movies about their institutions that may be rented or borrowed. It should be remembered that these institutions do not have unlimited funds; care should be used not to ask for too much nor to use their materials carelessly.

SIXTH GRADE. In the sixth grade the range of social understanding spreads to neighboring countries. The work of artists who interpret a culture can enrich the study of that culture. There are excellent descriptive films that have high artistic value. The Canadian National Film Board's "The Romance of Transportation" and "Klee Wyck" are excellent examples. The consulate offices of neighboring countries may have information of sources for free and rental films and prints of art work, including crafts and industrial design.

These social studies activities in the arts can enrich the art learning and self-directed art activities. They can increase children's appreciation and acceptance of art, and in many ways give them a broader base for their own creative activity.

DIFFERENCES
AMONG
CHILDREN

over-all growth
intellectual ability
perceptual ability
creative potential
cultural training
past experiences
attitudes and values

MOTIVATION

—has meaning for children of
many backgrounds
—is varied to allow for differences
in visual and intellectual com-
prehension
—begins where the children are
in over-all development
—is sequential so one experience
leads on from the preceding

CLASSROOM
EXPERIENCES

perceptual training
reward for exploration
and invention
individual expression
exploration in design
opportunities to explore
many media
study of art in the envi-
ronment
study of cultures through
art

MAJOR OBJECTIVES

sensitive perceptual
awareness
creativity, fluency, flexibility, originality
ability in individual ex-
pression and commu-
nication
independent aesthetic
judgment
appreciation of art
self-direction and self-
evaluation

FIGURE 10–6. A SUMMARY OF DIFFERENCES, EXPERIENCES, AND OBJECTIVES

INTERMEDIATE GRADE SCIENCE

During the intermediate years the science program expands
to more areas. The educational trend is to help children see the
patterns of relationships between things rather than just learn
facts.[7] The perceptual skills developed in art can be used for
critical observation in science. Training in the perception of subtle
variations in form, color, texture, repetition and variation in pattern give children a better framework in which to categorize new
information. Learning to see things clearly in three dimensional
form as it moves in space gives children a better basis for ordering
and remembering three dimensional systems in science.

Because of our cultural tendencies to separate the sciences and
arts we may have to help children learn that it is possible to see

beauty under a microscope as well as in a meadow; that beauty of form and pattern can be found in all of nature's structures.

SUMMARY

The art program at both the primary and intermediate grades should consist of *art learning, self-directed,* and *integrated activities.*

Art learning activities provide the child with motivating experiences to encourage his creative development of ideas for expression in art. His perceptual sensitivity is increased by giving him help in learning to organize complex visual information. He becomes familiar with the uses of many materials and tools.

During *self-directed activities* the child can exercise his ability to make choices and act upon them at his own speed.

During *integrated activities* art is used to complement learning in other areas—relationships, sequences, summaries in units of learning can be organized in visual communication. The role of the arts in the life of pupils' own and other cultures is part of social studies. Design in nature is part of learning in science.

Particular care should be taken to make the intermediate years as effective in art as the primary years. The sequence of learning should depend on what the children have learned before. Basic perceptual awareness must come before more advanced tasks are attempted in any grade.

REFERENCES

1. Helen Borten, *Do You See What I See?* (London: Abelard-Schuman, 1959).

2. Henry Schaefer-Simmern, *The Unfolding of Artistic Activity* (Berkeley: University of California Press, 1948).

3. Yvonne Whitehurst Seidel, unpublished material used with permission.

4. Walter A. Woods and James C. Boudreau, "Design Complexity as a Determiner of Visual Attention Among Artists and Non-Artists," *Journal of Applied Psychology,* XXXIV (1950), 355–366.

5. Lee J. Cronbach, *Educational Psychology* (New York: Harcourt, Brace and Company, Inc., 1954), pp. 256–257.

6. Margaret Mead, *The School in American Culture* (Cambridge: Harvard University Press, 1951), p. 41.

7. Jerome S. Bruner, *The Process of Education* (Cambridge: Harvard University Press, 1960).

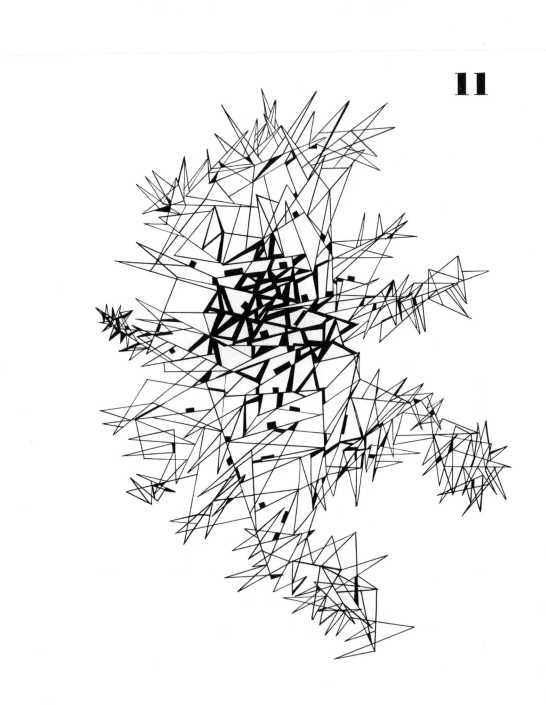

11

Design for the Classroom Teacher

As a teacher you are a designer. You arrange bulletin boards, chalkboards, and display tables; you organize tools, materials, furniture, and equipment. You wear clothing. You teach "art" by the kind of environment you create. You are concerned with teaching art directly to children; but much of their learning about it does not happen during an art lesson, nor even when art is used for science or social studies. All through the year the children are exposed to a major art form—an interior of a room. Their experience depends on the quality of your designing.

THE NATURE OF DESIGN

"What is design?" or more specifically, "What does a designer do for his viewers?" We know that the individual uses only a small quantity of the visual stimuli he receives. The designer's role is to select and organize from the environment those things that will assist him in expressing an idea or enhancing an object.

The designer works in two ways. (1) He works with the *functions* (purpose and operation) of the object he is designing. (2) He works with the *visual elements* of design. These are form, line,

243

color, texture, and space. With these in mind, he creates an arrangement that has balance, rhythm, dynamic unity, and integration. These are some of the *qualities* of design. They are the aesthetic essence of design—those qualities that give man a sense of resolution and beauty. Design is the language of the arts; it is the paragraphing, punctuation, and over-all organization that communicates the ideas clearly and interestingly to others. Visual symbols without design are like words without sentences.

The functions and the visual elements are important in architecture, city planning, product design, painting, sculpture, fabric design, industrial design, the setting of a table, the arrangement of furniture in a room, a teacher's bulletin board, and a science display. *Whenever we give order to objects, we are designing.* Whether the design is satisfying depends on how well we integrate the function and the visual elements as they operate together to create aesthetic effects (balance and rhythm, dynamic and organic unity).

The function of an object is part of its design. Let us use a chair as an example. If its function is to provide something to sit on, then part of its beauty is the way it fulfills this purpose. Many chairs have been designed as ornaments first and as chairs second. As an object designed to support us in a seated position, the ornamental chair is often inadequate. According to contemporary concepts of good design, difficulty in use detracts from aesthetic as well as from functional quality, these two being considered inseparable.

The visual elements—form, line, color, texture, and space—are used according to the function. Forms are selected that are suitable for the functional purpose of the chair. The line effects are usually developed in the structure. If the chair is structurally sound—considering the materials used—an aesthetic effect is usually achieved. Texture may be determined by the materials, color, form, and the uses to be made of the chair. A chair for a public place may require a texture different from a chair for a family living room. The element of space is judged by the chair's appearance from many viewpoints.

The combination of all these factors contributes to the aesthetic effects produced. A designer has to evaluate all the different decisions he makes to see whether all of them contribute to the aesthetic whole. Is there a sense of balance, symmetrical or asymmetrical? Do all the tensions produced by suggestions of movement, contrasts in colors, angle lines, and space result in an effect of dynamic unity? Do all the parts contribute to, rather than detract from, the whole organic effect? When all of these are accomplished the designer can feel that the object will be unified, thus aesthetically effective to the viewer.

PSYCHOLOGICAL BASIS FOR DESIGN

The designing process is based on visual organization—we organize the many stimuli we receive so that we can respond to them. We do this in several ways: (1) by dealing with *similar things as a unit,* such as calling a meadow *green,* when it actually has many variations of color; (2) by taking an *average of different things,* as when we look at a crowd of people and deal with them as a group even though they are all somewhat different visually; (3) *by continuation,* when we complete to wholes those things we see in part, according to our past experience with them.[1]

FIGURE AND GROUND

To recognize a visual pattern we divide the visual impressions into "figure" and "ground," that is "subject" and "background." Have you ever watched in a crowd for someone you know and seen only the crowd? The instant you see your friend, the crowd becomes background and your friend stands out. Forms, to be seen clearly, need space around them to create a sense of edge that defines their shape. Sometimes a line will suggest figure or ground on either side of it. Figure 11–1 can represent two faces or a lamp base, depending on what areas you see as figure and what areas as ground.

RELATING PROCESSES

We group similar things, relating them even though they are separated in space. The following figures based on Gestalt psychology show how this relating is done.[2] Figure 11–2* illustrates the *principle of proximity.* The dots in *A* are closer together in the

---

*Figures 11–2, 11–3, 11–4, and 11–5 from *Introduction to Psychology* by Ernest R. Hilgard, © 1953, 1957, by Harcourt, Brace and Company, Inc.

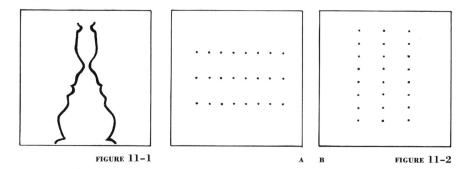

A   B   FIGURE 11–2

horizontal, so we get the visual effect of horizontal lines. In *B* the dots are closer together in the vertical, and we get the impression of vertical lines. The line effect is achieved by our grouping of the visual information according to the principle of proximity. No actual lines are present, only dots. We make the lines by grouping.

In Figure 11–3 we tend to see three narrow columns with a line left over at the right, rather than three wider columns with a line left over on the left. Notice how hard it is to make yourself see the wide columns.

In Figure 11–4 the principle of *similarity* rather than proximity is in operation. The dots are all equidistant. But, because we tend to group similarities, we see horizontal lines of the two sizes of dots. In the same way we relate similar forms, lines, colors, and textures that are farther apart, as we will see when we put these principles to use.

Another Gestalt principle is that of *continuity*. We tend to follow a line in its most easily perceived direction. Figure 11–5 has three parts. *A* shows a combination of lines; *B* and *C* show two ways

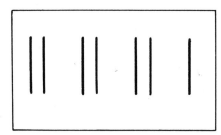

FIGURE 11–3   FIGURE 11–4

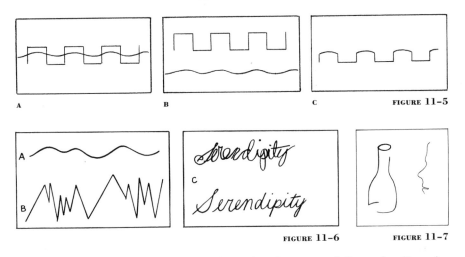

A   B   C   FIGURE 11–5

FIGURE 11–6   FIGURE 11–7

of following the lines. It is much easier for us to follow the lines in
B than in *C* because the lines in *B* are continuous rather than shifting from rounded to square lines. In Figure 11–6, why is line *A*
more restful than line *B?* Which handwriting is easier to read in
C? Our eye can follow the flow of line in the lower example much
more easily. Another form of continuity is *closure*—seeing the
whole from a suggested part (see Figure 11–7).

Each of the visual tendencies described gives us clues as to how
we can design our environment so that it is well organized yet interesting. Figures 11–8 and 11–9 are examples of two designs.

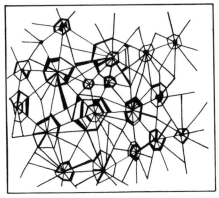

FIGURE 11–8

FIGURE 11–9

Both are interesting, but 11–8 is more unified, while 11–9 lacks integration of the different symbols.

These principles should help you in presenting visual material to children. You can make information easier to understand by grouping related ideas. Since children have to make averages of visual information, do not give them so much material that making the average is too difficult. How do the Gestalt principles apply to the organization of spelling words on the chalkboard? Arithmetic problems? Science displays? If you have a collection of fifty pictures on the Westward movement, how would you effectively display them? You would, of course, make selections according to topics you want to emphasize. At the same time, you would choose sizes, shapes, colors, and mounting papers that can be organized into groups to make the relationship between ideas clear. Some relationships can be shown with lines of colored string. A *few* lines that connect a *few* pictures will teach more than will a network of lines that try to show all relationships.

A symphony is a carefully designed group of musical ideas that are improvised upon and organized through time. To the listener who is unfamiliar with the parts of a particular symphony, the composition may seem strange and overwhelming, but if he hears it several times he begins to recognize repetitions and variations of basic themes. In a complex visual design such as a non-objective painting, the parts and subthemes are not always readily comprehensible, but through exposure and opportunity to study, the parts and their relationships become understandable to us.

A confident person may say, "I design intuitively—I just know when it's right, but I can't tell you why." A small child, who is certainly not intellectually aware of principles of design, can make a pleasing, balanced composition. Does intuitive designing differ much from intellectual planning according to the relationships described above? Consider the millions of visual stimuli you receive all the time your eyes are open. If you look out the window, every detail, including the window frame and every leaf of a nearby tree, will be reflected on the retinas of your eyes. But to respond to this information you will have to group it in some way. You will need to see leaves as parts of forms that make up trees. To recognize perspective you will need to see how the size of a road changes as it moves away from you. To recognize your friend in the crowd you have to separate him visually from all the other people. This is separating figure from ground. *Every time you look, you are in some degree designing—organizing all the information so you can handle it cognitively.* Most of this perceptual designing activity is done at a precognitive level, that is, without conscious thinking. What artists call intuitive designing (changing relationships until they "feel" right) appears to be this same process—the process that most of us use at Point III in P-D—organizing visual information. They carry it on to Point IV of the process as this information is organized and grouped in an art form. Those people who have not developed this intuitive skill can still design creatively by using cues from the psychology of perception.

Understanding design will help you organize what the children in your classroom see. When you apply design principles, your pupils are not learning design as such, but are living in an environment that is designed for easier learning. Every time you present visual information, you will need to group it so that the children will be able to assimilate it easily. Good design will also help hold their interest.

Children cannot learn to use principles of design until they have discovered design elements all around them. The elements are abstract, and some children are not able to organize them or to see relationships between them until they are taught. Other children are able to deal with abstractions very easily. Most children benefit by analyzing ways to make things clear and interesting, rather than by learning formal rules.

The following principles of design are given to you mainly for your own understanding. Introduce them to children in simplified forms when you feel that the children can be receptive. The way you introduce them is almost as important as what you introduce.

PRINCIPLES OF DESIGN

The principles of design we are going to explore have developed from experience with students' problems in design. These principles help a student think through those factors that might limit his ability to give form to his materials or express his ideas clearly. A designer generally tries to create an arrangement that has balance, pattern, and dynamic unity. Application of principles helps him achieve these qualities.

PRINCIPLE 1. A DESIGN SHOULD BE RECOGNIZED AS AN ORGANISM IN WHICH EVERY ELEMENT IS IN OPERATION IN TERMS OF EVERY OTHER ELEMENT. If you change any of the elements—form, line, color, texture or space—you change, to some degree, the over-all impact of the design and the function of any single element. This principle should sound familiar to you. It is similar in operation to the organismic concept of child growth—each factor is important and can change in some degree by itself, but its characteristics and change are also related to all the other factors.

While a formal principle usually cannot be taught to elementary school children, they can learn that wholes or groups change when something new is introduced. For example, most children can understand what happens to a group who are playing happily when an older child or "bully" tries to interfere—the whole game is changed by the impact of the intruder.

Your display boards, likewise, can be a harmonious group of ideas. If you add more ideas without integrating them into the total arrangement, you will destroy in part the effective teaching of the original design. When you design a bulletin board consider the other colors, forms, and amount of detail in the classroom, the way it is seen by most of the students, the kind and color of light that illuminates it. The bulletin board is a subdesign within the design of the whole classroom, just as a movement is part of a whole symphony.

PRINCIPLE 2. THE PROPORTIONS BETWEEN RELATED ELEMENTS SHOULD BE CONSTRUCTED SO THAT THE EYE CAN CLEARLY SEE A REAL DIFFERENCE, YET NOT SO EXTREME A DIFFERENCE THAT THE RELATIONSHIP BETWEEN THE ELEMENTS IS LOST. Look at Figures 11–10, 11–11, 11–12, and 11–13. Choose the one that is most pleasing to you. The figures contain the same shapes—squares. The relationship between any two squares depends on size and proximity (nearness in space). Figure 11–10 shows two extremes. The difference in size is so great and the squares are so far apart that they are difficult to organize as a single design.

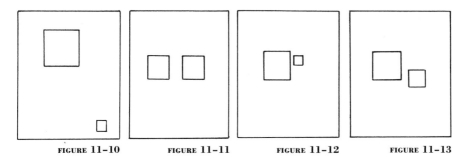

FIGURE 11-10   FIGURE 11-11   FIGURE 11-12   FIGURE 11-13

In Figure 11–11 we see the two squares as a unit because of their proximity. But we are not certain whether they are identical or not. Our eyes cannot measure so small a difference. We need more contrast in size to be sure of what we are seeing.

The contrast in size is evident in Figure 11–12. And the squares are near each other. But the value of the proximity is lost because, if we stand away from the page, we cannot be certain whether the forms actually touch or have space between them.

The squares in Figure 11–13 are clearly, but not extremely, different in size. They are near enough to each other to be easily grouped together and different enough so the difference is easily recognized. This figure then is stronger in its design than are the others. Possibly you chose it as the one most pleasing to you. The next time you plan a design, keep the principle of proportion in mind.

Figure 11–14 shows the range of proportionate relationships that are clearly identifiable, yet not too distant to remove the

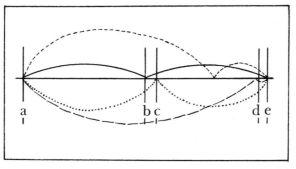

FIGURE 11-14

operation of the visual principle of proximity. Lines *a-b* and *b-e* are equal. Lines *a-b* and *c-e* are so close in size that a real difference is not easily identified. Line *a-d* is so much longer than *d-e* that the latter becomes only an accent. But on the line between *c* and *d* are many points where the line *a-e* could be divided with a strong relation between the two parts.

PRINCIPLE 3. ORGANIZED VARIATION OF SIMILAR THINGS IS MORE INTERESTING THAN ORGANIZED REPETITION. The least interesting way to break up a square is to divide it both ways in half. Figure 11–15 shows two squares, each broken by two lines. Which design follows Principle 3? Do you prefer it?

Rhythmic patterns of lines or shapes need some repetition to give a sense of unity, but exact repetition makes the design tedious. In Figure 11–16, *A* shows exact repetition, *B* shows inconsistent repetition, and *C* shows a rhythmic repetition and variation. This sets up a tension between what is repeated and what is varied. The variation makes it interesting, the repetition gives it unity. Children can learn to feel differences through auditory rhythm. We seldom feel like dancing to music that has a steady unvarying beat; we cannot dance to music that has no beat. But a Strauss waltz, designed with a steady beat and variations in rhythm, virtually compels us to move with the music. *Rhythm is a grouping of similarities and differences.*

A design that is made up of identical forms the same size is more tedious to observe than is an arrangement of various forms.

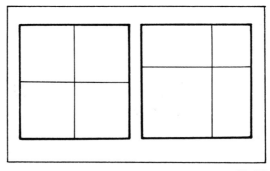

FIGURE 11–15

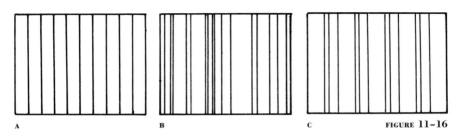

A   B   C   FIGURE 11-16

Figure 11–17 shows the interest created by variation of the sizes of similar objects.

PRINCIPLE 4. THE SUM TOTAL OF DYNAMIC ACTION IN A DESIGN SHOULD CONTRIBUTE TO THE UNIFICATION OF THE DESIGN. Dynamic action is the feeling of movement within a design. Draw a triangle with one short side. In what direction does the figure appear to be moving? Angular forms appear to be more outgoing than circular forms. The designer, if he is aware of the dynamic action of angular forms, can use his knowledge to keep the design integrated, not "flying off in all directions." He can, instead, lead the viewer's attention from one form to another. He can produce tension or resolution, according to his purposes. Tension can be produced with jagged lines, vertical forms, bright colors, sharp contrasts. The use of too many tension-producing devices, or the use of them without regard to principles of design, will fail aesthetically because the viewer cannot organize what he sees. It is the organization of the total that gives us a sense of resolution or unification.

FIGURE 11-17

We spend our lives resisting the force of gravity. The way we walk, the way we swallow, our major physical orientation is in terms of this force. Our tendency to give symbolic meaning of strength to vertical lines is not then surprising. We may feel strength in a line drawn on a page which is actually lying flat. In Western culture the top-to-bottom orientation in reading may influence our equating top to "up" and bottom to "down." Figure 11–18 shows two identical drawings printed with a vertical and then a horizontal dominance. The meaning we give to it varies with the two positions. Vertical forms symbolize strength, resistance to gravity. Horizontal forms suggest acceptance of gravity. Notice that, although the dominant motion in the first design is vertical, there is a relationship among the various horizontal edges.

Straight or curved lines that do not follow the horizontal and vertical also have symbolic dynamic quality. Figure 11–19 shows differences in the strength of such lines as they change from being more toward the vertical or the horizontal. Observe how the strength of line changes in the two positions. When we assess the balance or unity of a design, the total *impact* of vertical, angle, or horizontal lines should be considered.

Color has tension-producing quality. We see some colors as cool and receding and others as warm and advancing, giving us a

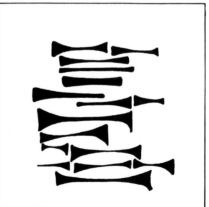

FIGURE 11–18

FIGURE 11-19

feeling of three-dimensional space. A small warm color equals a larger cool color in the impact it has upon us.

Through the use of perspective, three dimensions can also be suggested. It takes fewer objects in the immediate foreground to balance larger objects in the distance.

PRINCIPLE 5. THE ORGANIZATION OF ALL THE ELEMENTS AND OPERATIONS OF ELEMENTS IN A DESIGN SHOULD RESULT IN AN EXPRESSION OF DYNAMIC UNITY. This principle involves all the other principles. The interaction of all the visual elements, the proportions, rhythms, horizontal and vertical balances, contributes to the overall unity of the design. Dynamic action in the design is necessary because seeing is an active, not a passive, process. At Point III in the P-D process, all the relating processes—grouping by proximity, similarity, continuity, etc.—are in action. If the designer has done some of this relating, it is easier for us to respond to the visual elements. In other words, the design must produce enough tension to be interesting to look at, and it must achieve resolution. The progression from tension to resolution is used in other arts. In music a dissonance is usually resolved into a consonance. In drama, suspense may be followed by denouement.

Certain conventional systems of tension-building and resolution can be found in the art forms of most cultures. Children can observe these conventional forms, but they should be able to experiment with other forms. One way to achieve resolution or unity is by repetition. In some historical forms of design, as seen in the Baroque period, and again in the nineteenth century, extreme ornateness was unified by direct reverse repetition. Figure 11–20 is an example of such symmetrical design. Other kinds of unity are achieved without dependence on exact repetition. Figure 11–21 is an asymmetrical design that holds together as a unit. The dynamics produced by the small forms balance the size of the larger forms. The symbolic drawings at the beginning of each chapter are complex asymmetrical designs that have organic unity rather than repetition of identical organization. All the parts are somewhat alike, yet different in character and organization.

Now we are back to Principle 1, the recognition that all elements interact with all other elements of a design—which, in Principle 5, we find must be dynamically unified (the total impact of all the elements and their relationships to each other should produce a unified whole).

THREE-DIMENSIONAL DESIGN

THE PRINCIPLES THAT OPERATE IN TWO-DIMENSIONAL DESIGN ALSO OPERATE IN THREE-DIMENSIONAL DESIGN. In the perceiving process we do not actually deal with two-dimensional design. The design may be on a flat surface, but through the very act of seeing

FIGURE 11–20

FIGURE 11–21

forms, by separating figure from ground, we are dealing with the third dimension—forms in a sense of space.

A three-dimensional object should appear organized and interesting from the standpoint of any one viewing place. In judging an automobile, you walk around it to see how it looks from every angle. If you like it from every side in terms of what you know about design, then you have made a design judgment and this is part of the designing process. When children make a mobile, they can judge its design qualities from several different views. If the parts appear to belong together from each view point, we say it has strong three-dimensional design.

ELEMENTS OF DESIGN

The elements of design—form, line, color, texture, and space —operate within the principles of design. Also each element in a given design operates in proximity or similarity to, or continuity with, the other elements.

A design *element* is a part of the visual quality of anything seen. The visual world is composed of form, line, color, texture, and space. A landscape painting can be a very accurate representation of the real visual world. The artist uses form, line, color, texture and space to tell us what he sees. The design quality, the organization of visual elements, depends on how well he selects the objects he will paint in the landscape. Artists often call this "composition" rather than design, but the same principles apply to both. The elements can also be used to express something not so directly related to nature. A work of art may be called "abstract" because the elements have been separated or *abstracted* from nature. Lines may function as lines *per se* rather than as the outlines of an object. The lines are *nonrepresentational* because they do not attempt to copy the visual world. Color, form, and texture may also be used nonrepresentationally.

FORM

Form in design is an area that is identified by shape. A line, a contrast in color or in texture, makes a form stand out from the area around it. A form has size, color, value, shape, background, and is related to the other forms and elements in the design. A clear difference from the other forms makes the form easy to deal with visually. If the difference is not clear, the task of visually defining the form is difficult. For example, a single leaf on a tree may be hard to see because it does not differ much from the other leaves. It may be distorted visually by the lights reflected and the shadows cast from all the other leaves. Thus, to draw the tree most artists have to abstract in some degree and use enough of the overall form, the general shape, and enough detail to tell us what kind of a tree it is.

Forms are divided into two types—geometric forms and free forms. Geometric forms are the circle, square, and triangle, and forms derived from them, such as the sphere, rectangle, cube and pyramid. Free forms are those that are not made up of geometric forms.

FREE FORMS. Free forms appear in nature in infinite variety. When an artist makes an arrangement of free forms, he can use the principles of design in relating one form to another. In Figure 11–22 we see an amoeba-type form. In Figure 11–23 a free form has been structured. The straight lines are the structure lines. A variety in length and a variety in direction of line has been used. Consideration is given to the sizes of shapes constructed. If we had

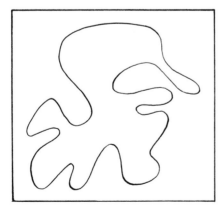

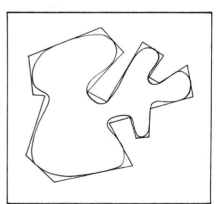

FIGURE 11–22   FIGURE 11–23

used parallel lines, our tendency to group similar things would focus our attention on those lines rather than on the design as a whole.

LINE

We may think of a line as something that is straight, curved, or wobbly. A line effect occurs whenever there is enough difference between two areas to give the appearance of an edge. A cast shadow can make a line effect. A sharp contrast in color or texture can make a line effect. If the transition is gradual (shading with lines, dots, or washes), our eye movement is smooth and, while we recognize a change, little line effect is made. Figure 11–24 shows the effects of shading with two uses of lines, (A) to show form, with sharp contrasts and line effects, (B) to show contour without sharp contrasts.

It is important for us to recognize line effects because a line leads our eyes in a direction. When we are using color and value changes to create forms, we must also consider the lines that appear and the directions they may indicate within the over-all design.

Lines have other qualities as well. Most lines have a beginning and an end. These create points in the area. Just as the line

A   B   FIGURE 11–24

is a divider, so where it begins and ends divides space. Figure 11–25 shows a single line in a rectangular form. The placing of the line, where it begins and where it ends, is important as it sets up the relationships within the rectangle. The dotted lines show the spaces a single line makes. Every time you use a line you do not necessarily stop and think about each of these elements of a design. You more often use your sense of liking or disliking the arrangement. But, if you are aware of the dynamics that a single line can create within a design, you can be critical of what you have made and able to make corrections.

COLOR

The perception of color is a very complex process, not yet completely understood. Individual differences in color perception exist. So-called color-blindness may affect the ability to distinguish between certain colors such as red and green, or green and blue. Even though some of your pupils may be limited in their color vision, they can develop more sensitive responses with the color vision they have by seeing more details of light and dark.

One of the newest theories of color perception has been developed by the physicist, Edwin H. Land.[3] He has evidence that the perceiving process involves making comparisons between different wave lengths of color rather than making a specific response

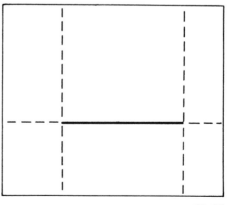

FIGURE 11–25

to each wave. This theory may lead to new insights into helping color-blind children develop their perceptual skills.

At present there is no color theory that completely explains color vision. Seeing color is a mechanical, physiological process, but it is also closely related to an individual's psychology. How color is reproduced in art work depends in part on the pigments available and the painter's skill in using them. The complex interaction of the physics of light, the chemistry of paint, and the psychology of perception has not as yet been exhaustively studied. The following simplified color system is suggested as one that will help children begin to see the dimensions of color as they use it in art. Color awareness should be part of perceptual training.

A SIMPLE COLOR SYSTEM. Most primary children can recognize the six basic colors most often used—yellow, green, blue, violet, red, and orange. They can experiment with colors to see how they can change them. What happens when they mix yellow and violet, orange and blue? What happens when yellow is mixed with blue or red? What can we do to make colors lighter or darker? What colors seem warm, what ones seem cool? Which colors come forward? Which go back? Discoveries made by the children themselves are more interesting to them than are facts told by the teacher. Rules are less valuable than are experiments with color mixing because such paints as tempera, most used in schools, have filler that tends to gray mixed colors. When children are asked to make precise color wheels, they are limited by their readiness (1) to control brushes, (2) to discipline themselves to wipe their brushes so that the colors will be pure, and (3) to mix paints with enough precision to get what they want.

In the upper grades children can explore color further. They can begin to see subtle changes of color in light. They will also need a more precise language to communicate about color. To the six color names they can add the intermediate steps of red-orange, yellow-orange, yellow-green, blue-green, blue-violet, and red-violet. *Value* is the lightness or darkness of a color. A color under direct light is lighter in value than a pure color and is called a *tint;* in shadow the color appears darker and is called a *shade.* With pigments, tints are made by adding white, shades by adding black.

A wheel of colored paper can be made by the advanced children to help all the children visualize the names they are learning.

COLOR EXPERIMENTS FOR THE INTERMEDIATE GRADES. In studying colored light, you will first want to show your pupils the effects of light focused on a prism. This can be done by making a small hole in a square of opaque black paper and setting it in glass for use in a slide projector. Your school district audio-visual office can make one easily. Hold a prism in the ray of light that comes from the hole in the black paper and a rainbow of colored light will show on the screen. A powerful flashlight, with a similar pierced card and a prism, will work in a darkened room.

A second demonstration to help children see how color changes in light is to cover a box with colored paper. Place the box on a large sheet of black paper. With the room darkened show a beam of light on the box, just off to one side of the top as shown in Figure 11–26. Pupils will see that the true value of the colored paper is seen on the near side. A tint is seen on the top, and a shade is seen on the side farthest from the light. After the class has seen this, you can put large sheets of colored paper under the box so that the effects of reflected light can be seen.

Put a colored glass in front of the white light so that the light is colored. You see a mixture of the color of the box and the color of the light on the top of the box. You see the complement of the colored light on the darkest side of the box.

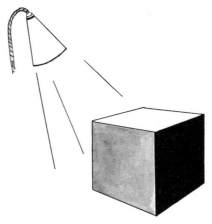

FIGURE 11–26

A third experiment with color is that of seeing after-image. Place a square of intense color on a large sheet of white paper. Ask the children, five or six at a time, to come up close to the sheet and close one eye while they concentrate on the color, counting to 20 slowly. After the count of 20 they should shift their gaze to the white paper. Soon they will see the complementary after-image of the color.

These experiments should help both you and your students see some of the properties of color and light.

COLOR IN DESIGN. The principle of similarities is important in using color. In a painting we may see all the reds as a single pattern, and the blues as another pattern. Too much of one color in an area may cause imbalance. Similarities in value may be grouped, the dark colors making one pattern, the light colors another.

Intensity is the purity of the color. Pure or full-intensity color is strongest and brightest. A grayed or diluted color is weaker in intensity. The most intense colors in a design may form a pattern. Because we sort our stimuli according to value and intensity, we may see patterns of lines and forms that give us the sense of three dimensions of figure and ground. Bright colors may come toward us, weak or dark colors may recede.

The amount of contrast between colors may contribute to the unity of a design, or it may cause conflict within the design. Black and white are strongly contrasting in value and are easy to deal with visually. Full-intensity red-orange and blue-green are strong contrasts in color, but they are the same in value; neither color dominates, and a conflict is set up that is hard to deal with visually. Placing black, white, or a grayed color between the two may reduce the conflict and make it easier to separate them. Some full-intensity colors, such as yellow and violet, are so different in value that it is easy to deal with them visually.

TEXTURE

Textures are the three-dimensional qualities of surfaces. If you take some colored tempera and brush it evenly on smooth paper, then rough paper, sandpaper, or terry cloth, you will see that the surface affects the appearance of the color. The rough paper makes slight shadows that change the value of part of the color. Textures can create tiny squares, lines, or mounds of light and shadow. Textures in pictures are not always made by three-dimensional surfaces, but their effects may be suggested by paint or other media.

In a design, the textures should contribute to the over-all unity. If all the rough textures are in one corner, that corner will appear to be the heaviest. The dominance of a form can be heightened with contrasting texture. A color can be grayed or muted by the surface shadows cast by rough paint. Figure 11–27 is an example of different kinds of texture effects that can be made with pen and ink.

SPACE

The final element of design we will consider is space. *Perspective is a system for symbolizing three-dimensional space on paper.* The simplest form of perspective is that of a figure with a ground, the figure appearing to come forward and the ground to go back. Man

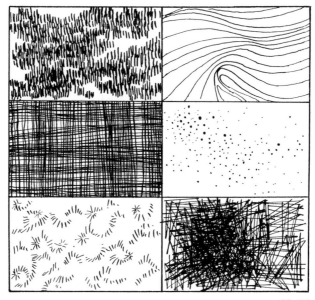

FIGURE 11–27

has invented different ways of showing objects in space. One of the simplest is that of overlapping two forms. A second is drawing things larger or smaller to show nearness or distance. We may use weak intensity, light value colors, less contrast in things that are at a distance compared with things that are close to us. The experiment with the colored box shows that value change can suggest three-dimensional form. The tendency to see things the same color, regardless of their distance from us or the light they are in, is a color constancy. If children can learn to see how colors and forms change in space and light, they will not be limited to a flat perspective for long.

A formal perspective system was invented during the Renaissance, but examples of drawing in perspective are also found in primitive groups. The drawings of the Orotchen children in Siberia show perspective and foreshortening (see p. 86).

Some children want to learn to draw in formal perspective. A perspective system, if taught in an authoritarian manner, before children are ready, will inhibit their use and understanding of it. Also, if they learn the mechanics without learning to *see* perspective, the system will have little meaning for them. It is much better to help them see how forms change in space. Then, *if they ask for it,* give them a simple system of perspective. Figure 11–28 shows a perspective system most intermediate grade students can learn— *if they have first learned to see perspective in their environment.* It should be clear to them that the mechanical system is but a way to sym-

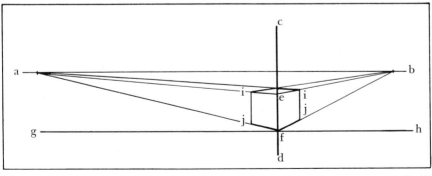

FIGURE 11–28

bolize perspective, just as the word *dog* is a symbol that means the friendly household pet.

Line *a-b* is the horizon line when we are looking straight ahead. Line *c-d* is the direct line from our eye (line of vision) to the closest vertical edge of the nearest object (in this case a cube) being drawn. We observe the position of the cube in relation to us, noticing which side of it is turned more toward us. This position determines where on line *a-b* the vanishing points are. Because the side of the cube to our left is slightly nearer, the vanishing point on that side is farther away from line *c-d*.

If we can see the top side of the cube, we know that the whole cube is below the horizon line. We mark off a segment of line *c-d* below the horizon line, and call it *e-f*. This is the closest corner of the cube. To make the sides of the cube, we connect point *e* with *a* and *b*, and then point *f* with *a* and *b*. We must estimate how far back the sides (*i-j*) go. We know that because the side to our left is nearer, it will be bigger than the right side. To show the top side of the cube, connect each point *i* with the vanishing point on the *opposite* side of the drawing.

Figure 11–29 shows how the cube can be multiplied so that you can make an object of different proportions, such as three times as long as it is wide. We are working with one side of the cube. Points *i* and *j* are the points at the back of the side of the cube. We need to find the midpoint of the line *i-j*. So we draw the crossed lines *i-f* and *e-j*, and a line through the point where the lines cross to point *b*. This puts a midpoint on *i-j*. Now we are ready to find the side of the second cube. Draw a line from point *f* through the

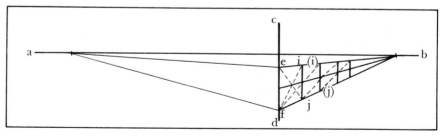

FIGURE 11–29

midpoint of *i-j* and continue it until it touches the long line *e-b*. At this point we draw a vertical line down to line *f-b*. This is the side of the second cube. Now we can complete the object by connecting the new point *i* with *a*, or we can draw more cubes to the right. When we transfer this procedure to the drawing of a house, midpoints will help us locate the peak of the roof and the centers of doors and windows.

Some advanced fifth and sixth graders can handle the process described. Be sure that they understand that it is only a *tool* to use in art and *not art itself*. Encourage them to do creative things with the use of perspective. Help develop their perceptual awareness of things in space to give them a broader base of information with which to be creative in art.

Another way to help older children see perspective is to draw on the classroom windows. If you mix a window cleaner like Glass Wax with powdered tempera paint children can draw on the glass and see how lines converge on objects outside the window. When the paint is dry, it can be wiped off, leaving the window clean.

To be of value in the process of designing, perspective must be seen as an element of the over-all unity. If we use perspective that carries our eye far back in space, we need to balance this with objects in the foreground to achieve a feeling of unification, and a left-right balance. If our design is relatively flat in all parts but one, we need to compensate for this, either by adding more depth in the other flat parts, or making the whole design on the same plane, so that we get a sense of balance of the space, as well as of all the other elements of design.

SUMMARY

When children's more intuitive sense of design appears to be waning, they can learn to analyze design cognitively. They can learn to look for ways designs are held together by similar spots of color, by similar kinds and sizes of forms. They can follow the lines made by forms to see whether they lead them out of the picture, or carry them around within the picture frame. In the upper grades, actual design problems can be used. The structured sequence of design problems, given for teachers, would not be appropriate unless considerable emphasis was made on "playing" with the forms to see what they might do. The important part of the problems is the kinds of exploring experiences the children have with them. If these are presented in an authoritarian way the children's freedom to experiment, to make many trials, to analyze and reanalyze might be lost.

Form, line, color, texture and space are all around you. Look at the way nature uses them—organizing them into dynamic and organic wholes. Artists and designers use the visual elements of design, and the principles of design, to make things have an aesthetic impact upon us. Sometimes they use design to communicate ideas, at other times to enhance the visual qualities of things. Sometimes the communication is highly symbolic; at other times the pure beauty of design as a structure, in itself, is the message the designer communicates. Look through the drawings and paintings in this book. Each artist was communicating something to you through the language of design.

DESIGN ACTIVITIES

These activities have been selected to help you become more familiar with the elements of design and the dynamic interaction they have with each other. Each problem has many possible solutions. To achieve an over-all sense of unity or order with variety, various types of grouping—of forms, of sizes, or of colors —can be used. Similar things that are close together have more relation than those that are far apart. Forms similar in shape, size, and color can be related even when quite far apart. Variety can be obtained by grouping by form or size or color, and making the other two elements different.

Remember that your role as a designer is to take unorganized elements and make them easier to handle visually; at the same time you make unusual arrangements to hold attention and interest. To do this your arrangements must be clear. You can direct eye movement by separating figure from ground, by using forms and organizations of forms that create line direction. You can balance your design asymmetrically by making bright colored forms smaller, and weak colored forms larger. One large form can be balanced by a number of smaller forms. You are balancing the amount of *impact* the different elements have on the viewer.

In the last problems you will be designing form, line, and color while you increase the variety in kinds of forms. It is suggested that you start with the simpler assignments first and gradually work your way into the more complex problems. These problems have been selected to enable you to use the elements of design without having to develop a high degree of skill in art media. You will need only a package of 9 by 12 inch colored construction paper, a paper cutter, scissors, and rubber cement.

1. Select two colors that you think go well together. Cut one of them in rectangular pieces with variety in the shapes from almost square to almost lines. Vary the sizes. Arrange the pieces on the other sheet of paper, and experiment with many different arrangements until you feel you have achieved a satisfying design. Check it to see whether you have interesting variation of spaces between the forms. See what grouping system you have used to give the design unity. When you are satisfied with your results you can cement them down. Put the rubber cement on the end of a small strip of paper and slide it under each form to get the cement on the under side. Then pull the strip out carefully and your form will not be shifted. Rubber cement allows you to change things even after cementing them, but pull them up slowly to avoid tearing.

2. Use rectangular forms again, this time in three colors. See how complex a design you can make without losing unity. Use subgroups (of color, of size, of shape) and relate them to the over-all design.

3. Use triangles instead of rectangles. Try placing an obtuse triangle (with unequal sides) within a large rectangle. What differences do you find between the ways it cuts up space and directs your eyes, and the ways an equilateral triangle functions in space? Use several triangles of various shapes and sizes and organize them into a unified design. Ask yourself whether the design leads your attention out of the rectangle or keeps it dynamically within it. How does the over-all design made with triangles differ from the designs made with rectangles?

Finally combine rectangles and triangles into a complex design using a variety of colors. Remember that the use of two parallel lines is one of the ways to visually group somewhat similar things.

4. Cut circles in a variety of sizes using three or more colors. Try many arrangements until you get one that you feel is resolved. See whether you can analyze why you like your final solution. What problems do you have with circles that you do not have with other forms?

5. Construct a design of three or more colors, using rectangles, triangles, squares, circles, in which the sum total of all the forms, colors, and lines appear to balance, no matter which side of the design is on top.

6. Construct three free forms of different sizes. Construct them first in straight line form with a variety of length, of line, of angle, and of shape. See how you can relate the free forms to each other in a rectangular space. What changes do you need to make in any of the forms to fit them into the total design?

Are you beginning to see that any one form changes as you add other forms, shapes, colors, and sizes? Design is not the sum total of the design elements but the total of the interaction of the elements. Solving design problems is like solving other complex problems where many variables are involved. Now you are ready to use this new language to "say" something in art. Whether you are arranging a landscape or a still life, creating an abstract painting, building a table, or designing clothes and jewelry, the functions of the design elements will be in operation.

7. Select a task that you have some readiness for and a medium that you have used before. See whether you can create an expression of a feeling or idea using design as your language. Do not be discouraged if your first attempts do not come up to your expectations. You may find you need to do a great deal of experimenting, to find symbols for your ideas and ways to design them into a well-composed art expression.

These skills you have been developing will help you not only in expression, but also in the practical task of making your classroom more effective for the visual learning of your pupils. It will help you clarify, organize, and direct children's learning processes.

REFERENCES

1. Fred Attneave, "Some Informational Aspects of Visual Perception," *Psychological Review*, LXI (1954), 183–193.

2. Ernest R. Hilgard, *Introduction to Psychology*, 2nd ed. (New York: Harcourt, Brace and Company, Inc., 1957), p. 371.

3. Edwin H. Land, "Experiments in Color Vision," *Scientific American*, CC (1959), 84–94.

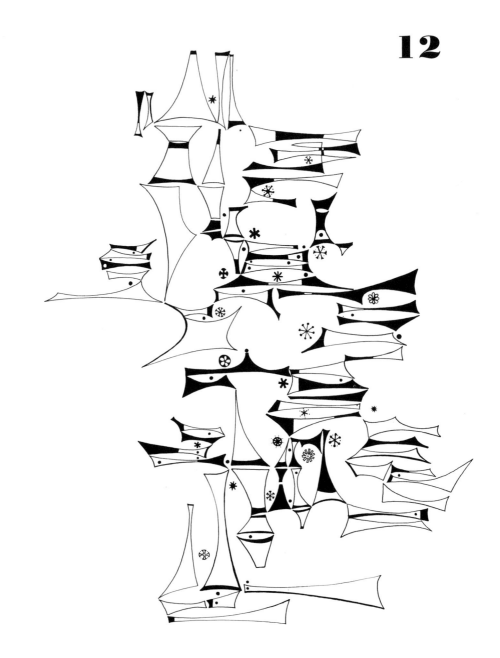

12

Classroom Procedures for New Teachers

Some compromise is usually necessary between your ideas and those of the school in which you begin to teach. Find out the philosophy and objectives of the principal and of the school district. If there is an art consultant find out what his objectives are and help him to understand yours. This is much easier if you know what your general objectives are. A study of the school environment will help you to decide how fast you can implement your own ideas. If your school is quite rigidly managed and you are required to follow the clock very closely, you will not want to defeat your ultimate purpose for good teaching by moving too quickly in changing the established curriculum and time patterns. If you can demonstrate the values of small changes you may be given more freedom to develop your own program. You will not always find agreement among teachers. Mutual understanding and respect for others' points of view usually result in cooperation.

THE ART CONSULTANT

The duties of the art consultant vary from one school district to another, depending in part on the size of the district, the number of consultants, and the attitudes of the school and community toward the arts as part of elementary education.

In large districts an art supervisor may direct the long-range planning for elementary and secondary schools. Working with the supervisor may be specialists in elementary art education who serve as consultants, who order and provide materials, films, art objects, and prints. They may organize field trips, contact resource persons, and arrange for loans from museums. They also serve as in-service teachers to elementary classroom teachers.

Some school districts insist that the consultant visit the classroom only on invitation; others insist that the consultant visit each classroom regularly to check on progress. Some consultants teach demonstration lessons in the classroom; others do not.

In other districts the duty of the art consultant is to carry out a curriculum planned for the whole district. Such a curriculum may prescribe the content for days and weeks. The consultant provides the materials and tells the teacher what to teach. Such a system does not allow for individual differences in either teachers or pupils.

In some districts there is the general elementary consultant who includes the arts as part of his work. Some of these consultants are well trained in the arts; but when they are not, or do not understand the educational values of art, the art program may be neglected.

The use of the art consultant as a special teacher of art in a district, where he spends an art period with each class, in an art room or in the classroom, has been found to be effective, particularly in the upper grades. The success of the plan depends on two important factors: (1) that the consultant knows enough about the children to allow for individual differences and (2) that the teacher utilizes this art learning activity in self-directed and integrated art activities. It is important in this system that the art consultant not limit his work to art learning activities, but that he help the teacher coordinate art with other activities in the classroom.

A fairly new system that appears to have merit keeps a specialist working within each school building. Each teacher in the building is well trained in all elementary fields, *plus an area of specialization.* Within each building one of the teachers is an art specialist, part of whose duties is to plan the general scope and sequence for the school and to serve as a consultant to other teachers in their art programs. Other teachers do the same for him in arithmetic, social studies, reading, music, and other subjects.

Probably the best system includes a well-trained classroom teacher and an art consultant who enriches the art program by providing a flow of material and new methods, by handling difficult educational problems, and sometimes by teaching the class.

Another important function of the consultant or supervisor is to introduce into classroom practice the implications from new research in art education, methods of teaching, and techniques with materials. The classroom teacher cannot always attend professional meetings where new ideas are discussed, but the consultant can keep abreast of all such developments.

Any system is dependent on the training, experience, and attitudes of teachers, consultants, and administrators. A young teacher interviewing for a position should ask about the roles of consultants and supervisors in that district to help decide whether or not the situation is one in which he can work effectively.

TOOLS AND MATERIALS

School districts usually have handbooks that tell about general supplies. The person responsible for ordering them will tell you how much you may spend on art supplies. Conant and Randall[1] give examples of the amounts and descriptions for ordering supplies for your classroom.

Check your equipment. Do the brushes hold their shapes when wet? Are the scissors sharp enough? Is the paper cutter sharp and is the spring strong enough to be safe? Does the drain in your sink work? Check all other permanent equipment, and find out the procedure for having repairs made.

LARGE EQUIPMENT. Check your furniture and storage areas. These large items are desirable: (1) at least four easels, (2) an art work table, (3) storage space for current projects, (4) long-term storage space, (5) a sink, (6) a bin for wet clay, (7) storage space for dry clay.

In classrooms where the art program has not been considered, teacher ingenuity can overcome inadequacies. If there are no easels and no room for them, part of the chalkboard can be used to set up easels. Set a lightweight piece of 24″ × 30″ × ¾″ wallboard in the chalk tray. Cover the chalk tray with oilcloth. Small tables or boxes covered with the same material can be placed between two easel boards. Two children can share the table for their tote trays of paints.

If the sink is in a corner or near traffic to the door, a cart on wheels can help a great deal. Large cans or jars may be obtained from the lunchroom or from the maintenance man. Water for cleaning brushes, for painting, and for washing hands can be placed on the cart.

If your work table is also your library table, cover it with pressed board or other heavy material. An art table whose major use is storage and supply of current materials is necessary. Many classrooms have tables surfaced especially for clay and paint.

Clay requires both dry and moist storage. If you do not have a clay cart for storage and drying, heavy crockery or ten-gallon galvanized refuse cans with tight lids will keep clay adequately. These are heavy to handle. If possible they should be placed on a low cart so that they can be moved by both pupils and teachers. If drying must be done on a counter top, protect the top with a

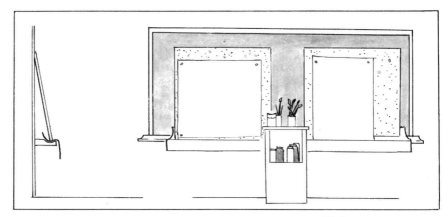

FIGURE 12–1. CHALKBOARD EASELS

moisture-proof material. A portable kiln may be shared by several classes.

Often several grades will share woodworking equipment in a fitted portable tool chest that can be wheeled from room to room. Find out whether such tools are available and how to arrange to use them.

STORAGE AREAS

The year's supplies may be in a general storage room from which you keep your room supplied. Space should be ample for assorted poster boards, colored papers, newsprint, and, if possible, a tear-off fixture for butcher paper.

Some tools are kept on the art table, so that they are readily accessible. Scissors and pen holders should be stored so you can quickly see at the end of the day that all are returned. A tool holder made of a board and base with holes drilled for each tool will quickly help you see whether any are missing. Erasers, crayons, chalk, and sponges should be in boxes suitable for small groups of children working at small tables.

Special tools and craft materials should be stored in cabinets or drawers and brought out as needed. They should be covered after every use to protect them from dust.

Storage and the handling of materials can be the stumbling block to effective teaching. Badly arranged storage interferes with effective self-directed activities; it takes time from teaching; and it does not contribute to children's sense of design. It also interferes with their learning to cooperate in management of the classroom.

The storage areas should be considered in terms of general classroom traffic. If they are too close to cleanup areas or in the direct line of classroom doors, they become stumbling blocks. This problem is particularly acute in overcrowded classrooms.

STORING CHILDREN'S ART WORK. Find a place to store work made by each child for your evaluation and anecdotal records of the child's growth. If no large picture files are available, you and the children can build one. A double thickness cardboard carton approximately the size of your larger sheets of paper can be covered with butcher paper and decorated with cut paper or

FIGURE 12-2. SAVING CHILDREN'S WORK

paint. Tagboard dividers with name tags for each child will keep the folders in order. A similar kind of box can be made to file resource materials of art prints from which children can select paintings they want to become acquainted with.

DISPLAY AREAS

Many classrooms have cork or wallboard areas for display. If wall display space is limited, you may be able to have a folding screen of pegboard or wallboard made. If it is supported by lightweight aluminum and is on glides or coasters, it is easily moved as classroom situations change. Display areas outside the classroom should be used as much as possible to integrate art work for the whole school. Hall displays are particularly effective with children who are accustomed to the visual appeal of advertising. These areas can be used to display not only school work but also American art and the art of other cultures. Short descriptions can be attached to displays.

Have available various kinds of T-shaped pins, straight pins, colored head pins and tacks, a tacking stapler, paper tapes, an assortment of wire, and pliers. Two excellent sources of ideas on bulletin boards and display are the Bailey film, Randall's "Bulletin Boards: An Effective Teaching Device," and the book by Kinney and Dresden, *Better Learning Through Current Materials.*[2]

Try to be in your classroom a week before school starts to get things organized and to create a well-designed classroom. The effect of the children's first day sets the stage for the whole year. If the children learn to enjoy the quality of the room and are encouraged to participate in its maintenance and in changing displays, your work will be easier. Many school districts require teachers to be on the job three or four days before school starts, but this time may be devoted to meetings and other planned activities.

AUDIO-VISUAL MATERIALS

Visual motivation, as well as experience with music, dance, and dramatic play, needs to be developed to keep growth continuing in art activities. Where possible, encourage the children to look for things on field trips and to explore their immediate environment. Within the classroom many exciting visual experiences can be used. The teacher with a camera can make slides of visual materials that will encourage inquisitiveness and develop perceptual awareness. Slides can be made that help children see how things change size in space. The relative sizes can actually be measured as they are reflected on the screen. Changes in form can be seen as an object is pictured from different viewpoints to help children respond to things as they see them *and* as they know them.

Slides are available of many of the great works of architecture, painting, design. Their advantage over prints is that there is less tendency for children to copy. The pictures can be exposed long enough for the children to react to them, and they can be repeated often enough for familiarity to develop.

The tape recorder can be used for stimulating motivation. Sounds from a film the children have seen can be repeated while children work. Tapes can be made of interesting sounds to encourage children to be responsive to their environment. Recordings of early morning birds, of a busy street, or of the noise at an airport, a train depot, or the docks, or of the children's own noise on the play field, make wonderfully exciting motivation for drawing and painting. Tapes made at the seashore with no sound but the pounding surf and the screech of gulls are stimulating. Crickets chirping at night, the clicking of a train on rails, factory noise, a house being built—these will increase children's awareness of their auditory environment and details in it that enrich their perceptual experience.

USE OF TELEVISION. Several research centers and schools are currently experimenting with television as a means of teaching. Most of this work has been done in the junior and senior high schools. In elementary schools where closed circuit TV is available, a teacher who is particularly able to motivate children to see and respond can be televised occasionally, but he does not replace the classroom teacher who knows the children's backgrounds and carefully selects tasks and media that will allow each child to develop at his own pace.

SELF-DIRECTED ART AREAS

A work area should be available for art activity by individual children throughout the day. In a class of thirty children, five or six may be working at a given time. Some activities can be carried out at the child's own table; others, like easel painting, require that he work in a special area.

An art table that has both current storage space, and a few places to work is ideal. The table should provide a range of media from which to select. In a first grade classroom, for example, the table should provide for:

easel painting
>—tote trays with containers of tempera and a container for water to wash brushes
>—brushes in a rack so they may be counted and bristles kept upright
>—small sponges
>—clean paint rags

crayons and chalks
>—assorted small boxes of unwrapped crayons and chalks

colored paper work
>—scissors stored in rack for easy counting and for safety
>—small jars of school paste with screw lids
>—paste brushes

Paper should be available in sizes ranging from 9″ × 12″ to long rolls. The *current paper* storage area should be easy to keep orderly.

Figure 12–3 shows a possible arrangement. At each grade level the arrangement will change as new media are introduced—depending on the scope and sequence planned for the whole school. Materials can be rotated on the table so that self-directed activity does not become monotonous.

BASIC ART MATERIALS

The best way to become familiar with art materials is to use them yourself. Never miss an opportunity to watch another teacher at work with a new material. Read books, pamphlets, and the art education magazines. Read labels and directions that come with your supplies. It is usually unwise to offer pupils a medium you have not tried.

EASEL PAINTING

PREPARATION. Easel painting is usually done on newsprint, inexpensive white or grey pulp paper, or butcher paper. Sheets are usually 18″ × 24″ or larger, because painting is done with large long-handled brushes. Tempera paint is most expensive if purchased in liquid form. The less expensive powdered tempera can be mixed with water and a drop of oil of wintergreen (for preservation), then stored in large jars with tight lids until needed. Tote trays of aluminum or reinforced cardboard can be filled with small cans of paint for each child. A child can select five or six cans for his tote tray from a wide range of colors. Older children should

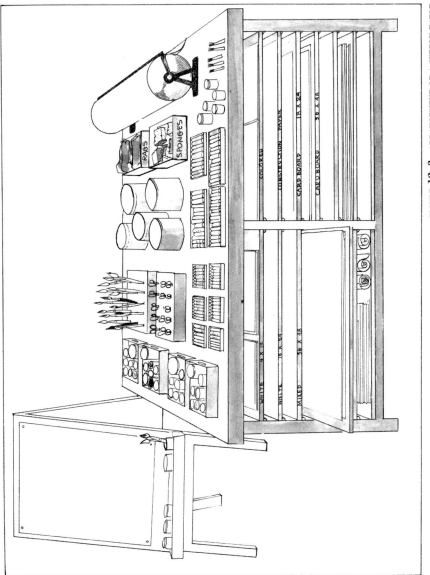

FIGURE 12-3.   ARRANGEMENT OF A SUPPLY TABLE

have more experience in mixing their own colors. Extra cans for mixing should be available.

EXPERIENCE. For many children easel painting is a satisfactory medium, particularly when they are making simple symbols of things. At an easel children can paint direct symbols with the least physical effort. They can make symbols fast, clearly, and in a variety of color. For children who are more inclined to make detailed and complex symbols, the use of easels and large brushes may be frustrating. For these children, working at a table with paper tacked to a drawing board may be appropriate. Using smaller, shorter brushes and being closer to their work will help them do the more detailed work for which they are ready. If a child's paints run when he doesn't want them to, add extender or precipitated chalk.

Children should be protected by smocks or aprons that fit well enough so that they are not burdensome. Shirts work very well, but long sleeves and tails should be trimmed.

FINGER PAINTING

Finger paint can be purchased in jars and tubes for direct use. Finger paint paper, which has a glossy finish, is also available. Glossy shelf paper can be used as a substitute. Liquid starch makes an excellent finger paint base. Large salt shakers can sift powdered paint into the starch, which the child has spread over the paper. Different effects can be obtained by sifting different colors in varieties of ways before painting.

Smocks are necessary for finger painting, and sleeves should be rolled high because they can easily be dragged through the paint. If children are working at a table, they can push their chairs up under the table and stand behind them. This arrangement protects girls' full skirts. Drying time is one of the problems of finger paint. Pictures take over an hour to dry. Use a collapsible clothes-drying rack or a multiple-shelf drying rack, or lay the paintings on paper in a play area.

EXPERIENCE. We know that children vary widely in their responses to finger paint depending on their readiness, which may be affected by cleanliness training. It is unwise to insist that every child finger-paint, but the freedom to work freely in this medium is an objective toward which the teacher can work.

Finger paint provides a child with a direct means of expression—his hands are his tools. If he is not inhibited, he can explore all kinds of effects, using fingers, palms, and the sides of his hands. Even his forearms are effective in manipulating the paint.

A child's behavior while he is finger painting will give the teacher more clues about the child's reaction to the paint than will an analysis of his work. If a child uses only one or two finger tips, is slow in getting involved with the paint, and tends to mix colors together when they touch, you may want to ask him if he would like to try something else. If he is strongly motivated to do what the rest of the class is doing and wants to stay with it even though he doesn't enjoy it, the teacher can give the child encouragement by participating in the work himself, by showing how much "fun" it can be.

CRAYON

Crayons come in varying degrees of hardness. Large-sized flat-sided crayons that are high in wax content are easier for young children to use. Children who are more developed in eye-hand coordination and in ability to see and respond to detail will be frustrated if they have only the big crayons to work with. This medium has been overused because it is easy and does not make a mess in the classroom. Sometimes teachers feel that children are being destructive if they take the paper off crayons. Actually the paper can inhibit freedom to work. The sides of short lengths are excellent for making different texture effects and for filling in surfaces.

Crayons can be used alone and in combination with other media such as tempera, India ink, and water color for creative work. Their restrictive use, like the coloring of adult symbols as in color books, or in coloring so many "rabbits" in arithmetic, can inhibit creative use of the medium.

Crayon can be used for an "etching." After coloring a piece of paper solidly with heavily waxed crayons, dust the surface with an eraser full of chalk dust. Paint the whole thing solidly black with

India ink. The chalk makes the ink adhere to the crayon. When the ink is dry, the children can use a sharp tool to draw through the ink so that the crayon color shows. Many texture and line effects can be made with different pointed tools.

Another use of crayon is as a *resist,* suitable for the intermediate grades. Make a crayon drawing. Spread rubber cement on the areas of the paper you wish to keep white. Leave some areas free of both crayons and rubber cement. Then wash the whole paper with water color. The crayon and rubber cement resist the water color. Water color is left in background areas where there is no resist. When the paper is dry, the rubber cement can be rubbed off to leave the fresh white areas.

EXPERIENCE. If crayons are heavy enough in wax content, children can use them quite freely. A child's success with them will depend on his prior experience as well as on the medium itself. One limitation is that it takes considerably more energy to make an area of solid color with crayon than with tempera. Some children are inhibited in their expression if they have to stop and fill in; other children who like smaller detail and are more patient can find crayons a satisfactory medium.

CHALK

Colored chalk is an excellent medium for direct expression. It can be used on wet or dry paper of any color. Strong bold lines and shading are easy to obtain. A fixative spray will make the drawing permanent. Because the spraying bothers some children it should be done after class hours, outside or in a well-ventilated room. A sprayed painting will retain its bright colors.

EXPERIENCE. Except for a few children who find the dusty quality unpleasant, most children are able to use chalk effectively. It goes on smoothly and easily; it can be spread with fingers or with a dry sponge, erased, and overlaid more successfully than crayon. In some respects it can give the child more varied experiences than crayon can. It is limited because it rubs off easily and drawings must be sprayed. Some children find it "messy" because they get their hands dirty.

TORN PAPER

Torn paper is a versatile medium with which to decorate a surface. It can be used for individual picture making. Also, it is easy to handle when several children are making a mural. They can plan together what they are going to do and each one can make parts. Together they can organize what they have made. Torn paper can be used to make posters and signs. It can be combined with paint or crayon for bulletin boards. If rubber cement is used instead of school paste, pieces can be moved after they are applied. Different textures of papers can be used. The heavier grade of colored construction paper is easier to control in tearing than is very thin paper.

Children can help gather interesting kinds of paper: butcher paper, Christmas papers, corrugated paper, sandpaper, cellophane, blotters, tracing paper, oil papers, colored aluminum foil papers, stiff paper, tissue paper, and printed papers from magazines. They can explore ways to use the different papers. Some can be scored, folded, or curled.

The same uses can be made of cut paper. Usually torn paper allows more freedom for children because when they use scissors they are trying to make an exact line and their inability to cut accurate forms is more noticeable. Torn paper forces them to deal in larger areas of color. Small details can be added with bits of paper.

EXPERIENCE. The medium allows children to explore different kinds of papers to see how they work, and to combine textures and colors more freely than they might be able to do with paint. The rough effects may be pleasing to older children who are frustrated by their inability to draw. The use of paper helps them deal with large areas rather than with fine detail. Children who have been strictly trained about the care of books may feel strange about tearing paper, but if you explain that we are careful not to tear paper in some instances and that we may tear it freely in others, they may overcome their timidity about using it. Also children who are destructive of books can be given an opportunity to tear paper for art while they are encouraged to respect and care for books.

WATER COLOR

The tendency to use water colors only in the intermediate grades has been a reaction to the rather restricted ways in which water color has been taught. You may want to save water colors for the intermediate grades, but younger children will not necessarily be inhibited by them if they are allowed to explore them. Water colors in cake form are adequate for elementary school use. A separate water color box should be available for each pupil. If possible, order the brushes separately, as the brushes in boxes may not hold their shape. An 8, 10, or 12 size sable or camel's-hair brush may be ordered for each child, and a few brushes of other small sizes should be available. In using water colors, plenty of water is needed to keep brushes clean and to mix colors. Soft rags for drying brushes are essential. Papers with various surfaces should be tried. Water color is most beautiful on clear white paper. It is often combined with crayons and inks.

EXPERIENCE. Water color is more useful than tempera for fine detail; it can also be used as freely as tempera. The transparent quality of water color may be hard for young children to deal with because bright colors in large areas are hard to make. Water colors require more care and greater motor skill, in mixing colors and in using a small brush to get paint from the small pans. Children who have enjoyed tempera and the bright opaque colors may find water color disappointing until they learn how to use it more brilliantly—that is, until they learn to get clear, clean contrasts between the strong color and the clean white paper.

PRINTING METHODS

Some of the easier printing devices are made by cutting potatoes, cutting rubber innertubes with scissors and pasting the designs on a block, cutting soft rubber erasers or corks, or by using assorted objects such as edges of cardboard, combs, nails, springs, etc. After cutting, use the same techniques you would use with linoleum blocks. A brayer (rubber roller) is rolled in ink, then rolled across the surface of the printing device, which is then pressed on a paper or cloth surface. When brayers are not available the ink can be spread on a masonite or glass surface and the device pressed in the ink and then on the surface to be printed. Oil-base inks are used on cloth and for permanent paper-printing; water-soluble inks may be used on paper. The water soluble inks dry much faster and are much easier to use in the classroom.

EXPERIENCE. Printing gives children an opportunity for invention and exploration in which almost every child can have some success. Printing processes are related to things they already know. There are direct uses for the things they make, products to show. Printing, like weaving, may cause less discontinuity for the child who has been trained to have something to show for his efforts. From more practical uses of printing, children can be led to more creative expression and more varied use of tools. Printing is particularly effective in the intermediate grades when creative behavior appears to decrease.

As in miscellaneous construction, tools and materials can be used in ways different from their original purposes. This shift can encourage flexibility in the uses of media. Figure 12–4 shows different tools that can be used for printing. Prints can be used as

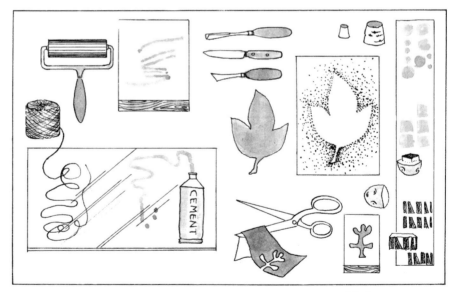

FIGURE 12–4. PRINTING TOOLS

illustrations for creative writing, for greeting cards and invitations to parents, for decorating five-gallon ice cream cartons to make waste baskets, for wallpaper and book covers. Most important of all, printmaking can be a form of artistic expression for its own sake.

CLAY

Large sacks of dry clay are most economical for schools. Sift the clay slowly into water, and stir it until thick. Let it sit for at least twenty-four hours before working it. Working clay means forcing out excess water and air bubbles by kneading and beating it on a hard surface until it is easy to manipulate and no longer sticky.

Clay that is moist and ready to use can be bought and kept in plastic bags; water is added as needed. This clay can be either fired or re-used.

Some clays come with an oil base so that they are always ready to use. Unless there is a high proportion of oil and the clay is warm, oil-based clay is too hard for small children to manipulate easily.

EXPERIENCE. Clay is a material that children become involved with physically, like finger paint. Some children will reject it as being "dirty." This is less likely to happen if the clay is not too moist. Some children will find that clay is drying to their hands and reject it without realizing why. Have moist terry cloth to wash the clay off as they are using it. A drop of lanolin on the hands before and after using clay will protect against chapping and make working with clay more pleasant.

Children getting acquainted with clay may first manipulate it without trying to make it into something. They need plenty of time for exploration. They may then try to make parts and put them together or squeeze the clay and manipulate it into the form they want. When they have succeeded with one method, encourage them to try others. If they are making pottery they can learn simple pinch methods and coil methods of preliterate people. If you have a potter's wheel, children in the intermediate grades can learn to use it. They can explore other methods such as making slabs and joining them together with slip (clay in liquid form). Intermediate grade pupils may make tiles, carving patterns in slabs of clay.

MOSAICS

Mosaic decoration has been a leisure-time activity for adults for some time. For children the mosaic form is important because it lends itself to simplification and analysis of basic forms in order to carry out ideas. Because drawing has to be quite primitive, children who are worried about adult standards may find more success.

Mosaics may be made of free materials, such as broken tiles from ceramic shops, vinyl and linoleum scraps, small polished pieces of wood, pebbles, cardboard, etc. These are glued to a surface material such as masonite, plywood, or heavy wallboard. Tile grout or plaster can be used for filler for hard materials. Filler is not needed if the mosaic will not be used for a working surface, such as a table or hot plate base. Instead of grout a liquid plastic can be poured over mosaics of assorted shape and size to get a smooth surface. New plastics are continually coming on the market that are easy to use.

EXPERIENCE. The manipulation of mosaics, the opportunity to arrange, evaluate, and rearrange, gives children excellent opportunities for creative problem-solving. They may work with a design until they are satisfied with it, and then glue it in place. Intermediate pupils can analyze the design intellectually. Paints and crayons do not have this flexibility. Once applied they are hard to change. But mosaics and cut or torn paper lend themselves easily to experimentation.

MISCELLANEOUS CONSTRUCTION

Elementary children are great gatherers of all kinds of materials. These materials, added to the teacher's collection, can provide children with opportunities to visualize multiple uses of things. For example, soda straws become hair, arms, and legs for bugs and people, branches of trees, fence posts, grass skirts, telephone poles, smokestacks, axles for wagons, etc. Milk cartons become bodies for dolls, trains, cars, houses, factories, wagons, animals. Egg cartons make wonderful reptiles, dragons, and worms. Anything that can be glued, wired, pinned, or stapled can be used for miscellaneous construction.

EXPERIENCE. Miscellaneous material encourages children to look at all things as objects with infinite possibilities for use. They can pool their discoveries and become increasingly observant of their environment.

Each child may see different possibilities in the materials. Encourage the children to look at the things not as objects but as materials to work with, to turn them upside down to get away from the accustomed view of them. Some children may find this kind of task quite difficult. If they are particularly rigid, and want everything in its "right" way, if disorder disturbs them, they need special help. They may not accept the task at first, some not at all. Often, after seeing other children's solutions to the problem, they will follow along. Do not be disturbed if they copy at first. Copying may be a way out of their rigidity. Your ultimate goal for every child is that he develop the flexible capacity to see tools, materials, and objects in many possible ways.

On rare occasions you may have pupils at the other extreme

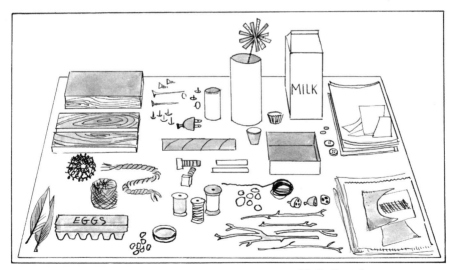

FIGURE 12–5. "JUNK" FOR CONSTRUCTION

—little sense of order—anything goes with anything. Instead of encouraging the free action of these children, you can help them more by structuring the activity. Let them experiment with only a few objects. Provide categories for them to order the objects into (smooth and rough; big, middle-sized, and small; light and dark).

PAPIER-MÂCHÉ

Papier-mâché has possibilities for three-dimensional work all through the elementary years. Three or four children working together can build large objects at little cost. A basic armature is required. Tightly rolled newspapers fastened with butcher or masking tape makes good "bones" for animals and figures. Use many dry strips of torn newspaper and pull them through a small tray of wallpaper paste to cover the armature. Build the strips ¼ inch thick around the armature. Use paper towel strips for the last coat for an excellent painting surface. The figures are strong when dry.

To make a mask, build a basic face-form of clay. Cover it with liquid soap and then use the strip method to cover the head ¼ inch thick. When the mask is dry on the surface, lift it off the clay and it is ready to be painted. Other masks can be made with rolled paper or screen wire as a base.

One of the most simple bases for a head is a stuffed paper bag. Stuff the bag with dry torn paper. Tie the end around a ¾ inch round wooden dowel. Then add layers of wet paper strips until the bag is solid. Carry the strips down around the neck so it will be strong, too. When it is dry, slip off the dowel, or use the dowel to hold the head up. Paint the face. Yarn, raffia, string, curled paper can be used as hair.

Papier-mâché masks, animals, and figures are useful in many dramatic play and social studies activities. They are excellent for sets for dramatic productions. They can be used instead of murals for culminating activities. Instead of each child making a drawing, he can contribute an object so that a whole village, or kind of animal life, can be portrayed. Papier-mâché can be manipulated at almost every level of competence.

EXPERIENCE. For many children three-dimensional work appears to have more meaning than painted or drawn symbols, perhaps because it is more closely related to their earlier tactile response to things. How often one hears parents say, "Just look at it, don't touch," when touching is a child's direct means of finding out about things.

WEAVING

Weaving, like papier-mâché, gives children an opportunity to make something "real." It is suitable as a self-directed activity, or it can be used by a group in a social studies unit. Some training is necessary for success. The process may be very simple, with a box or stick loom. Advanced pupils may use a table or a floor loom. The type of loom used must be suitable for the general ability level of the class in eye-hand coordination. Teach children the simple process of weaving. Once they have learned the basic principle of warp threads and how weft threads go over and under the warp threads, they can transfer this principle to different kinds of looms. They can watch a group demonstration, but often individuals need considerable help.

The simple tongue depressor loom shown in Figure 12–6 will give children experience in making a loom and actually weaving. The loom is made by lacing five sticks to two cross sticks. The sticks have holes drilled at the center (a). The warp threads are tied securely to a hook on the wall, then strung through the holes (a) and the spaces between the sticks (b), toward the person weaving. He can then tie the threads to his belt and control the tension by pulling back. He moves the loom up and down, laying the weft threads over and under the warp threads.

EXPERIENCE. Sometimes weaving can be a means for getting a very practical-minded child to be more interested in art, particularly if he can see that weaving is an art form. For a child whose dexterity has not yet developed, a weaving task can be frustrating. If he learns that weaving is art, he may "learn" that he isn't artistic, while in another medium he might have succeeded and learned a very different concept of himself.

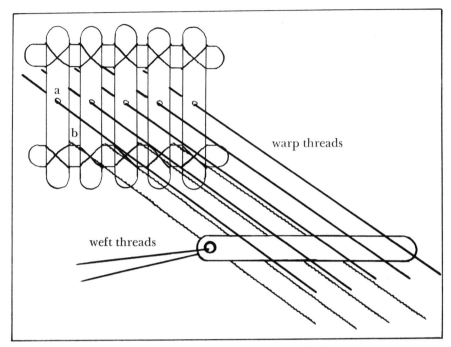

a

b

warp threads

weft threads

FIGURE 12-6. TONGUE DEPRESSOR LOOM

Weaving requires considerable planning, even on simple looms. Once a warp is ready, a child can experiment by trying different weft threads to make different patterns, giving him an opportunity for creativity. Sometimes a task in which there are few choices to be made can lead a less creative child into more experimentation. In painting, where the possibilities for choices are so much greater, such a child might be afraid to experiment.

MURALS

The basic media for making murals are tempera, torn or cut paper, chalk, and crayon. Several ways of organizing the children for the work can be used besides the one discussed on page 196, in which a whole class participated. If a mural is to be painted or drawn directly on the paper, not more than five or six children can work on it. The large paper can be mounted on the bulletin board and the children can work standing. Or the paper can be rolled out on the floor. In some schools the children paint directly on the walls. At times a group can paint a background while individuals make separate parts to be pasted on the background. Figure 12–7 is a mural made by teachers in training.

EXPERIENCE. Making murals gives children excellent experience in organizing ideas, seeing relationships, generalizing the most important ideas, and inventing symbols to communicate ideas with others. It gives them opportunity to design complex things so they can be easily "read." It contributes to their learning to work together. The teacher can gain insight into children's social skills when he watches them work in this kind of a group. Sometimes he will need to shift the membership in groups to be sure every child has an opportunity to contribute. Teachers can use mural groups to help bring an isolated child into interaction with the class. If he has a particular skill, his ability can be stressed so the group will let him participate. In discussing the merits of the finished work this child's contribution can be emphasized. Often the child himself will gain a sense of accomplishment that will mean more to him than his individual work.

MUSICAL INSTRUMENTS

Instruments that relate art to music can be made during art learning activities. Some that allow creative work are described here:

MARACAS. Use a dry ripe gourd. After soaking it in water,

FIGURE 12–7. PAINTED CUT PAPER MURAL MADE BY
TEACHERS IN TRAINING

scrape it clean with steel wool. When it is dry, sand it smooth. If seeds are not dry enough to make a sound cut the gourd in half and add small shot or pebbles, then glue the halves together. Fill cracks with wood putty. Decorate with enamels and lacquer for a permanent finish. Imitation gourds can be made of old light bulbs, using large and small ones for variety. Cover the bulbs with papier-mâché strips. When they are thoroughly dry, tap them lightly to break the glass inside to make them rattle. Then decorate and lacquer.

DRUMS. Many different bases can be used for drums. Five-gallon ice cream cartons and vegetable baskets can be covered with papier-mâché and allowed to dry. The best covering materials are real rubber sheeting or coated ticking materials painted with dope. Metal dot rings can be purchased in drapery shops. Use these to make holes around the edges of the rubber, so that it won't tear. Then it can be laced tightly to make a good drum. Drums can be gaily decorated. For more kinds of musical instruments see Timmerman[3] and Swanson.[4]

EXPERIENCE. Musical instruments the children have made and decorated themselves often enhance the experience of using them. The pattern of rhythm in music and their own art helps them learn from their own experience. Instruments that are gaily decorated become enjoyable art forms themselves. From rhythm a study of other patterns can be developed, such as visual patterns in nature. Relating similar elements in art and music can increase children's responses to both.

THREE-DIMENSIONAL BULLETIN BOARDS

The bulletin board can be used as a teaching device to show the relationships between things. The children can use it much as they do the mural to gather important information and then organize it to show how things relate to each other.

On three-dimensional boards pupils can organize samples of objects such as small rocks, plants in various stages, models of different methods of transportation, etc. If pegboard is available many variations of shelving and hooks can be used. Although efficient, this method does not challenge the children's ingenuity as much as working with paper, cardboard, wire, pins, and glue.

FIGURE 12–8. A THREE-DIMENSIONAL BULLETIN BOARD

Strong shelves can be made of cardboard. Have the intermediate children try to solve this problem. Discuss gravity and how the force of it can be used to hold a shelf in place. One solution is to use triangle cardboard supports, the top taped to the bottom of the shelf, the side to the bulletin board.

For small shelves, matchboxes can be tacked or stapled to the board. If needed, string supports can be used. Colored paper as a background behind them can help identify groups of related objects. Small cellophane bags can hold various samples so they can be easily arranged. Colored tacking pins can identify different types of wood, grass, cloth, etc. Corrugated or colored paper can be tacked to make vertical divisions to set objects off from each other. Wood dowels can be slipped through holes in the folds of the paper to support hanging objects.

EXPERIENCE. Encourage inventive construction, and discuss with the children how the organization of ideas can be made most clear and pleasing. Displays give many pupils opportunities to experience creative problem-solving, to exercise aesthetic judgment, to enrich their learning of the materials being displayed by encouraging research into the nature of the objects, and to increase their awareness of design as a means of communication.

An effective teaching technique is to ask pupils to put into words what is "said" in the bulletin board. Forming an awareness of the relationship of visual symbols to verbal symbols helps overcome two cultural prejudices: that art and knowledge are separated, and that learning involves reason while art involves emotion or aesthetic sensitivity.

OTHER MEDIA

As you learn of other media try to foresee the kinds of experiences the children will have with them. Will they be encouraged in real invention, or will a tricky process give them a showy effect with little creativity on their part? When you introduce anything new watch the children for clues that will help you decide whether to continue with it or not. An example of a trick that did not give children the experience they could have had was using egg shells for mosaic, gluing them down and *then* painting them. This gave no manipulating, problem-solving experience. Another type of trick is assembling prepared kits of moccasins or billfolds. *Almost any medium can be used in trite, uninventive ways.* Some processes, including most prepared kits, give children artificial feelings of accomplishment, but they have missed the valuable creative experience that leads to it.

ART LEARNING EXPERIENCES WITH THESE MEDIA

In Chapters 9 and 10 we discussed organizing art learning in the classroom, motivating pupils with individual differences, and the various kinds of experiences pupils might have. The next step is introducing new tasks into the classroom. In order to make the introduction of a new medium more specific, we will analyze basic steps that usually allow for more effective learning by many kinds of children.

1. Try to relate the new medium or tool to something the children already know. Show them how the new medium differs from the old ones. For example, if you are interested in helping children break away from a dependence on using brushes to paint with, you could introduce them to sponges and cardboard. Help them see that the brush is an instrument man has made for painting, but it is not the *only* painting tool.

Demonstrate just enough to get the idea across, by showing how the edge of thick cardboard can be used as a tool. Ask pupils to experiment with the cardboard by dipping the end in paint poured in a shallow dish. Encourage them to scrape with it, print with it, make lines with it, and see what other uses they can find.

2. After exploring with the new technique encourage pupils to put it to use, to say something with it, to describe something with it. Let them stay with the tool as long as it is fruitful and then make it available for self-directed art activities.

3. In the next art learning experience, build on the concepts and skills of the first lesson. You could next introduce the use of sponges for painting, showing how they are similar to, but different from, cardboard. Encourage exploration of the use of this tool as a means of expression.

4. For review and practice, give the children opportunities to use all three tools or combinations of them in the same drawing. A new kind of motivation may be needed to encourage further exploration and use of the techniques. A new live classroom pet, a chick, a white rat, a guinea pig, any furry or feathery animal can interest children in the kinds of feathery, furry qualities that can be expressed with brushes and sponges. A series of colored slides can be made of linear things, tall buildings, bare trees, rushes, telephone poles and wires, industrial plants, the halls of school buildings, to be used for motivation with the cardboard technique.

Once you have established that exploration can lead to a new kind of expression and communication, the child will be more willing to try new techniques. In each of these situations you may find reticent or inhibited children who do not want to try what the class is doing. Encourage them to try, but do not force them. Always have some substitute materials available. In each of the media, begin where these children are and bring in new concepts and skills as the children are ready.

RELATED TASKS FOR PART TWO

Planning for the Year. A flexible art program requires more careful preparation than a rigid sequence of activities. For this reason a "Planning Workbook" that includes all the information you need will be very useful for you. The workbook follows the sequence in Part Two of this book.

1. Define your objectives, as you see them at this time, in terms of the children and the community in which you plan to teach.
2. Observe an elementary school class similar to one you might teach. Get as much information on individual differences as you can. Organize this material so you can get a tentative picture of the ranges of abilities in the class. Watch behavior in class for clues about the children's tendencies.
3. Find out what art experiences most of the children had before they reached your grade.
4. Outline a *tentative* scope and sequence of units of activities that would allow for individual differences found in 2 and 3 above. Analyze the activities to see if they appear to lead toward your objectives. Will they develop the expressive, perceptual, and artistic awareness and the creativity of the children?

   a. Plan for each of the areas—*art learning, self-directed art,* and *integrated art.* Allow blocks of time so your plan is not too rigid. Identify the concepts and skills stressed in each unit of work to see that an orderly sequence of ideas is produced.
   b. Include what you will use for motivation—resource materials, audio-visual aids, bulletin boards, field trips, music.
   c. Collect information as you work with different media, and as you read art education periodicals, to help you with each task. The following outline is useful in describing media:

   Medium

   (1) Sources
   (2) Preparation and storage
   (3) Tools—number needed for art learning, for self-directed and for integrated activities
   (4) Ways of organizing tools for pupil use
   (5) Motivating pupils to explore the medium
   (6) Possible uses and possible combinations with other media
   (7) Means of displaying finished work

5. Draw a plan of a classroom as it is. Then draw several variations in organization of work tables, art tables, the

art corner, and storage areas. List the major limitations you see in the room design and ways you might overcome them.

Your art workbook should be started now. It can be so designed that you can add new ideas in any of the areas as you discover them. As you work with consultants, attend professional meetings, and have in-service training or more advanced college training, you will have many new ideas to add. A large ring notebook with dividers allows you considerable freedom in adding new ideas. It also makes it easy to remove materials that you find are not useful.

Start your collection of art prints and pictures of well-designed objects. Use rubber cement to mount them on stiff but lightweight cardboard. Spray them with a plastic spray and they can be wiped with a slightly damp sponge. A sturdy portable file is convenient for storage.

The planning you do ahead will make the administration of your art program much easier and leave you free for teaching.

REFERENCES

1. Howard Conant and Arne Randall, *Art in Education* (Peoria: Chas. A. Bennett Co., Inc., 1959), pp. 245–256.

2. Lucien B. Kinney and Katharine Dresden, *Better Learning Through Current Materials,* rev. ed. (Stanford: Stanford University Press, 1952).

3. Maurine Timmerman, *Let's Teach Music in the Elementary School* (Evanston: Summy-Birchard Publishing Co., 1958), pp. 149–172.

4. Bessie R. Swanson, *Music in the Education of Children* (San Francisco: Wadsworth Publishing Company, Inc., 1961), ch. 3.

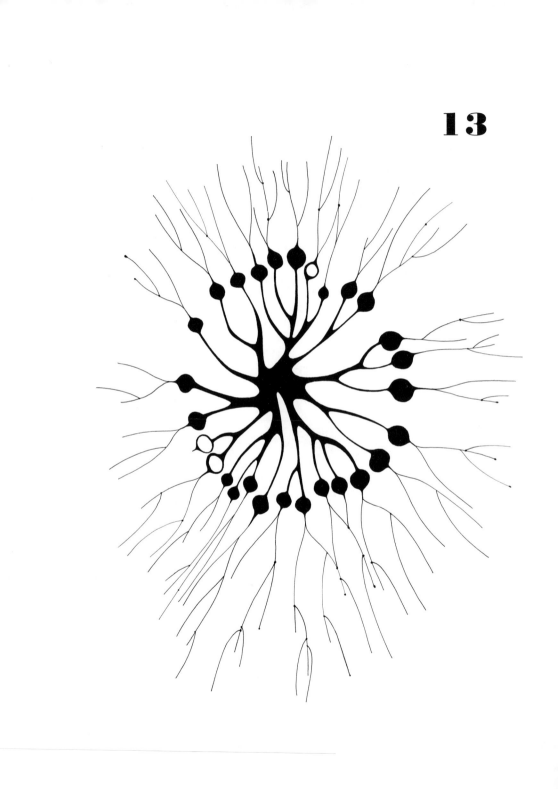

13

Summary:
Perception-
Delineation and
Art Education
Practice

In the last chapters we have looked at curriculum development in different ways: (1) objectives, (2) the learning situation, and (3) the scope and sequence of work through the elementary grades. In each discussion, and in the summary of basic materials in Chapter 12, we dealt with individual differences that need to be considered in teaching. To make this more clear we will summarize the basic generalizations from Part One and review the implications for practice described in Part Two.

POINT I: READINESS

A child's *readiness* for a task in art is made up of many constantly interacting factors. The more a teacher knows about a child the better he is equipped to see how these factors relate to each other. A child with a high I.Q. but with undeveloped motor skills and a background of strict cleanliness training will not react to art tasks in the same way as another child of high I.Q. whose motor skills are well developed and whose cleanliness training has been less inhibiting. If one of these children comes from a home where art is valued and the artist held in high esteem, and the other where art is negated as unimportant and "strange," still other differences in response are likely to emerge. If one child has had prior training that encouraged creativity and invention and the other has done only copy work, their differences will be even greater.

The categorizing systems that we have found so easy to use in labeling children, such as "gifted," "bright," "average," "slow-learning," may need clarification. Longitudinal studies of I.Q. development and the organismic concept of growth lead us to re-evaluate our age-based concepts of development, including development in art. We have found that at any age level a wide range of individual differences exist on any measurable factor. We need to consider the various stages of development of different capacities as they interact with each other. The individual differences we have identified that are most related to behavior in art are these:

1. *Flexibility-rigidity.* Children vary in their ability to respond to familiar things and to new things, and to shift from one motor-cognitive task to another.

2. *Orientation to space.* Children tend to learn a way of orienting themselves to their environment, depending on visual cues, bodily feelings, or both. The tendencies are related to child-rearing practice. Mothers who restrict self-direction tend to have children who depend more on visual cues. Those who foster self-direction tend to have more independent children who use bodily cues.

3. *Learning and the perceptual process.* Part of the perceptual process is learned. In Western culture the cognitive nature of things (what is known) is stressed much more than the visual (what is seen). Perceiving is an information-handling process in which visual stimuli are organized in order to make cognitive re-

sponses. The *ways* people group and organize information depend in part on their values and training.

4. *The perceptual constancies.* The tendencies to deal with size, shape, and color in terms of what is known about them rather than with the actual visual image, vary from person to person depending on learning and experience.

5. *Subcultures.* Attitudes and values about art depend on the subculture from which the child comes. Discontinuities can occur when the child does not understand why he is being encouraged and rewarded for one kind of behavior in one situation and punished and discouraged for the same behavior in another situation. The lack of understanding between some homes and the school art program may stem from differences in attitudes about art, artists, expediency, hard work, and aesthetic sensitivity.

6. *Prior learning.* In art or other activity, past experiences can produce "sets" that inhibit or increase children's readiness for art activities. Functional fixedness (learning limited uses) can inhibit creative use of tools and materials.

IMPLICATIONS FOR PRACTICE

The major implication for practice is that *the art program needs to be flexible and varied to provide for differences in readiness in children.* This is the reason for having three categories of art activities. *Art learning* periods are opportunities for the teacher to present tasks and materials that can provide motivation and progress for different groups of children in the class. The *self-directed activities* are avenues for each child to carry out his ideas within his own stage of development and interest. *Integrated art activities* help children understand the relationships of art to many other subjects.

This type of curriculum planning allows flexibility in the amount of time children have to adjust to the new methods, and in some degree it allows them to proceed at their own rate.

Perceptual training becomes part of the educational process. Cognitive and visual training can be developed together, thus strengthening the learning and relating process. *Critical analysis of one's perceptions is as important to critical thinking as analysis of one's ideas.*

Perceptions are the basis from which many ideas develop. Made uncritically they can lead to misconceptions. Learning in other areas is enriched by visual communication. Art helps both the advanced reader and the slow reader to develop better communication skills.

Children are better equipped to relate intelligently to their environment when they have learned to use both postural and visual cues, to see patterns that enable them to handle more visual detail, to see likenesses and differences, and to be aware of both the cognitive and visual qualities of things. If perceptual training takes place in art activities, dealing with the elements of art—form, line, color, texture, space—and their interactions, then aesthetic judgment will develop as well.

Art activities include expressing, designing, inventing symbols and forms, and developing skills in a variety of media. Children usually develop their abilities with more emphasis on one activity than on another. Part of the teacher's role is to help them become more ready for *all* art activities. Inhibited children need success in finding means for expression. Almost all children, particularly those in the intermediate grades, can improve their means of organizing or designing their expressions and inventions.

POINT II: THE PSYCHOLOGICAL ENVIRONMENT

The psychological environment has a great deal to do with the ways in which individuals behave in the perceptual process. Threatening situations can limit the amount of information that is used, its correctness, and its organization. Success and failure experience and the evaluation of one's ability by others change goal-setting behavior. Continued failure leads to unrealistic goal-setting, choosing goals way beyond one's ability to succeed or withdrawing from the situation and not trying at all. We found that praise and blame work differently on introverted and extroverted children. Extroverts are sometimes motivated to succeed more by *some* blame while introverts are inhibited by blame. It should be remembered that the terms "introvert" and "extrovert" describe only a part of the child's behavior and that they describe tendencies, not absolutes.

In studies of art in different cultures we found that the environment influences the amount of detail used. Sex roles are related to goals and to the development of skill in delineation. Cultural symbols influence the direction of drawing development. The values of the group and their specific needs direct the kinds of visual training children receive. When survival depends on keen observation, highly developed perceptual skills follow.

IMPLICATIONS FOR PRACTICE

The kinds of rewards a teacher establishes have a great deal to do with the psychological environment in which the children will be working. If the teacher rewards successes that only a few of the children can achieve, then most of the other children will experience feelings of inadequacy. If the teacher identifies certain children as artistic, calls on them to do most of the art for other subjects such as making posters and arranging displays, then the teacher is creating a negative environment for some members of the class. If representational drawing alone is encouraged and children are rewarded according to their skill in copying nature, or if mimeographed adult symbols are given them to copy, many children will experience anxiety and be less efficient in the perceptual task. Their concepts of art will be limited.

The studies of success and failure indicate that praise and constructive criticism may be the most effective tools in motivating children in art since this activity is in many respects a more personal or introversive activity. Constructive criticism should be used discreetly with the individual child. Usually comments should be made to the child alone rather than in front of the whole class.

Children who are isolates can be led into group art activities, and their particular talents in art can be emphasized. A flexible plan of art activities allows room for each child to find his own way of working in the classroom. New pupils who are well-informed about classroom procedures have little trouble in becoming accustomed to them.

In most cases it seems wise to let children know that there are three different kinds of art activities in the classroom, so that they will clearly understand the differences. In art learning they work together as a class, in self-directed art they can work on their own projects, and at other times they can use art to enrich other subjects. When the goals are clear there is less confusion, and the environment supports the different activities.

Part of the psychological environment of children in the classroom comes from anxieties and fears they bring from home or the playground. To help overcome these fears, try to make the children feel accepted in the classroom.

POINT III: INFORMATION-HANDLING

Individual differences in the ways people handle information result in part from differences in perceptual growth. Young children tend to see large outlines or forms and to learn to see smaller details as they grow older. Although there is an average growth tendency, individual differences in the amount of detail handled can be found among very young children as well as among older children and adults. Intelligence is found to be related to ability to handle detail and asymmetrical material (more complex organized detail).

Many other variables of experience, culture reward, and specific training influence this general trend. Ability to handle detail is in part learned, as we found in comparisons of the perceptual habits of artists and non-artists and comparisons of people from different cultures where differences in perceptual training exist. Intelligence tests based on children's drawings do not consider all the variables of experience.

IMPLICATIONS FOR PRACTICE

Motivating materials used in the classroom environment should be selected with the whole class in mind, with variations that will have meaning and stimulate interest in the slower as well as in the more advanced students. Generally speaking more detail can be used in the intermediate grades than in the primary, but considerable overlapping is found when individual cases are examined.

Apparently perceptual ability can be improved with motivation and opportunity to learn. Since, in other cultures we have studied, strong motivation to observe is accompanied by skill in drawing, drawing skill in the intermediate grades can be developed more easily by perceptual exploration than by exercising the hands. Ability to draw representationally has been a criterion of artistic ability for so long that children with this ability are most often rewarded. If drawing is considered as only one of the abilities in art and is used for both realism and the invention of new expressive symbols, it can contribute to a more flexible growth in art. Delineation is most dependent on a child's ability to observe and to organize the information he receives. But *each individual child's observations and organization are somewhat different. If these differences are recognized, many more children can learn to delineate skillfully and expressively.*

One of the bases of creativity is the breadth of information and experience that the child has to draw upon. Perceptual training can enrich a child's reservoir of possible combinations and reorganizations. It can make him much more aware of the functions of form, line, texture, and color in the world around him and give him a much richer "language" for expression in art.

POINT IV: CREATIVITY AND DELINEATION

Point IV of the P-D process is the point at which the three other teaching functions, assessing and improving readiness, developing a good working atmosphere, and helping children use their visual information, produce "art." The way children delineate, the symbols they borrow and invent, the freedom they have to express are outgrowths of their total readiness, the situation in which they work, and their ability to assimilate their perceptions of their environment. While we do not know much about the kinds of experiences that lead to creativity, analysis of the traits of creative people gives us clues about the kinds of abilities we should foster. Fluency, flexibility, and originality can be rewarded and encouraged. By logical analysis we can assess the kinds of experiences we give children to see that these behaviors are possible and that they are rewarded.

To achieve flexibility children need enough time to accept and use a wider range of materials and tools and to perform different kinds of tasks. Since children vary in their ability to shift tasks or in the time required to make responses, developing their creative potential takes longer for some children than for others. Many children may never develop much creativity because they rarely have time enough to shift tasks.

Originality can develop in a classroom where children have opportunities to come to their own conclusions and solutions to problems, as well as to get "right" answers. If the environment is one in which conformity is rewarded and deviation punished, originality is likely to burst forth in negative behavior rather than in constructive expression.

Self-directed activity gives those children who need time to develop more fluency an opportunity to do so. Often quite nonverbal children become fluent in art expression, because the causes of their lack of verbal communication may not be associated with drawing and painting. On the other hand, children who have been punished for drawing, or making "messes" with paint, have trouble being fluent in these media until the negative attitude is overcome.

Since creativity does not take place in a vacuum, children's creative work will be enriched if they have many real, direct, and stimulating experiences in exploring their visual world and in thinking about and expressing ideas and feelings. Motivation takes place at all stages of the P-D processes, and the teacher must be certain it is present at the time of creating.

Finally, creative work can be impeded if an avenue of expression is lacking or is not geared to a child's experience and manipulative ability. Part of the teacher's role is to expand the possibilities for experimentation with many different means of artistic expression.

CONCLUSION

The full range of experiences in the arts
recognized by the public and many educato
expression" was emphasized without clear def
art experience tended to have amorphous r
easily be disregarded as having no useful valu
reasons art may have been considered a "frill.

By contrast, when art is seen as a mean
and invention whereby the child can express
ganize and relate information), develop his p
exercise his creativity, art becomes an import
cative process. As a tool of education, it becc
spoken and written language. When art is t;
culture and is used to understand our own a
improves the communication among all memb

Art behavior, as we now see, is a primar
cannot be looked at in isolation. It is relate
separated from man's individual and social
his existence from the ordering of his immed
his search for aesthetic truth or order. It invc
tual and perceptual capacities, his complexes
attitudes, and values, his creativity, his goals
help each child develop his capacity for ae;
judgment we need to understand the child a;
ual in a complex environment, and the school
tion that can promote his growth. The purp
been to try to provide you with breadth c
human behavior in art as it applies to you an
your classroom.

SUGGESTIONS
FOR FURTHER READING

Art

Barr, Alfred H., Jr., *What Is Modern Painting?* rev. ed. New York: The Museum of Modern Art, 1956.

Daniel, Greta, ed., *Useful Objects Today: Teaching Portfolio No. 4.* New York; The Museum of Modern Art, 1955.

Edman, Irwin, *Arts and the Man.* New York: W. W. Norton and Company, Inc., 1939.

Faulkner, Ray, Edwin Ziegfeld, and Gerald Hill, *Art Today,* 3rd ed. New York: Henry Holt and Co., Inc., 1956.

Faulkner, Ray, and Sara Faulkner, *Inside Today's Home,* 2nd ed. New York: Henry Holt and Co., Inc., 1960.

Gardner, Helen, *Art Through the Ages,* 4th ed. New York: Harcourt, Brace and Company, Inc., 1958.

Gropius, Walter, *The New Architecture and the Bauhaus,* trans. P. Morton Shand. New York: The Museum of Modern Art, 1937.

Kaufmann, Edgar, Jr., *What Is Modern Design?* New York: The Museum of Modern Art, 1950.

Kepes, György, *Language of Vision.* Chicago: Paul Theobald, 1945.

Kuh, Katharine, *Art Has Many Faces.* New York: Harper & Brothers, 1951.

Mayer, Ralph, *The Artist's Handbook of Materials and Techniques,* rev. ed. New York: The Viking Press, 1957.

Mendelowitz, Daniel M., *History of American Art.* New York: Henry Holt and Co., Inc., 1960.

Moholy-Nagy, Laszlo, *The New Vision.* New York: Wittenborn, 1947.

Munro, Thomas, *The Arts and Their Interrelations.* New York: Liberal Arts Press, 1956.

Neutra, Richard J., *Survival Through Design.* New York: Oxford University Press, 1954.

Ozenfant, Amédée, *Foundations of Modern Art.* New York: Dover Publications, Inc., 1956.

Read, Herbert, *Art Now.* London: Faber and Faber, Ltd., 1948.

Seuphor, M., *Dictionary of Abstract Painting.* New York: Tudor Publishing Co., 1957.

Art in Culture

Boas, Franz, *Primitive Art*. New York: Dover Publications, Inc., 1955.

Havighurst, Robert J., and Bernice L. Neugarten, *American Indian and White Children*. Chicago: University of Chicago Press, 1955.

Keesing, Felix M., *Cultural Anthropology: The Science of Custom*. New York: Rinehart and Company, Inc., 1958.

Lerner, Max, *America as a Civilization: Life and Thought in the United States Today*. New York: Simon and Schuster, 1957.

Lynes, Russell, *The Tastemakers*. New York: Harper & Brothers, 1954.

Mead, Margaret, and Martha Wolfenstein, eds., *Childhood in Contemporary Cultures*. Chicago: University of Chicago Press, 1955.

Art Education

Barkan, Manuel, *Through Art to Creativity*. New York: Allyn and Bacon, Inc., 1960.

Borten, Helen, *Do You See What I See?* London: Abelard-Schuman, 1959.

Conant, Howard, and Arne Randall, *Art in Education*. Peoria: Chas. A. Bennett Co., Inc., 1959.

D'Amico, Victor, *Creative Teaching in Art,* rev. ed. Scranton, Pa.: International Textbook Co., 1954.

De Francesco, Italo L., *Art Education: Its Means and Ends*. New York: Harper & Brothers, 1958.

Jefferson, Blanche, *Teaching Art to Children*. New York: Allyn and Bacon, Inc., 1959.

Johnson, Pauline, *Creating with Paper*. Seattle: University of Washington Press, 1958.

Logan, Frederick M., *Growth of Art in American Schools*. New York: Harper & Brothers, 1955.

Reed, Carl, *Early Adolescent Art Education*. Peoria: Chas. A. Bennett Co., Inc., 1957.

Riley, Olive L., *Your Art Heritage*. New York: Harper & Brothers, 1952.

Wickiser, Ralph L., *An Introduction to Art Education*. New York: World Book Co., 1957.

Perception

Arnheim, Rudolph, *Art and Visual Perception*. Berkeley: University of California Press, 1954.

Hallowell, A. Irving, *Culture and Experience*. Philadelphia: University of Pennsylvania Press, 1955.

Hilgard, Ernest R., *Introduction to Psychology,* 2nd ed. New York: Harcourt, Brace and Company, Inc., 1957.

Krech, David, and Richard S. Crutchfield, *Elements of Psychology*. New York: Alfred A. Knopf, Inc., 1958.

Creativity

Anderson, Harold H., ed., *Creativity and Its Cultivation: Addresses Presented at the Interdisciplinary Symposia on Creativity.* New York: Harper & Brothers, 1959.

Ghiselin, Brewster, ed., *The Creative Process: A Symposium.* Berkeley: University of California Press, 1952.

Smith, Paul, ed., *Creativity: An Examination of the Creative Process.* New York: Hastings House, 1959.

Concept Formation

McDonald, Frederick J., *Educational Psychology.* San Francisco: Wadsworth Publishing Company, Inc., 1959.

Personality

Harsh, Charles M., and H. G. Schrickel, *Personality: Development and Assessment,* 2nd ed. New York: The Ronald Press Company, 1959.

Social Foundations of Education

Rugg, Harold, and William Withers, *Social Foundations of Education.* Englewood Cliffs, N. J.: Prentice-Hall, Inc., 1955.

Spindler, George D., ed., *Education and Anthropology.* Stanford: Stanford University Press, 1955.

GLOSSARY

Abstract. To separate out certain elements from a whole.

Aesthetic response. A sense of beauty and pleasure that is aroused through harmony in the organization of diverse elements into a unified whole.

Art. Man's attempt to make and organize the objects in his environment in order to enhance their visual quality (aesthetic value). *Fine arts* are those whose function is wholly aesthetic rather than practical.

Asymmetrical balance. Unity that is achieved without repetition of the left-to-right or top-to-bottom pattern.

Basic research. A study of phenomena made without concern for its possible application. *Applied* research uses basic research for specific purposes.

Behavioral sciences. Studies that deal with human behavior: psychology, sociology, anthropology, social psychology.

Categorize. To put into units of similar things, concepts, or percepts. In perception, to organize stimuli into categories of information that can be handled cognitively.

Clue. An idea, information that gives directions for behavior.

Cognitive. Consciously aware, thinking, knowing. *Precognitive organization.* The sorting of visual information that occurs before the information is brought to a conscious level of thought.

Concept. An organization of elements into an idea. A concept is made by learning or experience.

Cues. Stimuli that give bits of information. *Postural cues.* Stimuli obtained from the body about one's relationship to vertical and horizontal space. *Visual cues.* Stimuli obtained through the eyes.

Cultural anthropology. The study of the values, attitudes, beliefs, patterns of behavior, kinship systems, language of past and present organized groups of people.

Culture. The attitudes, values, beliefs, patterns of behavior, social organization, and concepts of reality of a group of people that persists through time. *Subculture.* A group of people who share in part the culture of a larger group to which they belong nationally, socially, or ethnically, but who have identifiable differences as a group. *Core culture.* That segment of a larger culture that is central to the culture, least deviant from it.

Design. The pattern of relationships between form, line, color, texture, and space that results in organic unity.

Deviant. One who is quite unlike the average or mode. A group that is different from a majority (or what is considered to be the majority) of other groups.

317

Discontinuity. The experience of a child who does not receive the same reward or punishment for the same behavior in two different situations.

Dynamic unity. The tensions created by contrast in value and color, between the degrees of depth in space, the varying directions of angular line contained within the whole of a design, maintaining a state of equilibrium. One of the factors that contribute to organic unity.

Enculturation. The process of a child's learning his own culture.

Eye-hand coordination. Ability to coordinate the directives gained from visual cues to the appropriate movement of the hand.

Field. *Visual field* is the area seen without moving the eye. *Psychological field* is the totality of the factors in a given situation that influence the individual's behavior (field theory). Field dependence means reliance on visual cues to get information.

Flexibility. An ability to accept change in the environment, to change one's behavior as needed, and to try new solutions for problems.

Inhibit. To hinder responses. *Inhibition* is the blocking of a response by other learnings.

I.Q. Intelligence quotient. The I.Q. is computed by dividing the mental age by the chronological age. Mental age is determined by a test that measures an individual's present general scholastic ability.

Kinesthetic response. Conscious awareness of bodily reaction to one's perceptions.

Mean. The arithmetical average, it is the sum of the scores divided by the number of scores.

Medium (art). The material used to communicate. Pl., *media*.

Motivation. A factor or a combination of factors that change behavior. Basic and learned needs that lead to goal-seeking behavior.

Motor skills. Skills that require movement and muscular control.

Nonobjective painting. An emphasis on the elements of art and the dynamics of design rather than on pictorial representation.

Objectify. Traditionally in art, to attempt to make things seem more real through representation or symbolism.

Objective. A goal to be worked toward.

Organic unity. The effect of completeness when all parts contribute to the unification of the whole.

Organismic growth. A concept of child development that deals with the child as a whole being in which all factors are interdependent.

Orientation. The process of relating oneself to the environment.

Primitive art. The work of an untrained person. Art of preliterate people. Anthropologists once used the term "primitive" but now the term preliterate (before writing) is preferred.

Process. A continuation of behaviors —a sequential operation.

Psychology. The study of the nature of man and animals.

Punishment. A form of penalty for less than acceptable behavior.

Readiness. The sum of all the factors of growth, learning, and capacity that contribute to an individual's ability to perform a given task.

Realism. In art, the attempt to reproduce objective nature.

Reinforce. To strengthen learning through further experience.

Rewards. Acceptance, recognition, and praise for a behavior.

Rigidity. A tendency to persist in familiar problem-solving behavior; resistance to novelty and change.

Schema. A rather habitual way to symbolize a concept.

Stereotypes. Limited concepts that are often assumed to be complete. *Cultural stereotypes.* Particular stereotypes about people that are part of a group's cultural tradition.

Symbol. A sign, a mark, a drawing, a form, or a style, which has cognitive meaning to a group of people.

Thinglike. Perceived in terms of the observer's experience.

Threat. A condition of impending bodily or psychological danger, which can arouse fear and anxiety.

Traditions. Customs, practices, art forms, and language that are handed down from one generation to another.

Value. A people's emotionally supported judgments of worth and importance.

Value. Lightness or darkness.

Visual information. Cues received through the eye.

Visual perception. The process of selecting, sorting and categorizing visual information.

Visual qualities. Characteristics of an object as it is seen, rather than as it is known.

INDEX OF AUTHORS

Page Symbol Key: Quotations appear on page numbers prefixed by *q*. Reading references appear on page numbers prefixed by *r*. Footnote references appear on page numbers prefixed by *f*. Page numbers with no prefix refer to discussion of the author's work.

Adams, B., r126, r144
Alper, T., 117–118, r126, 136, r144
Ames, L. B., r98
Anastasi, A., 37–38, r67, 86, q88, r98
Anderson, H. H., r315
Arnheim, R., 40, 48, r67, q82, r98, q151,
    155–156, r164, r314
Attneave, F., 39–40, r67, 78, r270

Baker, C. T., r97, 157, r165, r209
Barkan, M., r314
Barnhart, E. N., 157, r165
Barr, A. H., r313
Barron, F., r98
Bayley, N., 72–73, r97, 157, r165
Beals, R. L., r35
Becker, W. C., r68
Belo, J., 31, r35
Benedict, R., r126
Birch, H. G., r67
Blane, H., r126, r144
Boas, F., 87, r314
Borten, H., 215, r241, r314
Boudreau, J. C., r98, r241
Brown, D. R., r126
Bruner, J. S., r12, f37, r67, r241
Brunswick, E., r98

Conant, H., 275, r301, r314
Counts, G. S., q174, r182
Cronbach, L. J., r241
Crutchfield, R. S., r314

D'Amico, V., r314
Daniel, G., r313
De Francesco, I. L., r314
Dresden, K., 279, r301
Drevdahl, J. E., r144
Dubin, E. R., 204, r210
DuBois, C., 124, r127

Edman, I., 27, r35, r313
Eiduson, B. T., q134, r144

Faulkner, R., r313
Faulkner, S., r313
Foley, J. P., Jr., 37–38, r67, 86, q88, r98
French, J. E., 81, r98, 155, r164

Gabriel, R., r182
Gardner, H., r313
Gesell, A. L., 156, r164
Ghiselin, B., r315
Goodenough, F., r67, 104, r126, r154,
    158, r164, r165
Gorer, G., r127
Gropius, W., 177, r313
Guilford, J. P., 131, 141, r144, r209

Hallowell, A. I., 159, r165, r314
Harsh, C. M., q110, f110, r127, r315
Havighurst, R. J., r98, r314
Herskovits, M., q18, r35, r127
Hertzman, M., r67, r164
Hilgard, E. R., 48, r67, f245, r270, r314
Hill, G., r313
Hoebel, E. A., q19, r35, r182
Hoijer, H., r35
Honkavaara, S., r98
Hunnicutt, C. W., r127

Ilg, F. L., 156, r164

Jefferson, B., r314
Johnson, P., r314
Joseph, A., r98

Kaufmann, E., Jr., r313
Keesing, F. M., r314
Kepes, G., r313
Kinney, L. B., 279, r301
Kluckhohn, C., r35, r126, r127

Kluckhohn, F., r127
Kohn, H., 103, r126
Krech, D., r98, r314
Kuh, K., r313

Land, E. H., 269, r270
Lantz, B., 104, r126, 158, r165
Lark-Horowitz, B., 157, r165
Lawrence, M., r67
Lear, E., q92, r98
Learned, J., r98
Leighton, D., r35
Lerner, M., 29, r35, 108, r127, q178, r182, r314
Levin, H., r126
Lewin, K., r12
Lewis, H. B., r67, r164
Linton, H. B., 52–53, r67, r68, 156, r164
Livson, N., r98
Logan, F. M., r182, r314
Lowenfeld, V., q50, r67, 156, 157, 158, r165
Lunt, P. S., r127
Lynes, R., 29, r35, r314

Machover, K., r67, r164
Madden, W., q172, r181
McCandles, B. R., 159, r165
McDonald, F. J., q189, r210, r315
McFee, J. K., r67, r98
McFee, M., r127
Mayer, R., r313
Mead, M., f31, r35, r127, q177, r182, 238, r241, r314
Meissner, P. B., r67, r164
Mendelowitz, D. M., 207, r210, r313
Metreaux, R., r98
Moholy-Nagy, L., r313
Monroe, M., 204
Moreno, J. L., 192, r210
Mumford, L., 172, r181
Munro, T., 157, r165, r313
Murray, V. G., r98

Nelson, V. L., r97, 157, r165, r209
Neugarten, B. L., r98, r314
Neutra, R. J., r313
Newcomb, A. P., Jr., r98

Ozenfant, A., r313

Polyak, 39
Postman, L. J., r67, r126

Rabinowitz, H. S., r67
Randall, A., 275, 279, r301, r314
Read, H., r313
Reed, C., r314
Riley, O. L., r314
Rodrigues, J., r67
Rugg, H., r315

Sayers, E. V., q172, r181
Schaefer-Simmern, H., 217, r241
Schaie, K. W., r144
Schrickel, H. G., q110, f110, r127, r315
Schubert, A., r98
Sears, P. S., 104, r126
Seidel, Y. W., r241
Seuphor, M., r313
Slotkin, J. S., r98
Smith, P., r315
Sontag, L. W., 74, 82, r97, 157, r165, r209
Spiker, C., 159, r165
Spindler, G. D., q114, 114–116, q116, 120, r127, r315
Stewart, L. H., 119, 120, r127
Swanson, B. R., r301

Taba, H., 124, r127
Thompson, G. G., r127
Tilton, J. W., r12, 130, r144
Timmerman, M., r301
Tyler, R., r127

Veblen, T., q178, r182

Walker, R., r98
Wapner, S., r67, r164
Warner, W. L., r127
Welsh, G. S., r98
Whiting, J. W. M., r35
Whorf, B. L., r67
Wickiser, R. L., r314
Withers, W., r315
Witkin, H. A., 52–53, r67, r68, 156, r164
Woods, W. A., r98, r241

Ziegfeld, E., r313

INDEX OF SUBJECTS

Abstract art
Abstracting, 234, 257, 317
Fine arts, 96–97, 177, 179, 230–231, 232
Musical parallels, 89, 248
See also Design
"Acadian Suite" (Thomson), music, 222
Acculturation, 90
Administration, school, 169–170, 273–275
Adolescence, 119–120
Advertising, 19, 23, 89, 230, 231
See also Mass media
Aesthetic judgments
Aesthetic response, definition, 317
Bases, 4, 8, 23–26, 34, 96–97, 108–109,
124, 172–173, 199, 229, 230
Beauty, philosophy of, 175–176
Consumer/citizen use, 7, 171–173,
174–175, 230–231
Design criteria, 243–245
Drawing criteria, 119
Taste formation, 19, 23, 28–30, 34–35
African culture, 45, 90
After-image, color, 263
Age-based growth studies
Description, 72
Inadequacies, 37–38, 72–75, 156–160,
164
Personality and perception, 12, 37
Age differences
Design, 158, 199–200
Developmental stages, 156–160
Drawing symbols, 33, 87
Growth rates, 72–73, 77–78, 148–149
Mental development, 73–75, 77–78,
148–149
Originality, 132
Perceptual abilities, 49, 78–80, 96,
149–150, 155
Space orientation, 52–53
See also Theories, child art
Air Force Research, 50–51

Alert Bay Indians, 87–88, 89
Alphabet, 6, 60
American culture
Art forms, 18, 19, 22–23, 109
Art values, 27–28, 33–34, 35, 108–109
Core culture changes, 108–109, 113–
121, 125, 170–173
Definition, 17–18
Direction, perceptual training, 88–90
Economy, 178
Social organization, 171–175, 180–181
Subcultural composition, 90
Taste, social grouping, 29–30
See also Cultures (Indian); In-
dustrial society
American Indians; *see* Cultures
Anecdotal records, 75, 77, 160, 208, 227,
277–278
Animal symbolism, 84–88
Aniseikonic lenses, 55
Anthropology, art applications, 5, 6, 8,
37–38, 123–124
See also Case studies; Cultures;
Research studies
Antioch College, 74
Anxiety; *see* Feelings; Success/failure ex-
perience; Threat/non-threat
influences
Applied arts
Definition, 27
Fine arts conflict, 27–28, 33–35, 108–
109, 179–180
See also Industrial design
Architects, architecture, 18, 20, 22, 27–
28, 177, 229, 231
Arithmetic art patterns, 77, 178
Armatures, 292
Art
Cultural component, 8, 17
Definitions, 18–19, 317
See also Applied arts; Fine arts

Art abilities
  Definitions, 147, 163
  Evaluations, 93, 95, 104, 122, 206–209
    See also Creative potential; Crea-
    tivity; Pupil, understanding of
Art activities
  Evaluation, 10, 92, 206–209
  Functions, 8
  Kinds, 213, 241, 305–306
  Programming flexibility, 10, 63, 91–
    95, 106, 124, 305
  Relationships of learning, 240
  Teacher experience, 3–5, 96–97
    See also Curriculum planning,
    art
Art activities, art learning
  Intermediate, 230–240, 241
  Primary, 214–226, 241
  Purpose, 305
    See also Media, classroom ex-
    perience with; Motor skills;
    Perceptual training; Technique
    training
Art activities, integrated
  Classroom approaches, 203–206, 209,
    240
  Intermediate, 238–241
  Primary, 227–230, 241
  Purpose, 124, 305
  Role study, artist, 229, 231
    See also Curriculum, general
Art activities, self-directed
  Intermediate, 237–238, 241
  Primary, 226–227, 241
  Purpose, 238, 305
  Work areas, 280–281
Art appreciation
  Art learning basis, 172–173
  Self-development, 96–97, 268–270
  Separate study, 180–181
  Social values, 108–109, 171–173
    See also Aesthetic judgments;
    Attitudes, art; Fine arts; De-
    sign; Industrial design
Art attitudes; *see* Attitudes, art
Art communication
  Functions, cultural maintenance, 6, 8,
    17–18, 34–35
  Reality concepts, 20–22, 87

  Reflection of culture, 18–19, 20–27, 34
  Use of art "language," 7, 19, 22–23,
    71, 89, 134–135, 173, 178, 227,
    244
    See also Cultures; Expression;
    Mass media; Symbols
Art consultant; *see* Consultant, art
Art education
  Curriculum; *see* Curriculum planning,
    art
  Functions, 8
  Goals, teaching, 10, 118, 124, 129, 142,
    148, 172–173, 174–175, 176–177
  History, 179–180
  Ideal values, 172–173, 174–175, 176,
    178–179
  Integration, total education; *see* Cur-
    riculum, general
  Learning, relationships, 240
  Research applications, 5, 6, 7, 8, 10–
    12, 37–38, 71–72
  Scope, 6–8, 19
  Teacher orientation, 3–6
  Theories of; *see* Theories, child art
Art functions
  Comprehensive, 8
  Cultural, 20, 30, 34–35, 178–179
    See also Art communication;
    Cultural maintenance
  Expressive; *see* Expression
  Social; *see* Objectives
Art history, education, 179–180
Art learning; *see* Art activities, art learn-
  ing
Art library
  Classroom, 229, 277–278, 301
  Other, 97, 239
Artifacts, 22, 24–25
Artist
  Art abilities, 134, 148
  Art heritage use, 177
  Cultural evaluations, 33, 108–109, 114–
    116, 119–121, 190
  Education, 83–84
  Perceptual responses, 42, 81, 84, 231
  Personality problems, 115, 119–121
  Role-teaching, 229, 231
Asian culture, 27, 90, 133
Association theory, 12

Associational fluency, 132
Asymmetry; *see* Design (Qualities); Intelligence, measured
Attitudes, art
  Art value conflicts, 27–28, 33–34, 35, 108–109
  Core value changes, 113–121, 170–173, 305
  Ideal values; *see* Objectives
  Philosophy, 175–176
  Pupil response, 189–190
  Teacher response, 189–190
    See also Aesthetic judgments; Behaviors; Responses, emotional
Authority influences
  Discontinuity, 112
  Perception, 53, 56, 150
  Taste, 28–29, 35
  Teacher/pupil, 28, 35, 56, 108
Averages, child development, 72
Averaging, perceptual, 39, 245–248

Balance
  Color, 263, 268–269
  Design, 244–245, 250–257, 317
  Perspective, 267
Balinese culture, 30–33, 35
Barong, 31
Baroque design, 256
Bartók, music of, 222
Base line organization, 31, 60
Bauhaus school, 180
Behavioral science; *see* Psychology
Behaviors
  Age relationships, 159–160
  Art, 38, 71, 111–112, 207, 237
    See also Media, classroom experience with
  Averageness ideals, 114–115
  Creativity, 131–137, 143
  Goal-seeking, 74, 102, 112
    See also Rewards/punishments; Success/failure experience; Threat/non-threat influences
  Identification with adult, 174
  Likes/dislikes, 28–30, 34–35
  Trait formation, 55

Work value effects, 117–118
  See also Authority influences; Cleanliness attitudes; Dependency/independency; Feelings; Flexibility/Rigidity; Home influences; Perceptual readiness; Responses, emotional; Right/wrong behavior
Bella Bella Indians, 87–88, 89
Bella Coola Indians, 87–88, 89
Berkeley Growth Research, 72–73, 157
Better Learning Through Current Materials (Kinney and Dresden), 279
Blocks, nonsense, 55
Borten, Helen, 215
Braque painting, 177, Plate I
Brightness; *see* Color; Light
British Columbia Indians, 87–88, 89
"Broadway Boogie-Woogie" (Mondrian), painting, 230
Budget, art, 275
Bulletin boards, 187, 194, 250, 278–279, 296–298

Canadian Film Board, 193, 199, 239
Canadian Indians, 87–88, 89
Carolinians, Saipan, 86
Cartoons; *see* Mass media
Case studies
  Enculturation, home, 110–111
  Fluency, experience inhibiting, 134
  I.Q./Ability unevenness, 75–77
  Learning, home inhibiting, 26–27
  Rigidity, media usage, 57–59
  Symbolic fluency in mental retardation, 217–221
    See also Cultures; Research studies
Chalk, 281, 285, 294
Chamorros, Saipan, 86
Child art
  Abilities; *see* Art abilities; Perceptual readiness
  Behaviors; *see* Behaviors; Media, classroom experience with
  Creativity, 129, 130
  Cultural direction, 84–90

Developmental stages, 156–160, 164, 204

Dimensions, 157–158, 199–200

Evaluation, 92–93, 95, 104, 156, 186, 202, 206, 209

Fluency, 132–135

Originality, 132

Psychological inhibitions; *see* Home influences; Media usage, influences

Theories of, 37–38, 151–160, 164
See also Perception-delineation theory
See also Design; Drawing development; Expression; Media, classroom experience with; Perceptual readiness

Child art examples
Balinese, 30–33
Intuitive design, 199–200
Japanese, 133, Plate III
Orotchen, 85
Pacific Coast Indians, 87–88
Storm responses, 61–63
Trees, 205–206, Plate II
United Nations project, 59–60
Variable, first grade, 130

Child development/growth
Cultural direction, 84–91, 96, 151
Function of art, 8
Mental development, 72–78, 82–83, 96, 148–150
Perceptual growth, 78–84, 96, 148–150
Personality formation, 75
Physical growth, 72–74, 78–80, 148–150
Research, 71–75, 95
See also Creativity; Motivation; Motor skills; Perceptual readiness; Theories, child art

Child psychology; *see* Psychology

Child-rearing practices; *see* Cleanliness attitudes; Home influences

Churches; *see* Architecture; Religion

Citizenship development, 171, 173–175, 181

City planning, 27–28, 172

Classical culture, 27

Classroom physical arrangements; *see* Materials, art

Classroom, physical environment
Development, 9, 186–187, 194–195, 243, 244
Motivational use, 194–197
Overcrowding, 115

Classroom, psychological environment
Cultural dynamics, impact, 108, 112
Curriculum planning for, 185, 191–194, 209
Subcultural development, 9, 90–91, 92–93, 95, 96, 192–193
Threat source, 102–104, 112, 191

Clay
Storage, 276–277
Working, 289–290

Cleanliness attitudes, 4, 111, 117–118, 136–137, 283–284, 289

Cleveland Museum Study, 157–158

Closure, 40, 247

Clothing; *see* Costume

Coates, Eric, music of, 222

Collage; *see* Junk construction; Torn paper

Color
Design, 243–244, 250, 254–255, 268
Balance, 269
Perspective, 265
Textural effects, 264
Perception, 44, 47, 232, 260–263
See also Constancies

Color-blindness, 260

Comic books; *see* Mass media

Common man ideal, 114–117

Communication; *see* Art communication; Expression; Fluency; Language; Mass media

Community influences, 7, 8, 88–89, 90, 169–170

Composition; *see* Design

Conflicts; *see* Attitudes, art; Behaviors

Conformity; *see* American culture; Attitudes, art; Convergent thinking; Discontinuities

Constancies, perceptual
Brightness/color, 47
Definition, 47

Constancies, perceptual, *Cont'd,*
Learning, 60, 65, 80, 232, 305
Shape, 48–49
Size, 47–48
See also Color; Form; Perspective; Proportion
Consultant, art
Attitudes, 221
Classroom experiences, 26, 92, 187, 217–221, 223, 274–275
Duties, 273–275
Training, 169
Consumer education, 229
See also Aesthetic judgments
Continuity, perceptual, 40, 246–247
Contour; *see* Lines; Form; Shading
Convergent thinking, 141–142, 143
See also Attitudes, art
Copland, Aaron, music of, 222
Core culture
Definitions, 17–18, 317
Values, changing, 106–109, 112, 113–121, 125, 170, 171–173
See also American culture; Democratic society
Costume, 18, 19, 22–23
Crafts; *see* Media, classroom experience with
Craftsman; *see* Artist
Craftsmanship values, 114, 117–118, 125
Crayoning, 56–57, 93, 281, 284–285, 294
Creative experience
Pupil's need for, 176–179, 181
Society's need for, 171–173, 174–175, 180–181
Teacher's need for, 3, 4, 10
Creative potential, 129, 131, 140, 190–191, 228, 231
Creativity
Definitions, 129–130, 143
Factors, personality
Flexibility, 135–137, 143, 151, 190, 217
Fluency, 132–135, 143, 151, 190, 227
Originality, 131–132, 143, 151, 190, 234
See also Perceptual readiness
Increasing
Intermediate, 234–238

Primary, 216–223
Perceptual training, 62–64, 139–140, 143, 151, 306
Limiting factors, 143
Convergent thinking, 141–142, 234
Organizing ability, 138–139, 151, 163
Past experience, 138, 151, 163, 191
Skill inadequacy, 138–139, 151, 163
Pupil potential, 190–191
Summary, 240, 309–310
Teacher criticism, 122, 125
See also Environment, psychological; Motivation
Criticism, art; *see* Aesthetic judgments
Criticism, classroom use, 122, 125
Cubism, 28, 177, 179
See also Fine arts
Cues, bodily; *See* Receptors
Cues, postural; *see* Postural cues
Cues, visual; *see* Perceptual readiness (Information-handling and Space orientation)
Cultural change
Definition, 107
Discontinuity effects, 106, 107–109, 112, 125
Educational impact, 170, 171–172
Cultural confluence, definition, 107
Cultural dynamics, 106–109, 112
Cultural maintenance
Definition, 107
Functions, art, 8, 20–28, 178–179
Functions, art education, 19, 170–171
Historic record, 8, 22, 24
Reality concept communication, 20–22, 34
Reflection of culture, art forms, 8, 18, 19, 22–23, 24–27, 33–34, 109
Cultural reaction, definition, 107
Culture
Definitions, 17–18, 84, 107, 317
Functions of art, 8, 19–20
Cultures
African, 45
Balinese, 30–33, 35
British Columbian Indians (Bella Bella, Bella Coola, Haida, Kwakiutl, Nass River and Tsimshian tribes), 87–88, 89

Carolinians, Saipan, 86
Chamorros, Saipan, 86
Classical, 27–28
Egyptian, 22
English, 27
Eskimo, 193
Greek, 27
Hopi Indians, 89, 90
Japanese, 27, 133
Kwoma, New Guinea, 22
Migrant workers, 26
Navaho Indians, 20
Orotchen, Siberia, 85–86
"Pueblo Arts," film, 193
Zia Indians, New Mexico, 84–85, 95
    See also American culture
Curriculum, general
Art education, basic to, 7–8, 19, 30, 205
Art integration, 203–206, 213, 227–230, 231, 238–241, 248, 274, 278
Community impact, 169–170, 273
Humanities vs. practical education, 108, 170, 179
Pupils' needs, 160, 176–179, 180, 181, 206–209
Society's needs, 171–176, 180–181
Curriculum planning, art
Art consultant's contribution, 273–275
General objectives, 169–179, 273
    See also Art education, teaching goals
Kinds of activity, 213, 241, 305
Intermediate years, 230–241
Planning workbook, 299–301
Primary years, 214–230, 241
Sequential planning, 213, 241
Summary of factors, 241
    See also Art activities; Learning, teacher planning for; Media, classroom experience with; Media usage, influences; Motor skills; Technique training

"Dance of the Happy Spirits" (Gluck), music, 222
Decoration; *see* Ornamentation
Delineation, 38
    See also Drawing development; Motor skills; Perception-deline-

ation theory; Technique training
Democratic society, 7, 169–175, 180–181
Dependency/independency
I.Q. development factor, 74
Judgments, 172, 175–176, 181, 229
Space orientation, 52–53, 54, 60, 61
    See also Authority influences; Creativity
Design
Child art
Age differences, ability, 158, 199–200
Intuitive designing, 198–199, 248–249, 267
Definition, 317
Elements, methods of use, 257–267
Elements, visual, 243–244, 250–251, 257
Color, 243–244
Form, 243–244
Line, 243–244
Space, 243–244
Texture, 243–244
Function, basic concept, 24–25, 243–244
Principles, 249–257
Psychological basis, 245–249
Intuitive design, 198–199, 248–249, 267
Perceptual organization, 245–249
Qualities, 244–245
Balance, 244–245
Dynamic unity, 244–245
Integration, 244–245
Rhythm, 244–245
Teaching of, 236, 249, 268
Three-dimensional, 256–257
    See also Cubism; Industrial design; Perceptual readiness
Development studies; *see* Case studies; Research studies; Theories, child art
Dewey, John, 179
Discipline, classroom, 193, 237
Discontinuities
Definitions, 106, 318
Effects, cultural change, 107–109, 112–121, 125, 305
Overcoming of, 123–124, 125, 161, 193–194, 237

Dishes, art forms, 24–25, 109
Dislikes; *see* Taste
Display boxes, 196
Displays, school, 278–279
    See also Bulletin boards; Murals
Distance; *see* Perspective; Space
Divergent thinking, 131, 141–142
Do You See What I See?, Borten, 215
Dramatic play, 59–60, 197
Draw A Man Test (intelligence), 104,
    154, 158
Drawing development
    Criteria, 119
    Cultural direction, 30–33, 84–89, 96,
        202
    Design application, 249
    Developmental stages, 157
    Fluency, 132–133
    Originality, 132
    Past experience, effects, 134, 138–139
    Primary years, 214
    Realism, forced, 152–153
    Variation, classroom, 92–95
        See also Art abilities; Creativity;
        Media usage, influences
Dress; *see* Costume
Dreyfuss, Henry, 177
Drums, making, 296
Dynamic unity; *see* Design; Unity, dy-
    namic and organic

Eames, Charles, 177
Easel Age Scale Test, 104
Easel painting, 280, 281–283
    See also Tempera
Easels, 276
Education, general
    Artist, 83–84
    "Child-centered" emphasis, 179
    Cultural component, 17
    Democratic society needs, 169–171,
        173–175, 180–181
    Humanities vs. practical, 108, 170, 179
    Overcrowding, 115
    Teacher attitudes, 115–116
Egyptian culture, 22
Electrical Shock, Threat Test, 103
Electrical Switch, Testing, 43–44
Elementary school; *see* Intermediate
    grades; Primary grades

Embedded figure test, 52
Embellishment; *see* Ornamentation
Emergent values, 114–117
Emotion; *see* Feelings; Expression; Re-
    sponses, emotional
Enculturation, 30, 109–112, 123
English culture, 27–28, 90
Enhancement; *see* Ornamentation
Environment, classroom; *see* Classroom
Environment, cultural; *see* American
    culture; Perceptual readiness
    (Cultural influences)
Environment, home; *see* Home influences
Environment, psychological
    Cultural interaction, 101, 106–109,
        112–113, 124–125, 307
    Enculturation, home, 109–112, 123
    Value conflicts, 113–121
        See also Classroom, psycholog-
        ical environment; Motivation;
        Perceptual readiness
Equipment; *see* Materials, art
"Eskimo Arts and Crafts," film, 193
Europe, Western; *see* American culture
Evaluations; *see* Aesthetic judgments; Art
    abilities; Intelligence, meas-
    ured; Media usage, influences;
    Perceptual readiness; Personal-
    ity; Pupil, understanding of
Expediency values, 114, 117–118, 125,
    193
Experiments; *see* Case studies; Research
    studies
Expression, 60, 61, 89, 198–199, 209,
    217, 221–223, 231
        See also Creativity; Response,
        emotional
Expressionism, 179
Expressive fluency, 132
Eyes; *see* Sight

Family; *see* Home influences
Fashion; *see* Costume; Ornamentation
Fears; *see* Feelings; Threat/non-threat
    influences
Feelings
    Anxiety, 55, 57, 74, 76–77, 102–104,
        115
    Bias, teacher, 4, 108
    Bodily (receptors), 51–52

Fears, 102, 104, 112
Frustration, 57–58, 134
Like/dislike, 28–30, 34–35
    See also Behaviors; Environment, psychological; Media usage, influences; Motivation
Fels Research Institute of Human Development, 74, 157
Field definitions, 318
Field psychology; *see* Gestalt
Field, visual; *see* Perceptual readiness (Space orientation)
Films, 187, 193, 199, 239, 279
    "Bulletin Boards: An Effective Teaching Device," 279
    "Eskimo Arts and Crafts," 193
    "Klee Wyck," 239
    "Loon's Necklace, The," 199
    "Pueblo Arts," 193
    "Romance of Transportation, The," 239
Fine arts
    Classroom use, 91
    Definition, 27
    Programming basis, 177–179, 180, 181, 215, 230, 232
    Values conflict, 27–28, 33–35, 108–109, 179, 180
Finger painting, 4, 283–284
Fixatives, 285
Flexibility/rigidity
    In creativity, 131, 135, 137, 151, 190–191, 217
    Development, classroom, 45, 53, 56–59, 61–62, 65
    Media usage, 56–59, 65, 134, 135, 136–137, 188–189, 224, 225, 235
    Perceptual response, 43–44, 45, 54–55, 65, 150, 304
    In teacher, 10, 91, 137
    See also Art activities; Curriculum planning, art; Motivation; Perceptual readiness; Problem-solving
Fluency
    Creativity factor, 132–135, 190–191
    Definition, 132
    I.Q., influence on, 82–83, 133
    Vs. motor skills, 73, 75, 77–78
    See also Expression

Focus cards, 195
Folklore; *see* Cultural maintenance; Cultures
Folksongs, 222
Form
    Design elements, 243–244, 257–258, 268
    Design principles, 250–256
    See also Perspective
Free forms, 258
French art; *see* Cubism
Functional fixedness, 43–44, 45, 55, 56–59, 65
    See also Media usage, influences
Functions; *see* Art functions; Uses

"Gaieté Parisienne" (Offenbach), music, 222
Geometric form, 77
Geometry, perspective, 48, 258
Gestalt psychology, 12, 205, 245, 248
Gluck, music of, 222
Goal-seeking behavior; *see* Motivation
Goodenough's Draw A Man Test, 104, 154, 158
Gothic art, 20
Grade level sequence; *see* Curriculum planning
Grades, pupil performance; *see* Child art (Evaluation)
Greco-Roman democracy, 90
Greek culture, 27
Gropius, Walter, 177
Group common man, 114–117
Group planning, 114, 120, 175, 192
Growth studies; *see* Research studies

Haida Indians, 87–88, 89
Hanover Institute, 45–46
Haptic-visual theory, 50, 156, 164
Highbrow tastes, 29, 109
Home influences
    Classroom variations, 26–27, 90–91, 93, 107–109, 186
    Enculturation vs. art responses, 33–35, 109–112, 118, 123–124, 134
    Language skills, 82–83
    Space orientation, 52–53
    See also American culture; Attitudes, art; Taste

Hopi Indians, 89, 90
Hungarian folksongs, 222
Hypothesis vs. theory, 11

Identification behavior, 174
Illustration; *see* Mass media; Realism
Implements, 24–27, 109
    See also Cultural maintenance
Impressionism, 177
    See also Fine arts
Independence; *see* Dependency/independency
India ink, 284, 285
Indians; *see* Cultures; Projects
Individual artistic man; *see* Artist
Individual differences; *see* Behaviors; Creativity; Perceptual readiness; Pupil, understanding of
Individuality; *see* American culture (Core culture changes); Convergent thinking
Industrial design, 19, 27–28, 172, 177, 179–180, 230
    See also Applied art; Design
Industrial society
    Art values, 19, 27–28, 33–35
    Educational impact, 171–173, 175
    Work values, 114, 117–118, 125
    See also American culture
Information-handling; *see* Perceptual readiness
Inks
    India, 284, 285
    Print-making, 288
Inner tubes, print-making, 9, 287
Innovations, 107, 109, 115
Institute of Child Welfare, University of California, 119
Integrated art; *see* Art activities, integrated; Curriculum, general; Projects
Intellectualist theory, 153–155, 164
Intellectuals
    Social evaluation, 115–116
    Tastes, 29, 109
Intelligence, measured
    Age-based studies, 72–75, 158–159
    Child drawing tests, 103–104, 154, 158
    I.Q. vs. ability, 75–77, 133–134, 185–186, 209

I.Q. vs. personality, 74–75
I.Q., definition, 318
Perceptual effects, 78–80, 82–83, 91, 96, 150, 159, 186
Intensity, color, 263
Intermediate grades (4,5,6)
    Art learning activities, 230–237, 262–263
    Development variables, 75–77, 81–82, 104, 117, 234, 237
        See also Perceptual readiness
    Integrated art activities, 238–241
    Projects, 59–60, 92–93, 196–197
        See also Projects
    Self-directed art activities, 238–241
Inventions, cultural effects, 107, 109, 115
Isolates, social, 192

James, William, 179
Japanese child art, 133, Plate III
Japanese culture, 27, 133
Judaeo-Christian ideology, 90
Judgment; *see* Aesthetic judgments
"Junk" construction, 57–59, 290–292

Kinesthetic responses
    Definition, 318
    Perceptual use; *see* Postural cues
"Klee Wyck," film, 239
"Knightsbridge March" (Coates), music, 222
Kwakiutl Indians, 87–88, 89
Kwoma people, 22

Language
    Categorizing, 40, 161–163, 317
    Expressive fluency, 132
    Inadequacy, 22
    Learning, 82–83, 231–232
        See also Art communication; Fluency
Lantz's Easel Age Scale Test, 104, 158
Lear, Edward, poem, 92
Learning, art; *see* Art activities; Art communication; Curriculum planning, art; Media, classroom experience with; Media usage, influences; Perceptual training; Technique training

Learning, cognitive; *see* Perceptual readiness
Learning, integrated; *see* Art activities, integrated; Curriculum, general
Learning, prior; *see* Perceptual readiness
Learning, teacher planning for
  Classroom approaches
    Evaluation, pupil progress, 206–209
    Expression-prompting, 198–199, 209
    Integration of art, 203–206, 209
    Motivational stimulus, 194–197, 209
    Psychological environment, 191–194
    Skills guidance, 202–203
      See also Art activities; Curriculum planning, art; Classroom environments; Media, classroom experience with; Media usage, influences; Motivation; Teaching, practical applications
  Pupil evaluation, 185–186, 209
    Art attitudes, 189–190
    Creative ability, 190–191
    Perceptual readiness, 186–189
      See also Attitudes, art; Creativity; Perceptual readiness; Pupil, understanding of
Learning, visual; *see* Perceptual readiness
Leisure, influence of, 108–109, 171–173
Light, effect of, 45, 47, 195, 261–262
Light Test, authority influence, 53
Like/dislike behavior; *see* Taste
Lines
  Design element, 243–244, 250–257, 259–260, 268
  Perceptual distortions, 45–46, 245–247
    See also Perspective
Linoleum blocks, 9, 287
Longitudinal studies; *see* Psychology (Child growth studies)
Looms, weaving, 293
"Loon's Necklace, The," film, 199
Lowbrow, 29
Lower class, 83, 93, 136

Magazines; *see* Mass media
Man, nature of, 172
Maracas, making, 295–296
"Maria of San Ildefonso," film, 193
Marsalai idol, 22
Mask-making, 45, 199, 292

Mass media, art in,
  Cultural instructors, 23, 107, 170, 230
  Perceptual instructors, 89, 96
Massachusetts Normal School, 179
Materials, art
  Arrangements for
    Display areas, 278–279
      See also Bulletin boards
    Equipment, large, 275–277
    Storage, 237, 277–278
    Teacher responsibility, 275, 279
  Media needs
    Bulletin board work, 296–297
    Chalkwork, 281
    Claywork, 289
    Crayoning, 235, 281, 284–285
    Easel painting, 280, 281–283
    Finger painting, 283
    Inks, 284, 288
    "Junk" construction, 57–59, 290–291
    Mask-making, 199, 292
    Mosaics, 290
    Murals, 294–295
    Musical instrument, making, 295–296
    Paper, 281, 283, 286
    Papier-mâché, 292
    Print-making, 9, 287–288
    Prism, 262
    Self-directed art, 280–281
    Water color, 284, 287
    Weaving, 293
Materials, teaching aids, 239, 262, 274, 278–279
    See also Bulletin boards; Films; Slides
Measurements; *see* Intelligence, measured
Media, classroom experience with
  Bulletin boards, 187, 194, 250, 278–279, 296–298
  Chalk, 285
  Clay, 289–290
  Crayon, 226, 235, 285
  Easel painting, 223–224, 231, 261, 283
  Finger painting, 4, 283–284
  "Junk" construction, 57–59, 291–292
  Mask-making, 45, 199
  Mosaics, 235, 290
  Murals, 196–197, 286, 294–295
  Musical instruments, 296

Media, classroom experience with, *Cont'd*,
    Paperwork, 134, 226, 235, 286
    Papier-mâché, 293
    Print-making, 288
    Water color, 287
    Weaving, 293–294
        See also Drawing development;
        Media usage, influences;
Media usage, influences
    Confidence, 203
        See also Success/failure experi-
        ence
    Evaluation and introduction, 26, 63,
        163, 213, 224–226, 235, 236–
        237, 298–299, 300
    Flexibility, 56–59, 65, 134, 135, 136–
        137, 188–189, 224, 225, 235
    Psychological threats, 4, 56–58, 65,
        122, 135, 141
        See also Right/wrong behavior;
        Threat/non-threat influences
    Readiness; *see* Drawing development;
        Motor skills (Development);
        Perceptual readiness
    Variety, need for, 63, 95, 138–139, 163,
        225, 226–227
        See also Motivation; Expression
Median, definition, 140
Mental age; *see* Intelligence, measured
Mental retardation, 217–221
Middle class
    Cultural art use, 27, 109, 118
    Enculturation, 110–111, 118, 136
    Perceptual influences, 79–80, 82–83
    Taste, 29
        See also American culture; Dem-
        ocratic society
Models, artist, 42
Modern society; *see* American culture
Mondrian, painting, 230
Money, ornamentation, 24
Mother influence; *see* Home influences
Motherwell, painting, 97, 177, Plate III
Motivation
    Definitions and scope, 102, 240, 318
    Goal-seeking behaviors, 102, 112–113,
        150–151
    Planning considerations, 180, 190–191,
        209, 230–231

See also Curriculum planning,
    art; Media usage, influences
Psychological modification
    Cultural values, 113–121, 151
        See also Attitudes, art
    Reward/punishment, 102, 106, 112–
        113, 122, 125, 150–151, 161
    Success/failure, 73, 75–77, 104–106,
        112, 121–122, 125, 150–151,
        217
    Threat/non-threat, 102–104, 112
        See also Flexibility; Right/wrong
        behavior
Sources, 102, 112
Stimulus, 194–199, 209, 240
    Audio-visual materials, 279–280
    Cultural; *see* Drawing development
    Displays, 186–187, 194–196, 278–279
    Dramatic play, 59–60, 197
    Films, 199
        See also Films
    Media exploration, 234–235
    Murals, 196–197
    Music and sound, 199, 216, 222,
        235, 279–280
    Perceptual experiences, 205–206,
        215–216, 224, 279
        See also Perceptual training
    Postural cues, 53, 187–188
    Sensory, total, 216–217, 279
    Slides, 279
        See also Slides
    Suspense, 235
    Television, 280
    Verbal ideas, 92–93, 158, 187–188,
        189, 215, 216
    Variety, need for, 95, 96, 163, 216
        See also Media usage, influences
Motor skills
    Development, 57, 77–78, 138–139, 157,
        159, 202–203, 209, 223–226,
        234–237, 241
    Direction, cognitive, 136
    Naïve realism theory, 152, 164
    Perceptual theory, 155
    Vs. verbal skills, 73, 77–78, 202
Movies, public; *see* Mass media
Movies, school; *see* Films
Murals, 196–197, 286, 294–295

Museum of Modern Art (New York City), 231
Music
  Art parallels, 89, 222
  Instrument-making, 295–296
  Motivational use, 199, 216, 222, 248

Naïve realism theory, 151–154, 164, 215
Nass River Indians, 87–88, 89
Navaho Indians, 20
Negative responses; *see* Attitudes, art; Behaviors; Responses, emotional
New Guinea, Kwoma, 22
New Mexico, Indians, 84–85, 89, 90, 95
Nonliterate societies, 18, 84–86
Nonobjective painting, 318
    See also Abstract art; Cubism
Nonsense blocks, test with, 55
Nonsense poem, 92
Norms; *see* Age-based growth studies

Objectives, curriculum planning, 169–181
  Difficulty establishing, 169–171, 273
  Sources, 171
    Art heritage, 177–179, 181
    Citizenship needs, 173–175, 181
    Philosophical values, 175–176
    Pupil needs, 176–177, 181
    Social needs, 171–173, 180–181
  Summaries, 180–181, 240
    See also Art education (Goals)
Observation; *see* Perceptual readiness
Offenbach, music of, 222
Opportunity, social, 174–175
    See also American culture
Organic unity; *see* Unity, dynamic and organic
Organismic growth, 73–75, 149, 318
    See also Child development/ growth
Organization, learning; *see* Perceptual readiness (Information-handling)
Orientation, art teaching, 3–6
Orientation, space; *see* Perceptual readiness
Originality; *see* Creativity
Ornamentation, 18–19, 20, 24–27

Orotchen nomads, 85–86, 87, 160, 202, 265
Overleaf drawings, 201

Pacific Coast Indians, 87–88, 89, 199
Painting; *see* Easel painting; Tempera
Pantomime, 187
Paperworking, 286
Papier-mâché, 292–293
Pattern; *see* Balance, rhythm; Perceptual readiness
Perception
  Definitions, 64, 319
  Processes; *see* Perceptual readiness
      See also Theories, child art
Perception, color, 260–262
Perception-delineation theory
  Formulation, 11–12, 38
  Operational relationships, 38, 40–42, 64, 71, 91, 101, 112, 131, 147–148, 149, 151
  Summary, applications and factors, 303–310
      See also Theories, child art
Perceptual development/growth
  Brief summary, 91, 95–96
  Definition, 78
  Details; *see* Perceptual readiness (all * factors)
Perceptual learning; *see* Art communication; Perceptual readiness (Awareness, Cognitive and visual learning, Constancies, Cultural influences); Perceptual training
Perceptual organization (information-handling)
  Brief summary, 38–40, 65
  Details; *see* Perceptual readiness (Information-handling)
Perceptual processes; *see* Perceptual readiness
Perceptual readiness
    Note: * denotes a factor of Perceptual development and growth; † denotes a factor of Response sets
  † Authority influence, 53, 56, 150

Perceptual readiness

† Awareness (sensitivity), 38–39, 45, 49, 54, 56, 60, 63–64, 65, 90–91, 214–216

Lack of, 19, 33, 108

See modifications below: Cognitive/visual learning; Constancies; Cultural influences; Intelligence; Precognitive sorting; Prior learning

* Categorizing knowledge, 40, 63–64, 161–163

†* Cognitive/visual learning, 45, 46, 54, 56, 60, 63–64, 65, 66, 97, 231, 233–234, 305

†* Constancies, perceptual, 47–49, 60, 65, 80–81, 232, 305

See also Color; Perspective; Shape

†* Cultural influences, 46, 74, 84–96, 150, 159, 202

See also Environments; Motivation

Definitions, readiness, 42, 64–65, 91, 318

†* Detail/pattern perception, 39–40, 52–54, 61, 78–84, 96, 149–151, 159, 186, 201, 232, 245, 249

See modification above: Cultural influences

* Development and growth

Brief summary, 91, 95–96

Definition, 78

Details

See all * *items under* Perceptual readiness

Emotional modifications; *see* Behaviors; Feelings; Motivation; Environment, psychological; Responses, emotional

Evaluation, readiness, 186–189

† Flexibility/rigidity, 43–44, 45, 56–59, 65

Functional fixedness; *see* Flexibility *above and* Prior learning *below*

* Growth, physical, 43, 57, 64, 72–74, 78–80, 148–149

See also Child development

* Information-handling (organizing ability)

Abilities needed, 54, 65

Methods, visual, 38–40, 65

See all Development *factors* (*) *and* Response set *factors* (†) *under* Perceptual readiness.

* Intelligence, 72–78, 78–80, 82–83, 91, 96, 150, 151, 186

†* Precognitive sorting, 38–40, 64–65, 78, 151, 249

See also Prior learning *below*

†* Prior learning, 43–44, 45–46, 56–60, 65

See also Cognitive/visual learning; Constancies *above*

†* Resistance to visual field, 50–53, 60–61, 78–79, 96, 150, 187–188, 201, 245, 249

†* Response sets

Brief summary, 42–43

Details; *see all* † *items under* Perceptual readiness

†* Space orientation, 50–54, 60–61, 65, 150, 156, 187–188, 203, 304

Note: Affects Detail/pattern perception; Resistance to visual field *above*

†* Visual learning, description, 46

See also Awareness; Cognitive/visual learning; Constancies *above*

Perceptual rigidity; *see* Perceptual readiness (Flexibility)

Perceptual sensitivity; *see* Perceptual readiness (Awareness)

Perceptual theory, child art, 155–156, 164

Perceptual training

Art function, 8

Authority resistance, 56

Awareness; *see* Perceptual readiness

Cognitive/visual learning; *see* Perceptual readiness

Color perception, 260–263

Constancies; *see* Perceptual readiness

Cultural influences; *see* Perceptual readiness

Cultural need for, 33, 62, 63–64, 80–81, 175–176, 202

Detail and pattern perception; *see* Perceptual readiness

Flexibility; *see* Perceptual readiness

Information-handling, 44–45, 54, 62–64, 65, 80, 161–163, 176–177, 186–187, 209, 214–216, 232, 245–248, 304–305
Postural/visual cue uses, 53, 54, 60–62
Resistance to visual field
　　See Perceptual readiness
Stimulus for creativity, 62–64, 139–140, 161–162, 187–188, 306
Teacher's role, 7–8, 90–91, 248–299
　　See also Motivation
Personality
　Art response, 61–62, 237
　Development, 55, 74–75, 82, 109–111
　Difficulties, 115–116, 119–121, 192
　Evaluation, 75, 208
　　See also Creativity; Behaviors
Perspective
　Constancies, size and shape, 47–49, 232
　Formal system of, 264–267
　　See also Proportion
Pharaohs, 22
Philosophy, art, 176, 179, 180
Physical development, 43, 57, 64, 72–73, 148–149
Picasso, painting of, 96–97, 177, 232, Plate IV
Pictographs, 6
Pictorial art forms; *see* Mass media; Realism
Pilot training, space orientation, 50–51
Poetry, motivation of, 92–93
Polynesian culture, 90
Portraits, 42, 119
Postural cues
　Motor skills effects, 203, 223
　Space orientation, 50–54, 61, 65, 150
Potatoes, print-making, 9, 287
Potter's wheel, 289
Precognitive sorting; *see* Perceptual readiness
Pre-schematic art, 157
Preschool children
　Art expression, 157, 204
　Cleanliness training, 136
　Detail response, 79–80
　Enculturation, 109–112
　Success experience, 104
Primary grades (1,2,3)
　Art learning activities, 214–226, 241

Art responses, 60, 117, 138, 157
Integrated art, 227–230, 241
Perceptual abilities, 78–80, 81–82
Programming objectives, 214
Self-directed art, 226–227, 241, 280–281
Principal, school; *see* Administration
Print-making, 9, 287–288
Problem-solving, creative, 8, 116–117, 141–142, 148, 238
Problem-solving, teaching
　Background variables handling, 26–27, 46, 92–95, 108, 123, 160, 185–189
　Creativity, increasing, 138–142, 161–163, 190–191
　Discontinuity, overcoming, 112–113, 123–124, 125, 161, 193–194, 237
　Emotion, use with reason, 119, 123
　Interest, sustaining, 235, 249
　Media resistance, overcoming, 224–226, 235
　Personality adjustments, 115, 192, 237
　Rigidity, overcoming, 137, 188–189
　Successes, providing, 77, 104–105, 121–122, 124–125
　Threats, overcoming, 77–78, 121–123, 124–125, 161, 191, 237
　Work values, modifying, 118
　　See also Learning, teacher planning for; Motivation; Perceptual training
Product design; *see* Industrial design
Professional education; *see* Administration; Teacher training
Projects
　Art attitudes questionnaire, 189
　Art communication exploration, 89
　Bulletin boards, 194
　Classroom improvement, 9, 194–196
　Color perception, 44, 261–263
　Cultural institutions, exploring, 239
　Description, written, 64
　Design constructions, 269–270
　Dramatic play, 197
　Drawing county fair sounds, 235–236
　Drawing poetry ideas, 92–93
　Drawing self-portraits, 119
　Drawing story ideas, 187–188

Projects, *Cont'd,*
  Drawings, window, 267
  Field trips, 161, 193, 205–206, 224,
    229, 231, 239
  History and art, 238–239
  Indian study, 178, 186, 193, 199
  Junk construction, 57–58
  Mask-making, 45, 199
  Mass media discussions, 23–24
  Model house, 228
  Murals, 196–197
  Music/art relating, 89
  Paper effects, 143
  Perceptual organization tests, 78
  Perspective observations, 47–49, 65–66,
    232
  Table-setting, 26–27
  Textural observations, 66, 263
  Tree studies, 201, 205–206
  Two-string problem, 43–44
  United Nations study, 59–60
Proportion, 250–253
Proximity
  Perceptual principle, 245–246
  Proportion, 250–252
  Rhythm, 252–253
Pseudo-realism, 157
Psychological environment; *see* Environ-
    ment, psychological
Psychologist, school, 76, 77, 122, 208
Psychology
  Art education application, 5, 6, 8, 11–
    12, 37–38
  Association theory, 12
  Child growth studies, 71–75, 95
  Creativity behaviors, 131
  Personality and culture theories, 12
  Personality and perception theories, 37
    See also Behaviors; Research
    studies; Theories, child art
"Pueblo Arts," film, 193
Punctuality training, 111
Punishments; *see* Rewards/punishments
Pupil, understanding of
  Basis, curriculum planning, 171, 185,
    209
  Criticism, effects of, 122, 125
  Educational elements, 194
  Educational needs, 176–177
  Expressive needs, 198–199, 209

Pupil information, needs for, 9, 10, 12,
    38, 73, 160, 171, 185
Pupil information, sources, 185–186,
    209
    See also Attitudes, art; Be-
    haviors; Learning, teacher plan-
    ning for; Motivation; Percep-
    tual readiness; Problem-solving
Puppets
  Balinese, 30–33
  Class use, 188
  Speech therapy, 222
Puritan tradition, 20

"Quangle Wangle's Hat, The" (Lear),
    nonsense poem, 92

Randall, Reino, film of, 279
Reactionary attitudes, 107, 108
Readiness
  Basis, curriculum planning, 160, 177
  Basis, delineation, 151, 159
  Definition, 42–43, 64, 148, 318
  Details of; *see* Perceptual readiness
  Summary, 303–305
Realism
  Art revolt against, 179
  Artists' use of, 231
  Cultural direction, 87, 89, 159, 200
  Elementary pupil use, 59–60, 157, 200
  Forcing, effects of, 152–153
  Naïve realism theory, 151–154, 164
  Pseudo-realism, 157
Reality, concepts of, 20–22, 26–27, 30,
    34, 84, 87
Reason vs. emotion, 118–121, 125, 175
Receptors, 50–54, 60–61, 65
Recognition, reward, 227
"Red Pony Suite"
  (Copland), music, 222
Reindeer, Orotchen culture, 85–86, 87
Religion
  Art communication, 20–22, 30–33, 84
  Cultural component, 17–18, 90
Renaissance art, 20, 265
Representation, definition, 158
Representational unity, 158
Research
  Art educational application, 5, 10–12,
    37–38

Child growth, 71, 72–73, 95
Creativity, 131
Objectives planning aid, 170–171, 181
Research studies
  Art attitudes—Spindler, 115–116
  Authority influence, perception—Linton, 53
  Child art, environmental influence—Anastasi and Foley, 37–38
  Child art, preschool training—Dubin, 204
  Cleanliness training/art behavior—Alper, 136
  Color-matching—Bruner, 44
  Distortions, perceiving shape—Lawrence, 45–46
  Functional fixedness—Birch, Rabinowitz, 43–44
  Goal-setting/success-failure—Sears, 104
  Growth, Berkeley Growth Research—Bayley, 72–73
  I.Q./personality development—Sontag, 74
  I.Q./visual complexity patterns—Livson and Krech, 83
  Perceptual effects, success/failure—Postman and Brown, 105
  Perceptual effects, threat—Kohn, 103
  Perceptual information-handling—Attneave, 38–40
  Perceptual organizing ability—Honkavaara, 78–80
  Perceptual response/detail—French, 81–82
  Perceptual rigidity—Becker, 55
  Personality/artistic pattern—Stewart, 119–120
  Personality/ "ideal American boy"—Spindler, 114
  Space orientation—Witkin, 50–53
  Resistance, visual field—Linton, 52
"Resist" drawings, 285
Response sets
  Definitions, 42–43
  Details; see Perceptual readiness, all †
    factors
  Summary, 64–65, 91, 150, 151
Responses, emotional
  Capacity for, 215, 216

Expression of, 60, 61, 176, 198–199, 221–223, 234, 235–236
Fluency effects, 134
Vs. reason, 118–121, 125
Religious symbolism, 20–22
    See also Attitudes, art; Behaviors; Media usage, influences
Retinas; see Sight
Rewards/punishments, 101, 102, 106, 125, 227
    See also Discontinuities
Rhythm
  Color, 263
  Design quality, 244–245, 248, 250
  Principles, 252–256
    See also Music
Right/wrong behavior, 106–109, 112–113, 125, 135–136
Rigidity; see Flexibility
Rockefeller Center exhibition, 86–87
"Romance of Transportation, The," film, 239
Romanesque art, 20
Rorschach Inkblots, 79–80, 86

Saipan cultures, 86
Sand-paintings, Navaho, 20
Schema/schematic art
  Child usage, 157, 158, 159
  Definitions, 42, 160, 319
    See also Symbols
School; see Administration; Art education; Curriculum, general; Education
Science
  Professional
    Creativity needs, 8, 148, 175
    Perceptual needs, 64, 81, 148
  School
    Art integration, 81, 227–228, 240–241
"Scribbling" art, 157, 159, 204
Security values, 114, 117–118, 125
Self-directed art; see Art activities, self-directed
Sensitivity, perceptual; see Perceptual readiness
Sequential programming, 213, 241
Sex differences, art
  Balinese expression, 30–31

Sex differences, art
  Costume, 23
  Indian drawing, 84–85, 87–88
  Perceptual organization, 78–79
  Personality, artistic, 115, 119–121, 150
  Space orientation, 52–53
Shade, color definition, 261
Shading, line, 259
Shadow boxes, 195
Shadow, perceptual effect, 45, 47, 261
Shadow play, Balinese, 30, 31, 33
Shape
  Constancy, 48–49
  Perceptual distortions, 44, 45–46
      See also Constancies; Form;
      Lines; Perspective
Siberian Orotchens, 85–86
Sight, Physical
  Retinal capacity, 39
  Retinal projection, 48
      See also Space orientation
Similarity
  Color, 263
  Perceptual principle
    Design, 246
    Information-handling, 39
  Proportions, 250–252
  Rhythm, 252–253
Size
  Constancy, 47–48
  Proportions, 250–252
      See also Constancies; Perspective
Skills; see Art activities, art learning;
      Media, classroom experience
      with; Media usage, influences;
      Technique training
"Sleeping Beauty Waltz" (Tchaikovsky),
      music, 222
Slides, teaching aid, 187, 201, 232, 233–
      234, 279
Slip (clay), 290
Smith, Walter, 179
Social isolates, 192
Social organization; see American cul-
      ture; Cultural maintenance;
      Cultures; Democratic society;
      Industrial society
Social sciences, professional; see Anthro-
      pology; Psychology; Research
Social studies, school, 81, 228–230, 238–
      239, 241
      See also Curriculum, general;
      Projects
Society; see American culture; Cultures;
      Democratic society; Industrial
      society
Sociogram/sociometric technique, 192
Space
  Design element, 243–244, 245–249
  Design usage, 250–256
  Perception, spatial, 47–49, 60–61, 80–
      81
  Perspective, 264–267
Space orientation; see Perceptual readi-
      ness (Space orientation)
Spoons, ornamentation, 24–25
Stanford-Binet Test, 82
Stereotypes
  Definition, 189, 319
  Usage; see American culture; Attitudes,
      art; Cultures; Symbols
Stimulus; see Motivation (Stimulus)
Storage, 237, 277–278, 281
String Test, functional fixedness, 43–44
Structure; see Architecture; Form; Lines
Subculture
  Classroom, 90–91
  Complexity, American, 90
  Definition, 17–18
      See also American culture; Core
      culture (Changing values); En-
      vironments
Success/failure experience, 61, 73, 74,
      75–78, 101, 104–106, 112, 121–
      122, 124–125, 134–135, 217,
      234
"Suite for Children" (Bartók), music, 222
Supervisor; see Administration; Consul-
      tant, art
Supplies, art; see Materials, art
Surrealism, 179
Symbols
  Alphabet/pictographs, 6
  Line direction, 254
  Mass media, 89, 96
  Schema, 42, 157

Understanding, 45, 198
    See also Creativity; Cultural
    maintenance; Cultures; Draw-
    ing development; Stereotypes
Symmetry; *see* Design (Balance); Intelli-
    gence, measured

"Table, The (Braque), painting, 177,
    Plate I
Tables, artwork, 276, 280
Table-setting project, 26–27
Talent, 207
    See also Art abilities; Creative
    potential
Tape recordings, 279–280
Taste
    Formation, 28–30, 34–35, 177, 230, 231
    Mass media effect, 23, 89, 96, 230
    Perception of complexity, 81–82, 84
    See also Aesthetic judgments
Tchaikovsky, music of, 222
Teacher
    Attitudes, 4, 115–116, 123, 180, 237
    Authority figure, 56
    Creative approach, 130, 169–170, 181,
    204–205
    Cultural mediator, 8, 108
    Designer, classroom, 243, 244, 268
    Discussion leader, 9–10
    Major role, 7
    Model, child identification, 174
    Professional approach, 5–6
    Resource person, 9
    Taste-maker, 28, 35
    Visual responses, 81–82, 96–97
    See also Teacher training; Teach-
    ing, practical applications
Teacher training
    Art activity experience, 3–5
    Bauhaus school, 180
    Broad basis needs, 169
    Massachusetts Normal School, 179
    Orientation, art teaching, 3–6
    Self-analysis, 4, 10–11, 115–116, 123,
    171, 176, 180, 237
    Self-development activity, 47–49, 65–
    66, 96–97, 125–126, 134–135,
    143–144, 268–270

Teaching, practical applications
    Administrative relationships, 273–275
    Aesthetic judgments, developing; *see*
    Aesthetic judgments
    Anecdotal records; *see* Anecdotal rec-
    ords
    Art ability, evaluation, 206–209
    See also Art abilities
    Art communication, teaching; *see* Art
    communication
    Art integration; *see* Art activities, inte-
    grated; Curriculum, general
    Classroom, creating environment, 9,
    90–91, 121, 186–187, 191–194,
    209, 279
    Consultant's assistance, 274–275
    Creativity, increasing; *see* Problem-
    solving
    Criticism, uses of, 122, 125
    Cultural symbols, expanding, 89, 161,
    189–190, 231
    Expression, encouraging, 198–199, 209
    Information-handling, teaching; *see*
    Perceptual training
    Materials, appropriate selection, 138–
    139, 163, 189, 202–203, 209,
    216, 234–235, 237
    Materials, teaching aids, 239, 262,
    278–279
    Materials, visual presentation, 248–249
    Motivation; *see* Motivation
    Pupils, handling background vari-
    ables; *see* Problem-solving
    Research, utilizing, 11
    Response sets, broadening; *see* Percep-
    tual training
    Skills, teaching; *see* Art activities, art
    learning; Media, classroom ex-
    perience with; Motor skills;
    Technique training
    Social ideals, promoting, 174–175
    See also Curriculum planning,
    art; Learning, teacher planning
    for; Perceptual training; Prob-
    lem-solving; Pupil, understand-
    ing of
Technique training
    Color, 260–263

Technique training, *Cont'd,*
  Design, 249, 267–268
  Perspective, 265–267
      See also Art activities, art learn-
      ing; Media, classroom experi-
      ence with; Motor skills
Television, closed circuit, 280
Television, public; *see* Mass media
Tempera, 223–224, 261, 281, 284, 285,
  287, 294
Tension, design; *see* Unity, dynamic and
  organic
Texture
  Design element, 243–244, 268
  Design usage, 250, 263–264
Thematic unity, 158
      See also Unity, dynamic and
      organic
Theories, child art
  Age-based development 156–160, 164
  Association, 12
  Child art, general, 37–38, 151
  Gestalt psychology, 12, 155
  Haptic-visual, 50, 156, 164
  Intellectualist, 153–155, 164
  Naïve realism, 151–154, 164
  Perception-delineation; *see* Perception-
    delineation theory
  Perceptual theory, 155–156, 164
  Personality and perception, 12, 37
Theory, definition and function, 11
Thomson, Virgil, music of, 222
Threat/non-threat influences, 101, 102–
  103, 112–113, 122–123, 191,
  319
      See also Problem-solving
"Three Musicians, The," (Picasso), paint-
  ing, 96–97, Plate IV
"Tilt" perceptual tests, 51–52, 55
Tint, color, 261
Toilet training; *see* Cleanliness attitudes
Tool skills; *see* Motor skills; Media, class-
  room experiences with
Tools; *see* Materials, art
Torn paper, 134, 286, 294
Tote trays, 276, 280
Touch; *see* Haptic-visual theory; Motiva-
  tion (Stimulus)

Traditional values, definition, 114, 319
      See also Core culture; Cultural
      maintenance
Tsimshian Indians, 87–88, 89

United Nations project, 59–60
United States; *see* American culture;
    Democratic society; Industrial
    society
Unity, dynamic and organic
  Design quality, 244–245, 250
  Principles, 250–257, 263, 264, 267
University of California, research, 72, 119
University of Chicago, research, 204
University of Minnesota, research, 193
Uses
  Art; *see* Art functions
  Function in design, 24–25, 243–244
  "Thinglike" identification, 19, 33, 34,
    47, 109, 319

Value, color, 261
Value concepts
  Art; *see* Art functions; Attitudes, art
  Democratic society, 169–175
  Work; *see* Work values
      See also American culture; Core
      culture; Cultural maintenance
Verbal skills; *see* Fluency
Visual communication; *see* Art commu-
    nication; Mass media
Visual cues; *see* Perceptual readiness
    (Space orientation)
Visual elements, design; *see* Design
Visual field; *see* Perceptual readiness
    (Space orientation)
Visual learning; *see* Art communication;
    Mass media; Perceptual readi-
    ness
Visual responses; *see* Perceptual readiness
Visual training; *see* Perceptual training
Visualization
  Ideas, 92–93
  Shapes in space, 45, 80–81
  Wholes from parts, 40, 246–247
"Voyage, The" (Motherwell), painting,
  97, 177, Plate III

Wajang puppets, Bali, 30–33
Water color, 284, 285, 287
Weaving, 293–294
Wechsler, Children's Test, 76
Wechsler, Vocabulary Test, 83
Western culture; *see* American culture;
    Democratic society; Industrial
    society
Window size and perspective, 48–49

Work values
    Artistic vs. traditional, 108–109, 114,
       117–118, 125
    Social changes, 171–173, 180–181
    Work vs. play, 172–173, 180–181, 193
      See also Attitudes, art
Workbook, teacher planning, 299–301

Zia Indians, 84–85, 95, 202

p. 29 –   f. 2-6 – sources of taste
p. 41 –   f. 3-1 – P-D theory
p. 75 –   f 4-1 – organismic
      growth – the
      child and his
      environment
p. 96-97 – Bragne, Pecaro, etc.
p. 142 – convergent and
      divergent creation

p. 142 Our objectives in developing
      creativity are:

1–
2–
3–

chart 213 (c.10) scope and
sequence of an art program